KEN_

TOWN CENTRE MAPS

Street maps with index
Administrative Districts
Road Map with index
Postcodes

▬ Motorway	Every effort has been made to verify the accuracy of information in this book but the publishers cannot accept responsibility for expense or loss caused by an error or omission. Information that will be of assistance to the user of the maps will be welcomed.	∿ Stream / River
▬ 'A' Road / Dual		∿Lock Canal
▬ 'B' Road / Dual		→ One-way Street
▬ Minor Road / Dual		🅿 Car Park
▬ Track		🅲 Public Convenience
▨ Pedestrianized	The representation on these maps of a road, track or path is no evidence of the existence of a right of way.	🅸 Tourist Information
▬•▬ Railway / Station		✚ Place of Worship
- - - Footpath		● Post Office

Street plans prepared and published by ESTATE PUBLICATIONS, Bridewell House, TENTERDEN, KENT.
The Publishers acknowledge the co-operation of the local authorities
of towns represented in this atlas.

 This product includes mapping data licensed from Ordnance Survey®
with the permission of the Controller of Her Majesty's Stationery Office.

COUNTY RED BOOKS contain street maps for each town centre. The street atlases listed below are SUPER & LOCAL RED BOOKS, with comprehensive local covergae.

ASHFORD & TENTERDEN
including: Charing, St Michaels, Wye etc.

BROMLEY
including: Beckenham, Chelsfield, Chislehurst, Farnborough, Orpington etc.

FOLKESTONE & DOVER
including: Aylesham, Deal, Dymchurch, Eastry, Hythe, New Romney, Walmer etc.

GRAVESEND & DARTFORD
including: Greenhithe, Hartley, Meopham, New Ash Green, Swanley, Swanscombe etc.

MAIDSTONE
including: Bearsted, Ditton, Headcorn, Snodland, Staplehurst etc.

MEDWAY & GILLINGHAM
including: Chatham, Hoo, Rainham, Rochester, Walderslade etc.

SEVENOAKS
including: Borough Green, Kemsing, Westerham, West Kingsdown etc.

SITTINGBOURNE & FAVERSHAM
including: Leysdown on Sea, Minster, Queenborough, Sheerness etc.

THANET & CANTERBURY
including: Herne Bay, Margate, Minster, Ramsgate, Sandwich, Whitstable etc.

TUNBRIDGE WELLS & TONBRIDGE
including: Cranbrook, Crowborough, Edenbridge, Hadlow, Hawkhurst, Paddock Wood, Southborough, Wadhurst etc.

For a complete title listing please visit our website
www.estate-publications.co.uk

CONTENTS

MINISTRATIVE DISTRICTS: pages 4-5

AZETTEER INDEX TO ROAD MAP: pages 6-7

OUNTY ROAD MAP: pages 8-11

OWN CENTRE STREET MAPS:

ford	page 12	Marden	34
ldenden	13	Margate	36
chington	14	Minster	37
rough Green	13	New Romney	38
adstairs	15	Northfleet	39
nterbury (Enlarged Centre)	16	Paddock Wood	40
aring	17	Queenborough	41
atham	18	Rainham	42
tonville	19	Ramsgate	43
nbrook	20	Rochester	44
rtford	21	Royal Tunbridge Wells (Enlarged Centre)	56
al	22	Saint Margarets at Cliffe	41
ver (Enlarged Centre)	23	Sandwich	45
enbridge	24	Sevenoaks	46
versham	25	Sheerness	47
lkestone (Enlarged Centre)	26	Sittingbourne	48
lingham	27	Snodland	49
avesend	28	Southborough	50
eenhithe	29	Staplehurst	51
dlow	17	Strood	52
mstreet	30	Swanley	53
rrietsham	30	Swanscombe	29
wkhurst	31	Tenterden	54
adcorn	31	Tonbridge	55
rne Bay	32	Westerham	57
the	33	Westgate on Sea	58
nham	32	Whitstable	59
dd	34	Woodchurch	60
idstone	35	Wye	60

DEX TO STREETS: page 61

Scale of street plans: 4 Inches to 1 Mile (unless otherwise stated)

COUNTY RED BOOKS

This atlas is intended for those requiring street maps of the historical and commercial centres of towns within the county. Each locality is normally presented on one or two pages and although, with many small towns, this space is sufficient to portray the whole urban area, the maps of large towns and cities are for centres only and are not intended to be comprehensive. Such coverage is offered in the Super and Local Red Book (see Page 2).

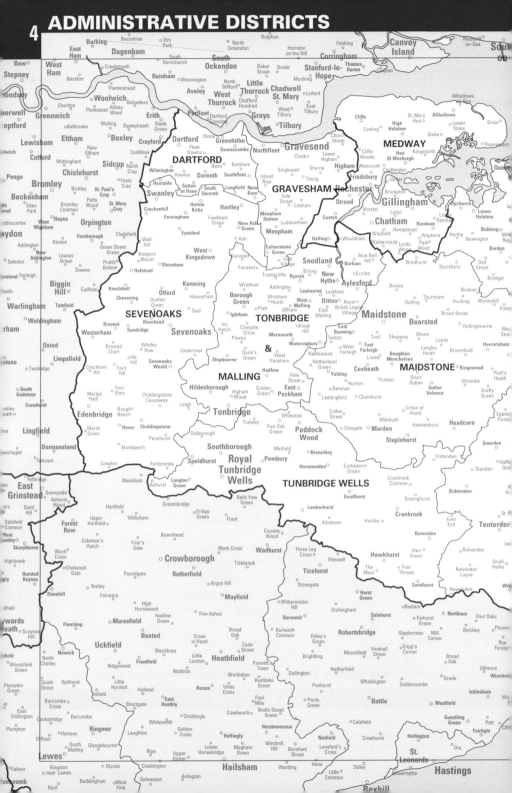

eeburyness

Minster
Warden
Eastchurch
Leysdown-on-Sea

Margate
Cliftonville
Birchington
Kingsgate
Westgate
-on-Sea
Reculver
St. Peter's
Broadstairs

Herne Bay
Tankerton
Hillborough
St. Nicholas
at Wade
Acol
Manston
Dumpton
Whitstable
Swalecliffe
Beltinge
Broomfield
Sarre
Ramsgate
THANET
Chestfield
Herne
Marshside
Monkton
Minster
Cliffs End
Seasalter
Maypole
Chislet
Conyer
Clapham
Hill
Hoath
West-
bourmouth
Teynham
Oare
Graveney
Yorkletts
Broad
Oak
Hersden
Upstreet
East
Stourmouth
Goodnestone
Dargate
Honey
Hill
Westbere
Grove
Preston
Westmarsh
Ospringe
Faversham
Hernhill
Tyler
Hill
Sturry
Ware
Great
Stonar
Painter's
Forstal
Blean
Stodmarsh
Elmstone
Hoaden
WALE
Boughton
Street
Dunkirk
Rough
Common
Fordwich
Wickhambreaux
Ash
Sandwich
ewnham
CANTERBURY
Littlebourne
Ickham
Wingham
Marshborough
Stone
Cross
Sheldwich
Harbledown
Staple
Woodnesborough
Eastling
Chartham
Hatch
Canterbury
Worth
Throwley
Selling
Old Wives
Lees
Thanington
Patrixbourne
Goodnestone
Eastry
Ham
Finglesham
Badlesmere
Chartham
Nackington
Bekesbourne
DOVER
Stalisfield
Green
Shottenden
Shalmsford
Street
Lower
Hardres
Bridge
Adisham
Chillenden
Knowlton
Betteshanger
Northbourne
Sholden
Leaveland
Chilham
Aylesham
Deal
Molash
Petham
Bishopsbourne
Kingston
Nonington
Tilmanstone
Great
Mongeham
Challock
Godmersham
Sole
Street
Upper Hardres
Court
Barham
Womenswold
Barfreston
Elvington
East
Studdal
Walmer
Charing
Boughton
Aluph
Bilting
Crundale
Waltham
Bossingham
Derringstone
Woolage
Green
Eythorne
Shepherdswell
or Sibertswold
Sutton
West
Langdon
Ripple
Ringwould
Kingsdown
Westwell
Boughton
Lees
Wye
Hassell
Street
Bodsham
Stelling
Minnis
Denton
Coldred
Lydden
Whitfield
Martin
East
Langdon
Martin
Mill
Hothfield
Kennington
Brook
Hastingleigh
Elmsted
Lymbridge
Green
Elham
Wootton
Temple
Ewell
Guston
West
Cliffe
St. Margaret's
at Cliffe
Ashford
Hinxhill
Brabourne
Rhodes
Minnis
Swingfield
Minnis
Ewell
Minnis
Buckland
Great Chart
Willesborough
Stowting
Alkham
West
Hougham
HFORD
Sevington
Brabourne
Lees
Lyminge
Densole
Dover
Mersham
Paddlesworth
Kingsnorth
Smeeth
Postling
Hawkinge
Cheeseman's
Green
Sellindge
Etchinghill
Channel
Tunnel
Terminal
Capel-
le-Ferne
Shadoxhurst
Stanford
Aldington
Frith
Newington
Cheriton
Aldington
Bromley
Green
Bonnington
SHEPWAY
Saltwood
Folkestone
Hamstreet
Bilsington
Lympne
Sandgate
rdington
Ruckinge
Hythe
Warehorne
Newchurch
Burmarsh
Snave
Dymchurch
idore
Snargate
St. Mary
in the Marsh
Brenzett
Ivychurch
St Marys Bay
Brookland
New Romney
st
ford
Old
Romney
Littlestone-on-Sea
Greatstone-on-Sea
Lydd
Camber
Lydd-on-Sea
Dungeness

County Boundary
District Boundary

Place	Ref
Acol	10 E3
Addington	8 D4
Adisham	10 D4
Aldington	11 C6
Aldington Frith	11 B6
Alkham	11 D5
Allhallows	8 E2
Allhallows-on-Sea	8 E2
Appledore	11 A7
Ash	8 C3
Ash	10 E4
Ashford	11 B5
Ashurst	9 B6
Aylesford	8 D4
Aylesham	10 D4
Badgers Mount	8 B3
Badlesmere	10 B4
Bapchild	10 A3
Barfreston	11 E5
Barham	11 D5
Bean	8 C3
Bearsted	8 E4
Bekesbourne	10 D4
Beltinge	10 D3
Benenden	9 E6
Benover	9 D5
Bethersden	11 A6
Betsham	8 C3
Betteshanger	10 E4
Bicknor	8 F4
Bidborough	9 C5
Biddenden	9 E6
Bilsington	11 B6
Bilting	11 B5
Birchington	10 E3
Birling	8 D4
Bishopsbourne	10 D4
Blean	10 C4
Blue Bell Hill	8 D3
Bobbing	8 F3
Bodsham	11 C5
Bonnington	11 B6
Borden	8 F3
Borough Green	8 C4
Borstal	8 D3
Bossingham	11 C5
Bough Beech	9 B5
Boughton Aluph	11 B5
Boughton Lees	11 B5
Boughton Monchelsea	8 E4
Boughton Street	10 C4
Boxley	8 E4
Brabourne	11 C5
Brabourne Lees	11 C5
Brasted	8 B4
Brasted Chart	8 B4
Bredgar	8 F4
Bredhurst	8 E4
Brenchley	9 D5
Brenzett	11 B7
Bridge	10 D4
Broad Oak	10 D4
Broad Street	8 E4
Broadstairs	10 F3
Bromley Green	11 B6
Brompton	8 E3
Brook	11 C5
Brookland	11 B7
Broomfield	8 E4
Broomfield	10 D3
Buckland	11 E5
Burham	8 D4
Burmarsh	11 C6
Canterbury	10 D4
Capel-le-Ferne	11 D6
Chainhurst	9 D5
Chalk	8 D3
Challock	11 B5
Channel Tunnel Terminal	11 D6
Charing	11 B5
Charing Heath	11 A5
Chart Sutton	9 E5
Chartham	10 C4
Chartham Hatch	10 C4
Chatham	8 E3
Chattenden	8 E3
Cheeseman's Green	11 B6
Cheriton	11 D6
Chestfield	10 C3
Chevening	8 B4
Chiddingstone	9 B5
Chiddingstone Causeway	9 B5
Chilham	10 B4
Chillenden	10 E4
Chislet	10 D3
Church Street	8 D2
Clapham Hill	10 C3
Claygate	9 D5
Claygate Cross	8 C4
Cliffe	8 D2
Cliffe Woods	8 D2
Cliffs End	10 E3
Cliftonville	10 F3
Cobham	8 D3
Coldred	11 E5
Collier Street	9 D5
Conyer	10 B3
Cooling	8 E2
Cowden	9 A6
Coxheath	9 D5
Cranbrook	9 E6
Cranbrook Common	9 E6
Crockenhill	8 B3
Crockham Hill	9 A5
Cross-at-Hand	9 E5
Crundale	11 C5
Culverstone Green	8 C3
Curtisden Green	9 D5
Cuxton	8 D3
Darenth	8 C3
Dargate	10 C4
Dartford	8 B2
Deal	10 F4
Densole	11 D5
Denton	11 D5
Derringstone	11 D5
Detling	8 E4
Ditton	8 D4
Doddington	10 A4
Dover	11 E6
Dumpton	10 F3
Dungeness	11 C8
Dunk's Green	8 C4
Dunkirk	10 C4
Dunton Green	8 B4
Dymchurch	11 C7
East Barming	8 D4
East End	9 E6
East Farleigh	8 D4
East Langdon	11 E5
East Malling	8 D4
East Peckham	9 D5
East Stourmouth	10 E3
East Studdal	11 E5
Eastchurch	10 B3
Eastling	8 B4
Eastry	10 E4
Eccles	8 D4
Edenbridge	9 A5
Egerton	11 A5
Egerton Forstal	11 A5
Elham	11 D5
Elmsted	11 C5
Elmstone	10 D4
Elvington	11 E5
Etchinghill	11 D6
Ewell Minnis	11 E5
Eynsford	8 B3
Eythorne	11 E5
Fairseat	8 C4
Farningham	8 B3
Faversham	10 B3
Fawkham Green	8 C3
Finglesham	10 E4
Five Oak Green	9 C5
Fleet Downs	8 C2
Folkestone	11 D6
Fordcombe	9 B6
Fordwich	10 D4
Four Elms	9 B5
Four Throws	9 E6
Frindsbury	8 D3
Frinsted	8 F4
Frittenden	9 E5
Gillingham	8 E3
Godmersham	11 B5
Golden Green	9 C5
Goodnestone	10 B4
Goodnestone	10 D4
Goudhurst	9 D6
Grafty Green	9 F5
Grain	8 F2
Graveney	10 C3
Gravesend	8 D2
Great Chart	11 B5
Great Mongeham	10 E4
Great Stonar	10 E4
Greatstone-on-Sea	11 C7
Greenhithe	8 C2
Grove	10 D4
Guston	11 E5
Hadlow	9 C5
Haffenden Quarter	9 F6
Hale Street	9 D5
Halfway Houses	10 A3
Halling	8 D3
Halstead	8 B4
Ham	1
Hamstreet	1
Harbledown	1
Harrietsham	
Hartley	8 D4
Hartley	9 E6
Hartlip	8 D4
Hassell Street	1
Hastingleigh	1
Hawkenbury	9 D5
Hawkhurst	
Hawkinge	1
Hawley	10 B3
Headcorn	10 B4
Heaverham	10 E4
Hempstead	8 D4
Herne	1
Herne Bay	1
Hernhill	1
Hersden	1
Hever	11 C5
Hextable	10 D4
High Halden	11 E5
High Halstow	11 D6
Higham	11 E5
Higham Wood	8 B3
Highsted	11 E5
Hildenborough	
Hillborough	1
Hinxhill	1
Hoaden	1
Hoath	1
Hollingbourne	10 E4
Honey Hill	1
Hoo Saint Werburgh	8 C2
Horsmonden	9 E6
Horton Kirby	9 B6
Hothfield	1
Hucking	
Hunton	
Hythe	1
Ickham	1
Ide Hill	
Iden Green	8 E3
Ightham	11 B5
Istead Rise	9 C5
Ivy Hatch	10 B4
Ivychurch	1
Iwade	1
Kemsing	10 C3
Kemsley	8 F2
Kenardington	1
Kennington	1
Kilndown	
King's Hill	10 E4
Kingsdown	1
Kingsgate	1
Kingsnorth	10 D4
Kingsnorth	11 E5
Kingston	1
Kingswood	9 C5
Knockholt	
Knowlton	1
Laddingford	8 D3
Lamberhurst	8 B4

gley Heath	9 E5	Newington	8 F3	Selling	10 B4	Tovil	8 E4
ton Green	9 B6	Newington	11 D6	Sevenoaks	8 B4	Toy's Hill	9 B5
field	8 D4	Newnham	10 A4	Sevenoaks Weald	9 B5	Trottiscliffe	8 C4
veland	10 B4	Nonington	10 E4	Sevington	11 B6	Tudeley	9 C5
ls	8 E4	Northbourne	10 E4	Shadoxhurst	11 B6	Tunstall	8 F4
h	9 B5	Northfleet	8 C2	Shalmsford Street	10 C4	Tyler Hill	10 C4
h Green	9 F6			Sheerness	10 A2		
ham	8 F4	**O**ad Street	8 F3	Sheldwich	10 B4	**U**lcombe	9 F5
ham Heath	9 F5	Oare	10 B3	Shepherdswell	11 D5	Underriver	8 B4
ourne	8 D4	Offham	8 D4	Shepway	8 E4	Upchurch	8 E3
down-on-Sea	10 B3	Old Romney	11 B7	Shipbourne	8 C4	Upnor	8 E3
on	9 E5	Old Wives Lees	10 C4	Sholden	10 F4	Upper Hardres Court	11 C5
Chart	11 A5	Ospringe	10 B4	Shoreham	8 B4	Upstreet	10 D3
ebourne	10 D4	Otford	8 B4	Shorne	8 D3		
stone-on-Sea	11 C7	Otham	8 E4	Shottenden	10 B4	**V**igo Village	8 D3
gfield	8 C3			Sibertswold	11 D5		
se	8 D4	**P**addlesworth	11 D6	Singlewell	8 D3	**W**ainscott	8 D3
ls Wood	8 E3	Paddock Wood	9 D5	Sissinghurst	9 E6	Walderslade	8 E3
er Halstow	8 F3	Painter's Forstal	10 B4	Sittingbourne	10 A3	Walmer	11 F5
er Hardres	10 C4	Park Wood	8 E3	Small Hythe	9 F6	Waltham	11 C5
er Higham	8 D2	Patrixbourne	10 D4	Smarden	9 F5	Warden	10 B3
er Rainham	8 E3	Pembury	9 C5	Smeeth	11 C6	Ware	10 E4
er Stoke	8 E2	Penshurst	9 B5	Snargate	11 B7	Warehorne	11 B6
desdown	8 D3	Petham	11 C5	Snave	11 B7	Warren Street	10 A4
on	8 E3	Platt	8 C4	Snodland	8 D4	Wateringbury	8 D4
d	11 B7	Platt's Heath	9 F5	Sole Street	8 D3	Wayfield	8 E3
den	11 D5	Plaxtol	8 C4	Sole Street	11 C5	Well Hill	8 B3
d-on-Sea	11 C7	Pluckley	9 F5	South Darenth	8 C3	West Cliffe	11 E5
bridge Green	11 C5	Postling	11 C6	Southborough	9 C5	West Farleigh	8 D4
inge	11 D5	Preston	10 D4	Southfleet	8 C3	West Hougham	11 E5
pne	11 C6			Speldhurst	9 B5	West Kingsdown	8 C3
sted	10 A4	**Q**ueenborough	10 A3	Stalisfield Green	10 B4	West Langdon	11 E5
				Standen	9 F6	West Malling	8 D4
dstone	8 D4	**R**ainham	8 E3	Stanford	11 C6	West Peckham	8 C4
mans Hill	9 F5	Ramsgate	10 F3	Stansted	8 C3	West Stourmouth	10 E3
ston	10 E3	Reading Street	11 A6	Staple	10 E4	West Street	10 A4
den	9 E5	Reculver	10 D3	Staplehurst	9 E5	Westbere	10 D4
gate	10 E3	Redbrook Street	11 A6	Stelling Minnis	11 C5	Westerham	8 B4
kbeech	9 B5	Rhodes Minnis	11 C5	Stockbury	8 E4	Westgate-on-Sea	10 E3
lpit Hill	9 A5	Ringwould	11 E5	Stodmarsh	10 D4	Westmarsh	10 E4
sh Green	9 A5	Ripple	11 E5	Stoke	8 E2	Westwell	11 B5
shborough	10 E4	Riverhead	8 B4	Stone	8 C2	Whetsted	9 C5
shside	10 D3	Rochester	8 D3	Stone	11 A7	Whitfield	11 E5
tin	11 E5	Rodmersham	10 A4	Stowting	11 C5	Whitley Row	8 B4
tin Mill	11 E5	Rolvenden	9 F6	Strood	8 D3	Whitstable	10 C3
field	9 C5	Rolvenden Layne	9 F6	Sturry	10 D4	Wichling	10 A4
rpole	10 D3	Rough Common	10 C4	Sundridge	8 B4	Wickhambreaux	10 D4
pham	8 D3	Royal British Legion Village		Sutton	11 E5	Wigmore	8 E3
pham Station	8 C3		8 D4	Sutton at Hone	8 B3	Willesborough	11 B5
eworth	8 C4	Royal Tunbridge Wells	9 C6	Sutton Valence	9 E5	Wilmington	8 B3
sham	11 B6	Ruckinge	11 B6	Swalecliffe	10 C3	Wingham	10 D4
bush	9 E5	Ryarsh	8 D4	Swanley	8 B3	Wittersham	11 A7
stead	8 F4			Swanscombe	8 C2	Womenswold	11 D5
on Regis	8 F3	**S**t Margaret's at Cliffe	11 F5	Swingfield Minnis	11 D5	Woodchurch	11 A6
ster	10 B2	St Mary Hoo	8 E2			Woodnesborough	10 E4
ster	10 E3	St Mary in the Marsh	11 C7	**T**ankerton	10 C3	Woolage Green	11 D5
ash	10 B4	St Marys Bay	11 C7	Temple Ewell	11 E5	Wootton	11 D5
nkton	10 E3	St Michaels	9 F6	Tenterden	9 F6	Wormshill	8 F4
		St Nicholas at Wade	10 D3	Teston	8 D4	Worth	10 E4
kington	10 C4	St Peter's	10 F3	Teynham	10 A3	Wouldham	8 D3
lestead	8 D4	Saltwood	11 D6	Thamesport	8 F2	Wrotham	8 C4
lestead Green	8 D4	Sandgate	11 D6	Thanington	10 C4	Wrotham Heath	8 C4
v Ash Green	8 C3	Sandhurst	9 E7	The Moor	9 E7	Wye	11 C5
v Barn	8 C3	Sandwich	10 E4	Thong	8 D3		
v Hythe	8 D4	Sarre	10 E3	Throwley	10 B4	**Y**alding	9 D5
v Romney	11 B7	Seal	8 C4	Thurnham	8 E4	Yorkletts	10 C3
vchurch	11 B6	Seasalter	10 C3	Tilmanstone	10 E4		
venden	9 E7	Sellindge	11 C6	Tonbridge	9 C5		

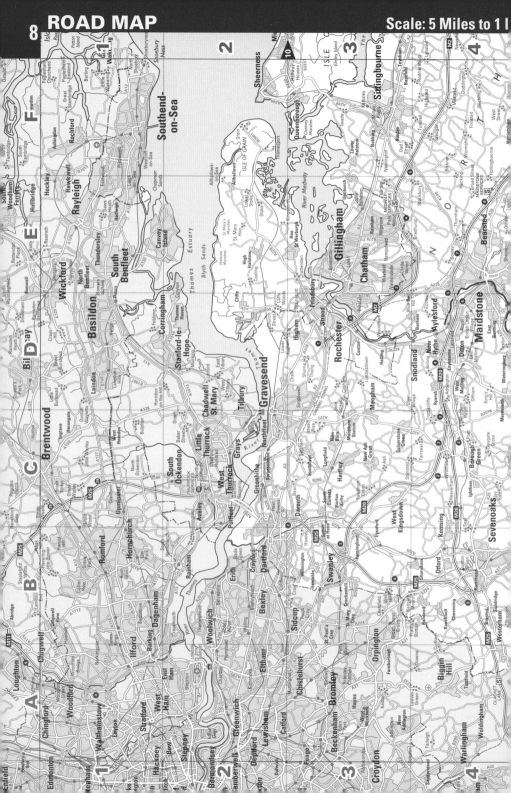

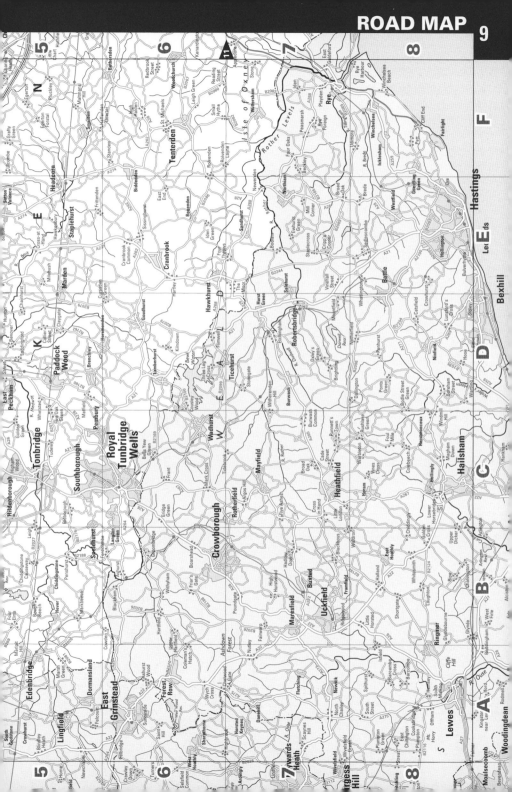

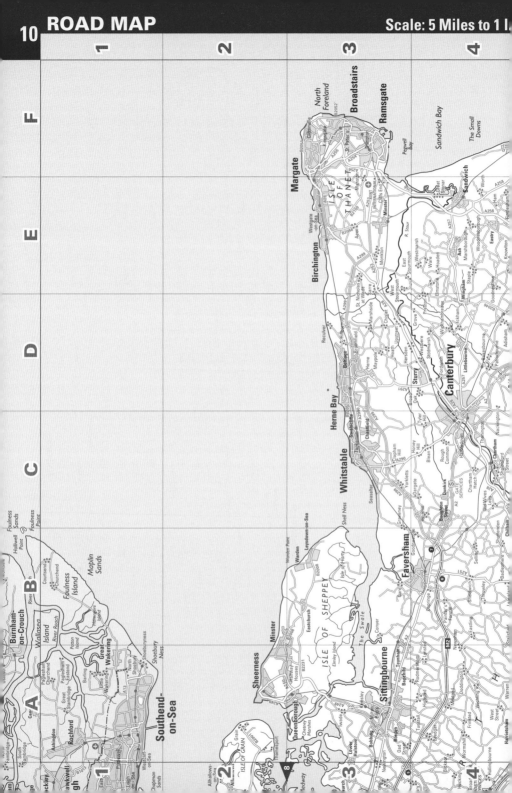

ZEEBRUGGE OSTEND DUNKIRK
CALAIS

South Foreland

Dover

CHANNEL TUNNEL

St. Margaret's at Cliffe
St. Margaret's Bay

Kingsdown

Sutton
West Langdon
East Langdon
Guston
Martin Mill
West Cliffe

Ripple
Maydensole

Whitfield

Buckland
Coldred

Temple Ewell
Ewell

Shepherdswell or Sibertswold
Colbred

Woolage Green

Wootton

Ewell Minnis

West Hougham

East Wear Bay

Folkestone

Denton

Alkham

Swingfield Minnis

Capel-le-Ferne

Lydden

Hawkinge

Denton

Drellingore

Ottinge

CHANNEL TUNNEL

Channel Tunnel Terminal

Elham

Newington

Hythe

Swingfield Minnis

Paddlesworth

Lyminge

Sandgate

Etchinghill

Rhodes Minnis

Stelling Minnis

Posting

M20

Saltwood

Dibgate

Elmsted

Lympne

Dymchurch

Stowting

Hastingleigh

Lymbridge Green

Stanford

Postling

St Marys Bay

Brabourne

Sellindge

Wye

Hinxhill

Brabourne Lees

Smeeth

Stanford

Littlestone-on-Sea

Boughton Aluph

Brook

Mersham

Bilsington

St. Mary in the Marsh

Greatstone-on-Sea

Crundale

Hothfield

Hinxhill

Aldington

Ruckinge

Lydd-on-Sea

Romney Marsh

Wye

Dungeness

Wythall

Boughton Lees

Kennington

Willesborough

Bromley Green

Newchurch

Hamstreet

Snave

Ivychurch

New Romney

Lydd

Walland Marsh

Ashford

Great Chart

Shadoxhurst

Warehorne

Brookland

Brenzett

Old Romney

Kingsnorth

Bethersden

Woodchurch

Appledore

Stone

Fairfield

East Guldeford

Rye

Little Chart

Redbrook Street

Reading Street

Kenardington

Witttersham

Playden

Rye Harbour

Winchelsea Beach

Pluckley

Leigh Green

Tenterden

Small Hythe

Isle of Oxney

Iden

Peasmarsh

Winchelsea

Cliff End

Egerton

High Halden

St. Michaels

Wittersham

Stone

Iden

Rolvenden

Playden

Camber

Egerton Forstal

Biddenden

Rolvenden Layne

Beckley

Rye Foreign

Udimore

Icklesham

Fairlight

Pluckley Thorne

R. Brede

Rother Levels

Fair Oaks

Smarden

Headcorn

Iddenden

Standen

Rolvenden Layne

R. Rother

Grafty Green

Boughton Malherbe

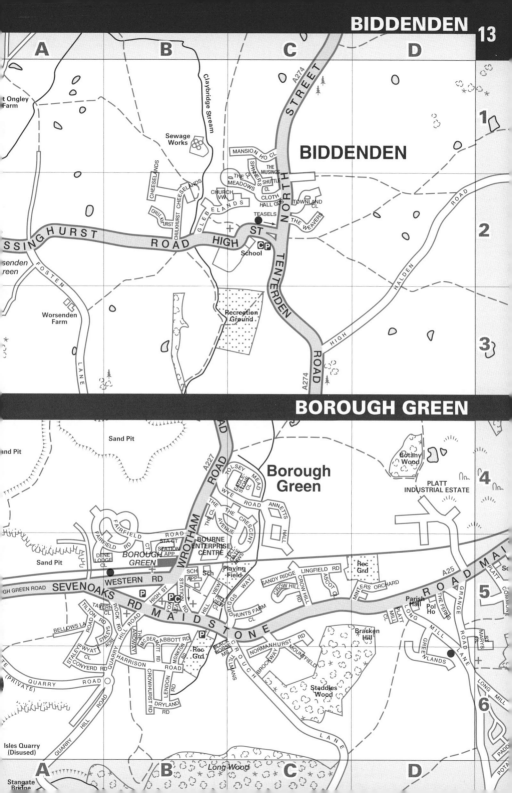

A B C D

1

2

3

BIDDENDEN

t Ongley
Farm

Claybridge Stream

Sewage
Works

MANSION HO CL

CHEESELANDS

CHILHURST
CHEESELANDS

CHILHURST
CHEESELANDS

GLEBELANDS

THE
MEADOWS

SPANTERS

THE
MUSINGS

SHUTTLE
CL

CLOTH
HALL GDNS

CHURCH
VW

TOWNLAND
CL

THE WEAVERS

TEASELS

ST

A274

STREET

NORTH

TENTERDEN

ROAD

HIGH

ROAD

HALDEN

senden
een

FOSTEN

SSINGHURST

ROAD

HIGH

CP

School

LANE

Worsenden
Farm

Recreation
Ground

A274

HIGH

**Borough
Green**

A B C D

4

5

6

and Pit

Sand Pit

A227

ROAD

WROTHAM

Botany
Wood

PLATT
INDUSTRIAL ESTATE

TOLSEY
MEAD

WYE
ROAD

THE
CL

ANNETTS

HALL

FAIRFIELD

FAIRFIELD
RD

ROAD

BOROUGH
GREEN

STA ST

STATION
APP

BOURNE
ENTERPRISE
CENTRE

THE
AVENUE

THE
CRESCENT

CL

DENE
LODGE
CL

Sand Pit

WESTERN RD

SCH
APP

Sch

VIEW
CL

VIEW
CL

Playing
Field

SANDY RIDGE

LINGFIELD RD

CROW HILL RD

ASCOT

Rec
Grd

MINTERS ORCHARD

A25

ROAD

MAI

PLATT

GH GREEN ROAD

SEVENOAKS

RD

MAIDSTONE

HIGH ST

STATION
RD

HILL

BIGGS WAY

WAY

HUNTS FARM

CROW HILL

Parish
Hall

Pol
Ho

THE FERNS

GRANGE ROAD

FLATT
MILL

LONG

GREENLANDS

MILL

ROAD

ST
MARYS

TAVERN
CL

ROCK RD

STEYNING

LANDWAY

MCDERMOTT RD

ABBOTT RD

MCMTN

BLACK
HORSE

Rec
Grd

NORMANHURST
RD

MOUNTFIELD

Bracken
Hill

LONG
MILL
LANE

BELLOWS LA

TILTON ROAD

SWYAT
CL

STALEY
CL

CONYERD RD

QUARRY HILL ROAD

HARRISON
ROAD

CROWHURST RD

LENDON
ROAD

DRYLAND
RD

CROUCH

ST
RICHMANS

BROOKWAY

Staddles
Wood

LANE

(PRIVATE)

QUARRY

ROAD

QUARRY HILL

Isles Quarry
(Disused)

Long Wood

POTT

PADD

Stangate
Bridge

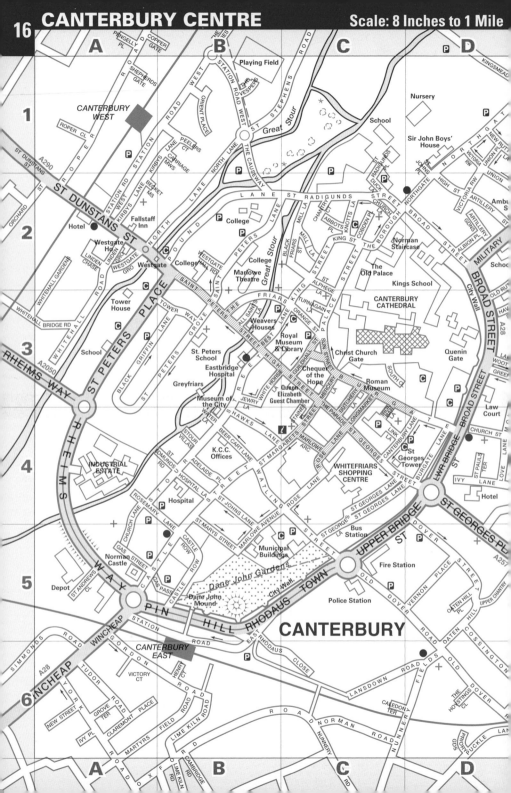

CANTERBURY

A **B** **C** **D**

Charing Hill

Pilgrim's Way

BOWL ROAD

THE WIND

A252

1

MAIDSTONE LANE

ROAD

NORTHERN BY-PASS

CHARING

HILL

PILGRIMS WAY

North Downs Way

CHARING HILL

SAYER ROAD

Fire Sta RD

WHELER

CENTENARY WAY

CLEARMONT DR

DOWNS ROAD

THE WIND

Charing

LANE

WAY

2

MAIDSTONE

SCHOOL ROAD

Cemy

Charing C.E Prim Sch

MONKS

HIGH STREET

PETT

MARKET PL

Library

P

WOODBROOK

TOLL

e Hook arm

Surgery

Hall

HITHER FIELD

P

CHARING

PLUCKLEY RD

STA

BURLEIGH RD

PILGRIMS CT

ASHFORD

OLD

THE MOAT

THE

Pavilion

Arthur Baker Recreation Ground

P

Pym House

WESTWELL LA

Pett Place

3

ROAD

A20

A **B** **C** **D**

COMMON ROAD

Hotel

LANE

BROADWATERS

STEERS PLACE

CARPENTERS

LOWEWOOD DR

VALLEY DR

PALMERS BROOK

MAIDSTONE

A26

ROAD

P

4

CEMETERY

Hope Farm

THE PADDOCK

Recreation Ground

HADLOW PK

NORTON

Cemy

Little Goblands Farm

Bourne Mill

CARPENTERS

MILL VW

FREEHOLD

HOPE AV

HOPE

Village Hall

MARSHALL GDNS

MARSH GDNS

GREAT ELMS

Pond

JAMES PL

PARK VILLAS

LANE

5

River Bourne

WATER

SLIPPER

TWYFORD

TAINTER

TWYFORD ROAD

THE CHERRY ORCH

SMITHERS CL

SPA CL

Hadlow

MONTENVIN CL

CAXTON LA

BROOK-FIELDS

CHESFIELD CL

Court Lane Farm

Bourne Grange Farm

Hadlow College of Agriculture & Horticulture

BOURNE GRANGE LANE

TOBY GDNS

THE MALTINGS

MALTINGS

MALTIN GS

LANE

KENWARD

School

MUS Lby

CHURCH SQUARE

HALSTOW

COURT

APPLE-TONS

THE COASTAL

COURT LA PL

CEMETERY

GOBLANDS FARM INDUSTRIAL ESTATE

Broadview Gardens

TONBRIDGE ROAD

HIGH ST

MAIDSTONE

CASTLE TER

COURT

LANE

VICTORIA RD

COURT

6

Faulkners Farm

A26

BLACKM

Bourne Bridge

HADLOW CASTLE & Folly Tower

Nurseries

LANE COURT

A **B** **C** **D**

RO D

A20

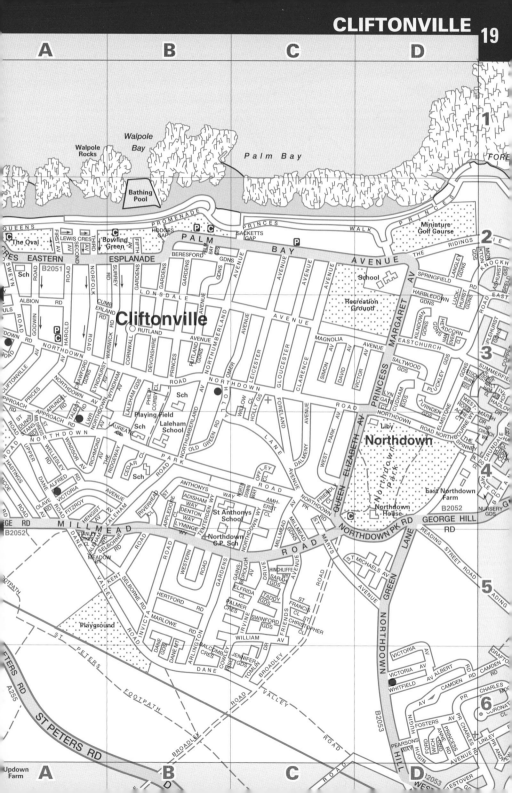

A   B   C   D

Walpole Rocks

Walpole Bay

Palm Bay

FORE

1

Bathing Pool

PROMENADE

QUEENS

The Oval

Miniature Golf Course

HODGES GAP

PALM

SACKETTS GAP

PRINCES WALK

THE RIDINGS

KNOCKH

2

FIRST AV

LEWIS CRES

THIRD AV

Bowling Green

FIFTH

BERESFORD

BAY

AVENUE

EASTERN

ESPLANADE

B2051

SCH

NORFOLK RD

SURREY RD

GARDENS

GARDENS

GARDENS

GDNS

BAY AV

GDNS

School

SPRINGFIELD

LANGLEY GDNS

HURST RD

MONKTON

EAST

ALBION RD

GODWIN RD

CUMBERLAND

LONSDALE

AVENUE

Recreation Ground

HARBLEDOWN GDNS

LUCK RD

ADCORN GDNS

KILNDOWN GDNS

IPLEHURST

SUMMERFIE

3

Cliftonville

RUTLAND

DEVONSHIRE

PRINCES

RUTLAND GDNS

NORTHUMBERLAND

AVENUE

LEICESTER

MAGNOLIA

GLOUCESTER

CLARENCE

SIMON AV

DAVID AV

VICTOR AV

AVENUE

EASTCHURCH

SALTWOOD GDS

PLUCKLEY GDS

CUDHAM GDNS

WEST-

MARSH

CHURCH

DOWN RD

NORTHDOWN AV

PRICES AV

CRAWFORD GDNS

LYNHURST AV

WARWICK RD

HAROLD RD

CORNWALL RD

PHILIP CL

CORBY CL

Sch

ROAD

WILLOW

HOLLY GS

FORELAND

Sch

Playing Field

Laleham School

LALEHAM GDS

OLD GREEN RD

NORTHUMBERLAND

PARK

Sch

LANE

DALMENY

WEST PARK

ROAD

LYN GATE

CUDHAM GDNS

NORTHDOWN

TURNDEN GDNS

ELMSTONE

Liby

Northdown

THE SPINNEY

CRUNDALE

4

NORTHDOWN

APPROACH

TALBOT RD

WYNDHAM RD

THE RIDGEWAY

CEDAR RD

LAUREATE

RICHMOND

Sch

ANTHONYS

ADISHAM WAY

DENTON WY

St Anthonys School

AMH-ERST CL

Northdown House

East Northdown Farm

B2052

APPLE CL

MAPLE CL

NURSERY GDS

WINDSOR RD

ALFRED RD

VICTORIA RD

FITZROY RD

RIVERHEAD

APPLEDORE

WAY

LYMINGE WY

TENTERDEN WY

Northdown C.P. Sch

MILLMEAD AVENUE

NORTHDOWN PK

QUEEN ELIZABETH AV

GEORGE HILL

George Hill RD

NORTHDOWN PK RD

READING STREET ROAD

5

OLAVE RD

MILLMEAD

HASTINGS RD

UPPER DANE RD

HENGIST RD

LALEHAM

DANE

SELBORNE RD

MEADOW

WESTERN

ROAD

HERTFORD

GARDENS

DRIVE

HINCHLIFFE RD

SARA GDS

ELFRIDA CL

TADDY CL

ST FRANCIS

ST CHRISTOPHER AV

ST MICHAELS AV

NORTHDOWN HILL

B2052

B2052

MILL

MEAD

VALLEY

KENT RD

SELBORNE RD

INVICTA

MARLOWE

DANE

DANE

ARLINGTON

DANE MT

BALCOMBE CRES

COWLEY

FISHER

JENNIFER

ROAD

PALMER CRES

RVINE

SWINFORD GDS

FRIENDS AV

WILLIAM

TOMLIN RD

BROADLEY

ROAD

VALLEY

VICTORIA AV

WHITFIELD

VICTORIA AV

CAMDEN RD

CAMDEN RD

CHARLES CL

Playground

ST PETERS

FOOTPATH

BROADLEY ROAD

REE

FOSTERS AV

HUGIN AV

PEARSONS WAY

ANNE RD

PRINCESS

EDEN

LINLEY RD

CORONATI

6

A255

ST PETERS RD

Updown Farm

A   B   C   D

Temple Hill

Dartford Fresh Marshes

RIVERSIDE
INDUSTRIAL
ESTATE

VICTORIA
INDUSTRIAL
PARK

New Town

WEST HILL

DARTFORD

Central
Park

River Darent

Brooklands
Lake

Leisure
Centre

Oakfield
Park

QUESTOR
TRADING
ESTATE

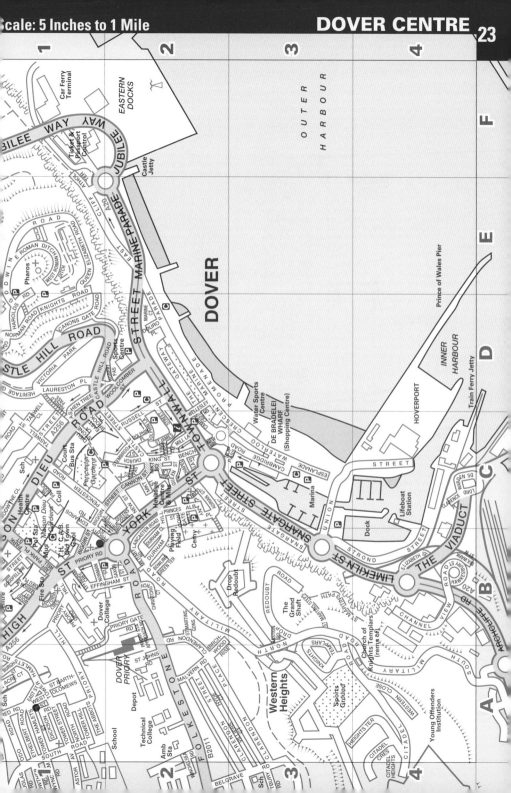

A B C D

Scamperdale

Gaywood Farm

1

HOMESTEAD RD

FAIRMEAD RD

Swan Lane Farm

Marlpit Hill

OAKFIELD RD

HILDERS CL

HILL CREST RD

HIGHFIELDS ROAD

ELM COTTS

ASHCOMBE DR

BROWN INGS

2

MARLHURST

HILDERS LANE

MEADOW LANE

SWAN LANE

MARLPIT WAY

RIDGE WY

SWAN

RIDGE

SWAN RIDGE

LANE ROAD

FOUR ELMS

Mowshur

Foc Gr

ALBION

EDENBRIDGE

SUNNYSIDE

CROWN ROAD

Breezehurst Farm

Hamsell Mead Farm

STATION WY

FIRCROFT

WY

MALLARD WY

HERON

KESTREL CL

OXFIELD STACKFIELD

ROWFIELD

STONEYFIELD

3

CROUCH HOUSE ROAD

St BRELADES CT Caravan Park

ENTERPRISE WAY

GREAT RD

INDUSTRIAL ESTATE

INDUSTRIAL ESTATE

COMMERCE WY

FIRCROFT WAY

WOODLAND

1

2

SPEEDWELL CL

BRIAR CL

FOXGLOVE CLOVER WY

WATERSIDE

SMITHFIELD

Sewage Works

Spitals Cross

NEWHOUSE TER

FOUR

PLOVER CL

3

4

WAYSIDE DR

FARMSTEAD

PLOUGH CL

HARROW

SKINNERS

HOPGARDEN CL

1 WOODPECKER CL
2 SORRELL CL
3 BROOK CT
4 TEMPLARS CT

4

GRESHAMS WY

CHILTERNHURST

GOODWIN CL

ORCHARD

TORCHARD

HOLLY COTTS

CROUCH HO COTTS

CEDAR

PARK

HAW THORN CL

MOLES MEAD

WELLINGTONIA WY

WESTWAYS

Eden Valley School

Skinners Farm

Edenbridge Golf & Country Club

CHESTNUT DRIVE

STANBRIDGE DRIVE

PINE GROVE

PARK VIEW CL

PENLEE CL

EDENBRIDGE TOWN

Edenbridge

Crouch House Green

Edenbridge Leisure Centre & Swimming Pool

Hall

STATION APPROACH

GORDON HENRY HO

HEADLEY GRANGE

CLOSE

GREENFIELD

Clinic

STANGROVE ROAD

RATLAND

Sch

CROFT LA

FORGE

FRANT CT

CROFT

CP

P

Cemy

CHURCH FIELD

QUEENS

CROFT

THE PLAT

5

SPRINGFIELD ROAD

CROUCH HOUSE ROAD

MANOR RD

MANOR

STANGROVE

SKEYNES FIELDED RD

MANOR GDNS

ASH CL

MANOR GDNS

LINGFIELD ROAD

BARN HAWE

THE LINES

Libry

Council Offices

LEATHER MARKET

S/store

Mkt

THE SQ

CHURCH ST

CHURCH STREET

RIVERSIDE CT

RIVERSIDE

STREET

Skeynes Park

TANNERS MEAD

COOMBE FIELD

LUCILINA DR

DOBBETS CL

COBBETS WY

PENN

MONT

AVIGNAN WY

Fire Sta

River Eden

C

6

LINGFIELD ROAD

Recreation Ground

Mill Race

KATHERINE RD

VICTORIA RD

VICTORIA CL

Mill Hill COTTS

ASHBY'S

ROBINS WAY

HEVER

MILL HILL

EDENBRIDGE TRADING CENTRE

WARSOP IND EST

RO

Kent Brook

WATERLAKES

HOSPITAL

B2026

MEAD RD

A B C D

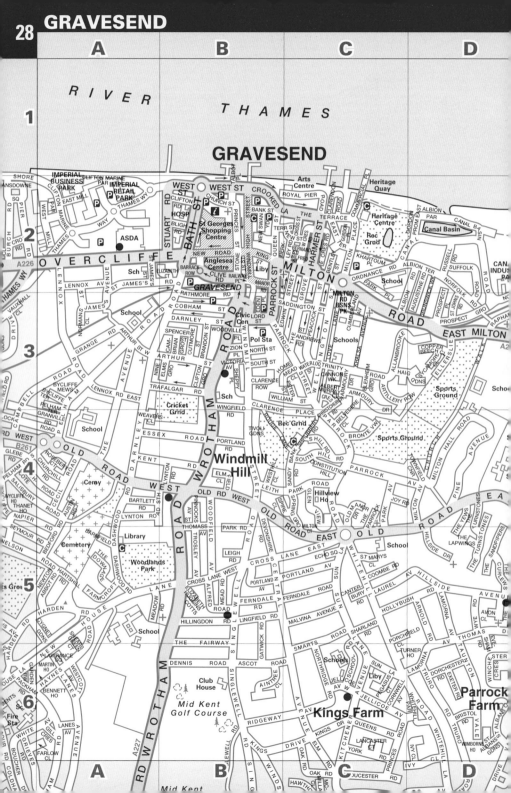

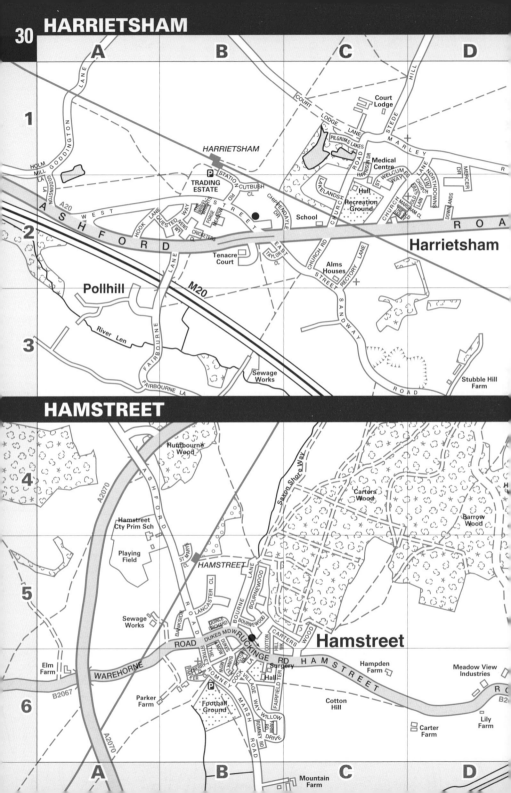

A **B** **C** **D**

1

HARRIETSHAM

Court Lodge

PILGRIMS LAKES

COURT LODGE LANE

STEDE HILL

MARLEY LANE

Medical Centre

TRADING ESTATE

STATION RD

CUTBUSH CL

CHIPPENDAYLE DR

LAKELANDS

Hall

Recreation Ground

WELCUM WAY

CHURCH LANE

NORTHDOWNS

MERCER DR

SONY WAY

HOLM MILL LA

GODDINGTON LANE

A20

WEST

HOOK LANE

DUESTED WAY

FORGE MEADW

THE WRIGHT

CRICKETERS

School

CHURCH RD

MARSHAM CL

ROA D

2

ASHFORD

Tenacre Court

EAST STREET

TAYLORS CL

CHURCH STREET

Alms Houses

RECTORY LANE

Harrietsham

Pollhill

M20

FAIRBOURNE LANE

SANDWAY

3

River Len

FAIRBOURNE LA

Sewage Works

ROAD

Stubble Hill Farm

Huntbourne Wood

ASHFORD RD

A2070

Saxon Shore Way

Carters Wood

Barrow Wood

4

Hamstreet Cty Prim Sch

Playing Field

HAMSTREET

BOURNE LANE

BOURNEWOOD

CARTERS WOOD

5

Sewage Works

BANKSIDE

ROAD

LANCASTER CL

DURICE ORCHARD

DUKES MD

BOURNEWOOD

WRUKINGE

COTTON HILL

CARTERS RD

Hamstreet

Elm Farm

WAREHORNE

ROAD

THE STREET

STEVENS

RUMWOOD

BOURNE

KNOCK

VILLAGE WAY

WILLOW

FAIRFIELD TER

Surgery

Hall

HAMSTREET RD

Hampden Farm

Meadow View Industries

R O

B2067

6

Parker Farm

Football Ground

ROMNEY STREET

MARSH ROAD

WILLOW DRIVE

Cotton Hill

Carter Farm

Lily Farm

B2

A2070

A **B** **C** **D**

Mountain Farm

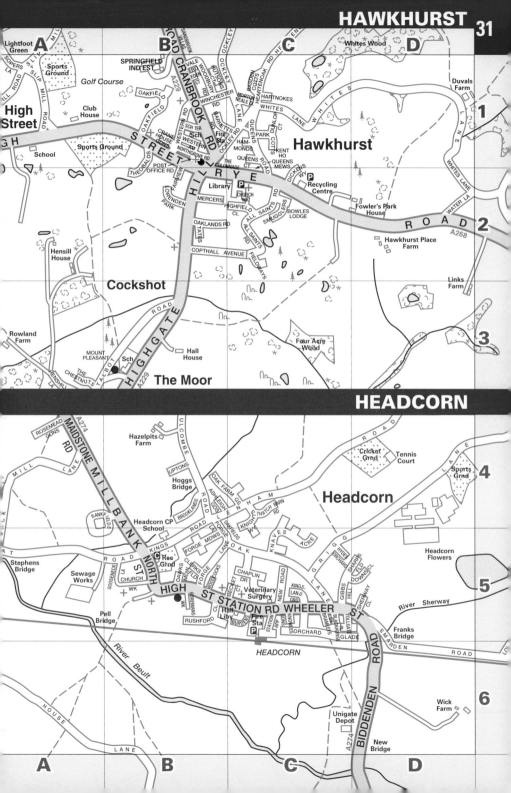

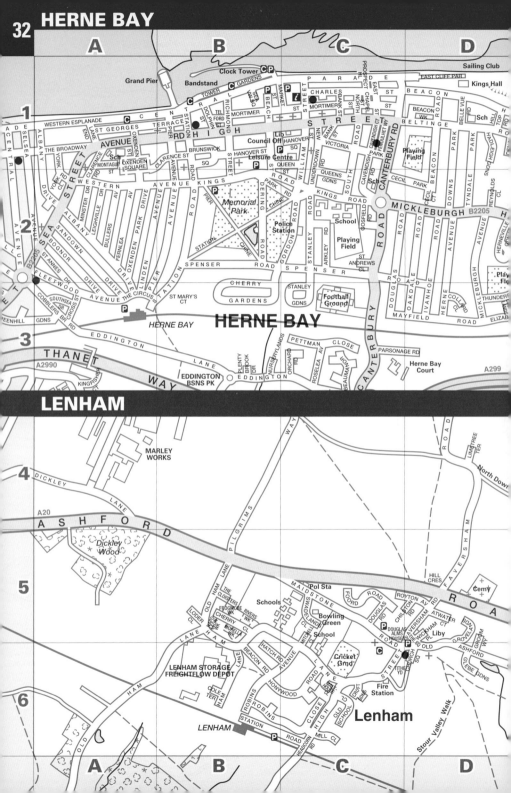

LENHAM

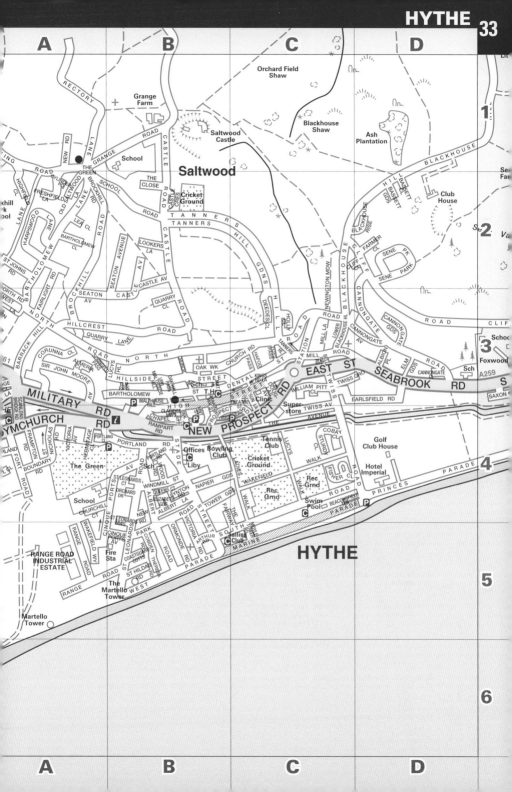

A **B** **C** **D**

1

Orchard Field
Shaw

Grange
Farm

Saltwood
Castle

Blackhouse
Shaw

Ash
Plantation

School

THE
GREEN

THE
CLOSE

Saltwood

Cricket
Ground

Club
House

2

Seaton Avenue

Quarry
Cl

Hillcrest

Quarry Lane

Newington Mdw

Sene Pk

Sene Park

School

Foxwood
Sch

3

East St

Seabrook Rd

Military Rd

Ymchurch Rd

New Prospect Rd

Dental

Clinic

Super
store

William Pitt

Earlsfield Rd

The Green

School

Offices Bowling
Club

Liby

Cricket
Ground

Tennis
Club

Wakefield

Rec
Grnd

Rec
Grnd

Golf
Club House

Hotel
Imperial

Parade

Swim
Pool

Parade

Princes

4

Range Road
Industrial
Estate

Fire
Sta

The
Martello
Tower

Sailing
Club

Parade

HYTHE

5

Martello
Tower

6

A **B** **C** **D**

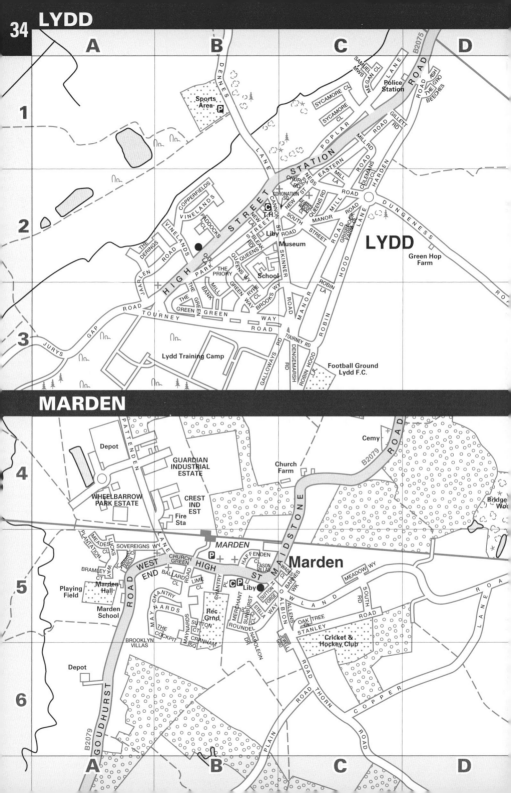

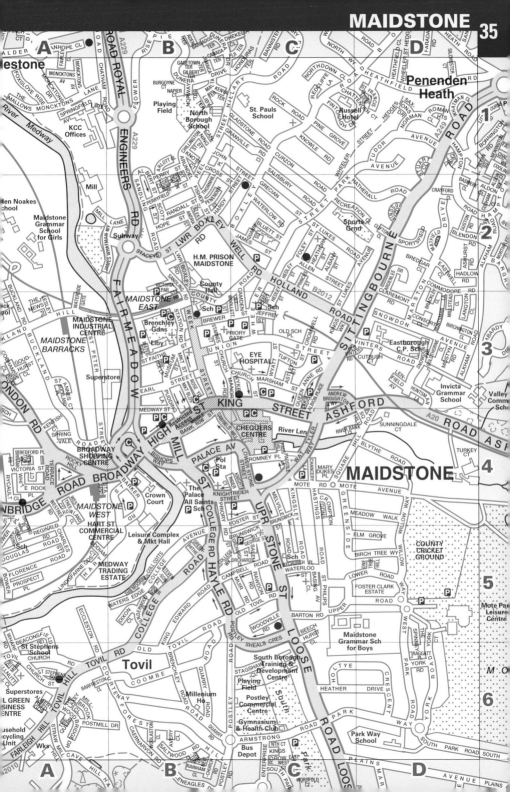

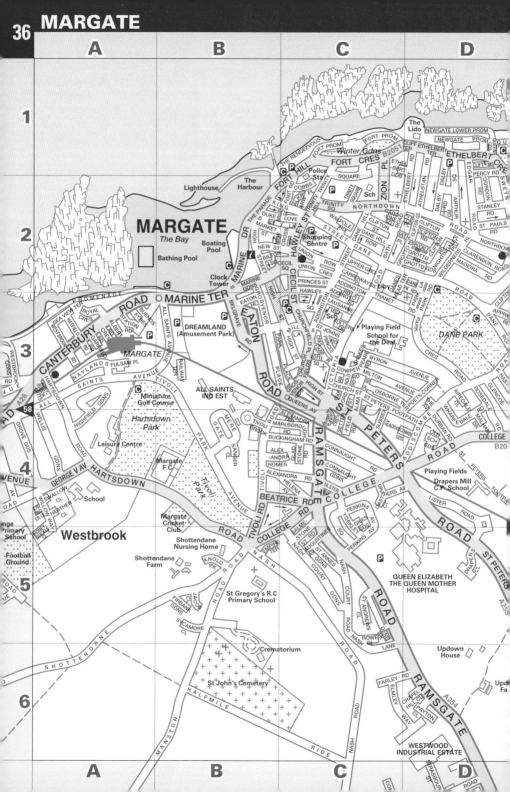

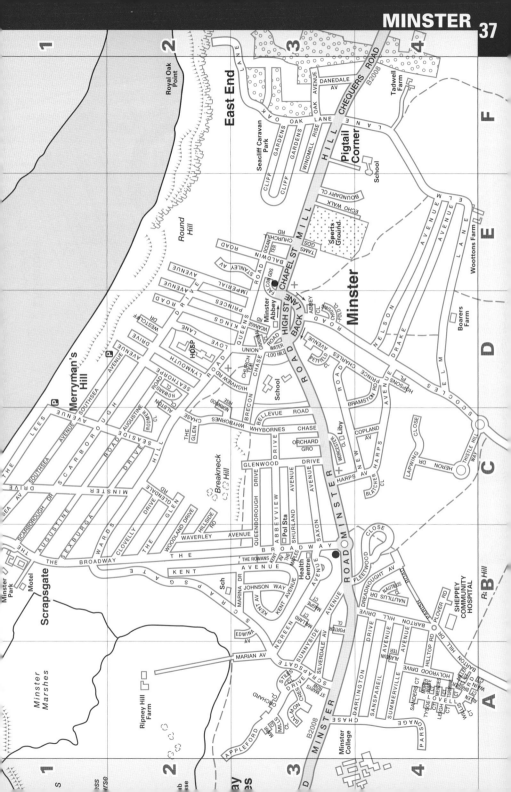

Minster

East End

Scrapsgate

Merryman's Hill

Pigtail Corner

Round Hill

Minster Marshes

Ripney Hill Farm

Breakneck Hill

Tadwell Farm

Woottons Farm

Boarers Farm

SHEPPEY COMMUNITY HOSPITAL

Minster College

Minster Park

Royal Oak Point

Seacliff Caravan Park

Sports Ground

Minster Abbey

Health Centre

Pol Sta

School

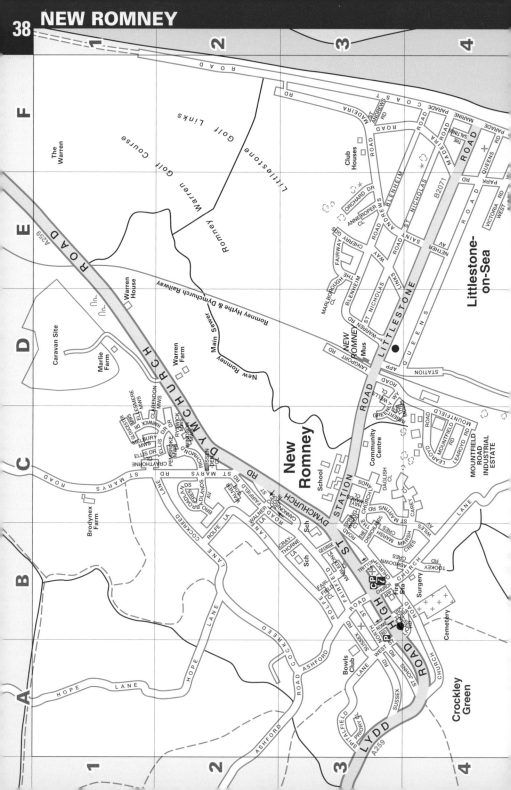

A **B** **C** **D**

R I V E R

T H A M E S

Wharf

Football Grnd

Gravesend Reach

Northfleet

1

Cement Industry Heritage Centre

GROVE RD

THE CREEK

Rosherville

STONEBRIDGE

FIELD EST

Huggens College

GROVE RD

WALLIS PK

COLLEGE RD

WARWICK PL

KINGSTON RD

FISHERMENS HILL

RAYNERS CT

HIVE LA

FISHFORD

Cement Works

CRETE

PORTLAND

HALL ROAD

CRETE

A226

FOUNTAIN

LOND

NORTHFLEET

RAILWAY ST

HAMERTON RD

HIGH

STATION RD

ROSE ST

FACTORY RD

LAWN RD

Sch

GRANBY ROAD

2

CHEVIOT HO
CLEVELAND HO
MALVERN HO
MENDIP HO
DE WARREN HO

ROSHERVILLE

RURAL VALE

GORDON RD

BERESFORD RD

BURNHAM

COLLINGTON CL

A226

EBBSFLEET WK

EBBSFLEET WK

STREET

A226

W KENT AV
N KENT AV
S KENT AV
COUN
CIL RD

HUNTLEY AV

BANKSIDE

CHURCH WALK

VICARAGE RD

THE HILL

DOVER

CHURCH PATH

LONDON

ROAD

THAMES

A226Q

Rec Grnd

Liby

LABURNUM GRD

LIME

AVENUE

ROBINIA AV

PLANE AV

MERMAID

MARITIME

GATE

WATERSIDE

CAPTAIN MWS

MARINERS WY

Sch

BEAUM

SPRINGHEAD ROAD

HARTFIELD

SHEPHERD ST

YORK RD

TOOLEY ST

BUCKINGHAM

School

VALE

DUDLEY RD

ROAD

B261

3

School

DOVER ROAD

DETLING

Sch

Perry Street

Depot

THAMES

WAY

COULTON AV

GOUGE AV

PRESTON RD

FIRST

AV

VALE

ROAD

AVENUE

PARK

AVENUE

ROSEBANK

DAVIS AV

FOXWOOD GRO

ALL SAINTS

PERRY

4

SPRINGHEAD ENTERPRISE PARK

Recreation Ground

Cemy

HALDANE

GDNS

CAMDEN

WATT

DALES

School

FALCON MWS

TUDOR

OLD PERRY ST

EARL RD

THOMAS MARGARETS

BEATRICE

MILROY AV

COOPER

SNELLING

ring head

MEADOW RD

ORCHARD RD

SPRINGVALE CT

SPRINGHEAD RD

GWYNN RD

MITCHELL

COLYER

Sports Centre

ROAD

Liby

Womwell Nursing Home

MILLFIELD

WOMBWELL GDNS

FORTHE

THE HEDGEROWS

SUMNERS

5

Superstore

WINGFIELD BANK

HALL

Wombwell Park

ROAD

COLYER

School

SAUNDERS CL

RIVERSIDE

CHIFFINCH

HATTON

WATLING

ST

WATLING

A2

NIACAE ROMAN TLEMENT (site of)

PEPPER HILL

HALL

ROAD

FLEET

VIKING

BOTOLPHS

PEPPER

DANES CL

JAMES PEPPER

SAXON CL

ROMAN

PAINTERS RD

MASEFIELD

CHAUCER CL

PICKWICK GDNS

PEP'S

DENNYSON

ASPDIN

MARCONI

JOHNSON CL

HOLM

DENE HOLM

COTS WOLD

CONSTABLE RD

PENNINE

CHILTERN WY

HOCKLEY

MAYER RD

TEN

6

B262

ROAD

STATION RD

HALL

ROAD

STREET

WATLI

School

HOG LA

GAINSBOROUGH

REMBRANDT

DRIVE

LANDSEER

ROMNEY

HILLARY

PARKFIELD

KENDAL

MULBERRY

CHERIN

HEN

A **B** **C** **D**

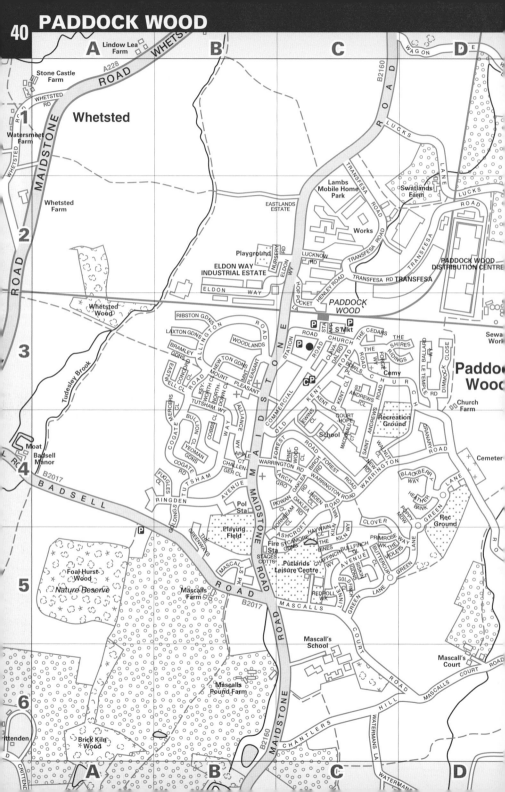

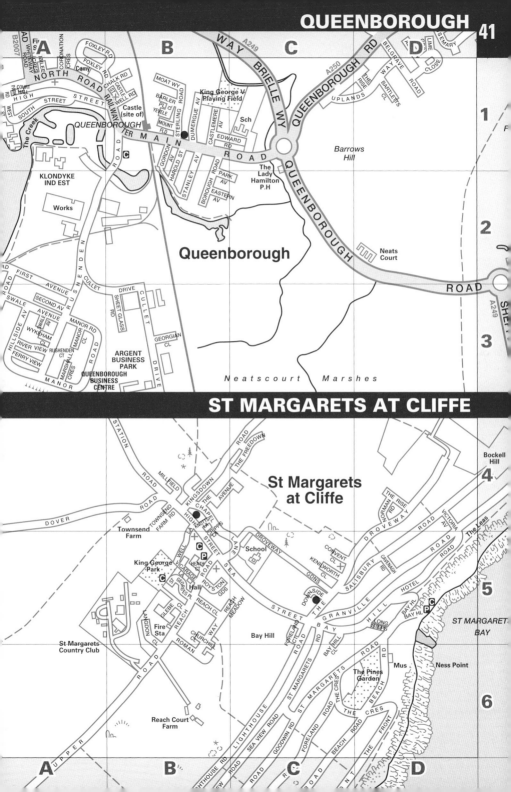

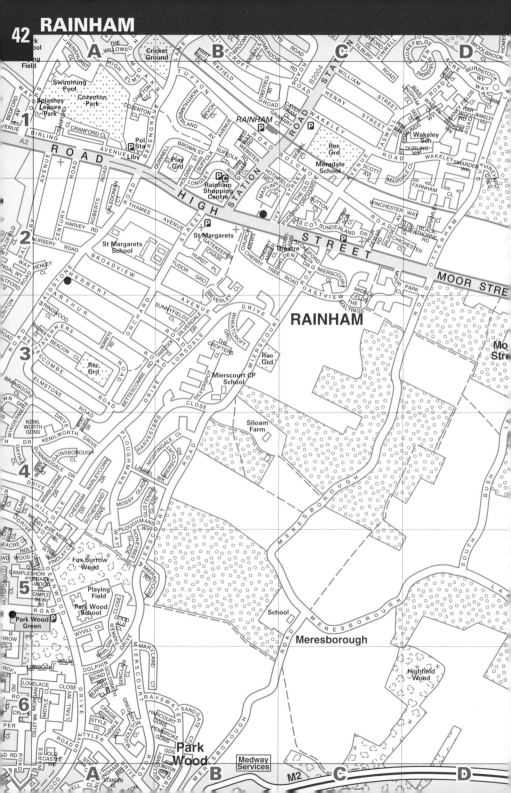

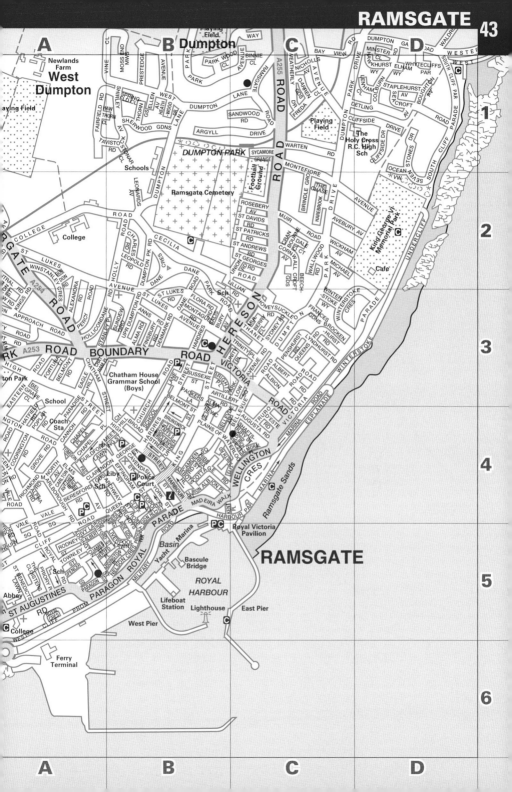

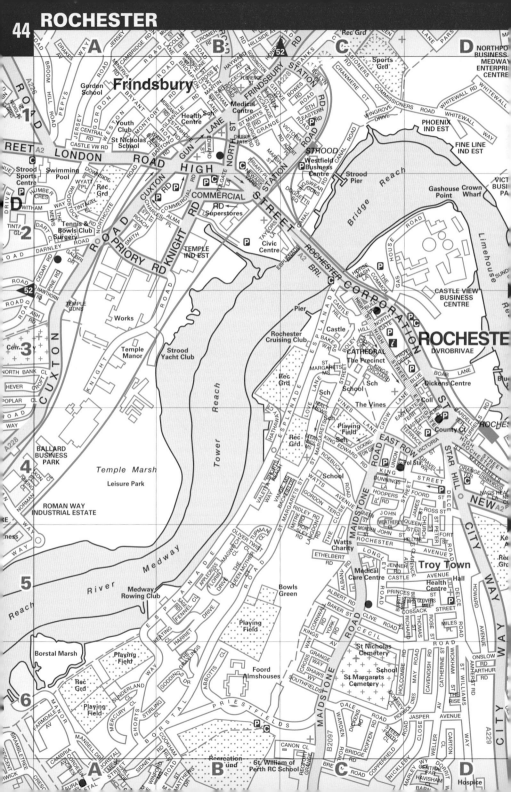

Sandwich

SANDWICH BY-PASS

SANDWICH BY-PASS

Stone Cross

Poulders Gardens

SANDWICH INDUSTRIAL ESTATE

Sports Ground

Playing Field

Sir Roger Manwood's School

Sandwich County Junior School

Sandwich Technology School

Sports & Leisure Centre

Little Sandown Farm

Little Temptye

Grove Manor Farm

The King's House

Fire Station

Caravan Park

Football Ground

Recreation Ground

Cemetery

Rope Walk Town Wall

White Cliffs Country Trail

White Cliffs Country Trail

South Poulders

Poulders

IND EST

A257

A258

A256

Coventon

A | B | C | D

1

Garrison Point

Garrison
Point
Fort

Lifeboat
Station

Docks

Jacobs
Bank

RIVER MEDWAY

GARRISON ROAD

BOAT HOUSE

SLIPWAYS RD

PADDOCK ROAD

ANCHOR LA

Blue
Town

MAIN

MORTUARY RD

GREAT BASIN RD

HIGH STREET

WEST LA ST

KINGS HEAD ALLEY

ST CHARLES ST

EAST LA

UNIONS

JETTY ROAD

Steel Works

BRIELLE WAY

SHEERNESS
ON-SEA

ESPLANADE

Superstore

Sheppey Park
College

Amusement

Sports &
Leisure Centre

Swimming
Pool

BRIDGE RD

Bus
Sta

HIGH ST

BROADWAY

MEYRICK RD

RANELAGH RD

BERRIDGE RD

NEPTUNE

BROADWAY

INVICTA

ALEXANDRA

BEACH ST

CLARENCE RD

DELAMARK RD

MILLENNIUM WAY

RAILWAY

SHORT ST

SHEPS AV

RUSSELL ST

HOPE ST

Pol
Sta

Lib

PC

Council
Offices
Lib

TRINITY RD

BROADWAY

WINSTANLEY

HIGH STREET A250

CAVOUR

CORONATION

ST HELEN

PARK

YELSELE

2

RIVER MEDWAY

Sheerness

Festival
Playing Fields

NEW RD
INDUSTRIAL
ESTATE

GRACE RD

NEW KENT RD

NORTH

MEDWAY ROAD

FLEET

ESTUARY ROAD

ROSE ST

AVENUE

SWALE

MORE CL

Sch

Mile
Town

HOLLAND CL

BOTANY RD

ST AGNES

GEORGES STREET

FIRST AV

VICTORIA ST

SECOND AVENUE

VINCENT GARDENS

VINCENT

MAPLE

GARDENS

ST HELEN

INVICTA

GALWAY RD

ACORN CL

GRANVILLE RD

AVENUE

3

The
Lappel

MILE TOWN
INDUSTRIAL
ESTATE

DORSET RD

BRENTA

MINTER

WATER RD

BONETA

CT

DIAMOND

CT

MONTAGUE

TRIBUNE

THE FLEET

DORSET RD
INDUSTRIAL
ESTATE

SHEARWATER CT

NELSON CL

CECIL AVENUE

CARLTON

AV

WHEATSHEAF
GDNS

Sports
Ground

VICTORIA ST

SOUTHVIEW

GARDENS

SHEPPEY COURT
MARSHES

4

West Minster

BRIELLE WAY

NEWLAND RD

QUEENS COATS AV

LINDEN RD

QUEENS DRIVE

HAWTHORN AVENUE

CHERRY TREE CL

ALMOND TREE CL

LARCH TER

ALDER CL

EDENBRIDGE

MILSTED RD

CHILHAM
CL

APPLEDORE AV

BRADHURST

BOXLEY DRIVE

HARTLIP CL

DETLING CL

EDENBRIDGE DR

GEORGES ST

DAVIE CL

RULE CL

Sch

Sch

5

Diggs Marshes

A249

BRIELLE WAY

B2007

Holm
Place

6

PIER ROAD

WHITEWAY RD

WHITEWAY

BRIELLE WAY

The
Mount

Recreation
Ground

Works

A | B | C | D

SITTINGBOURNE

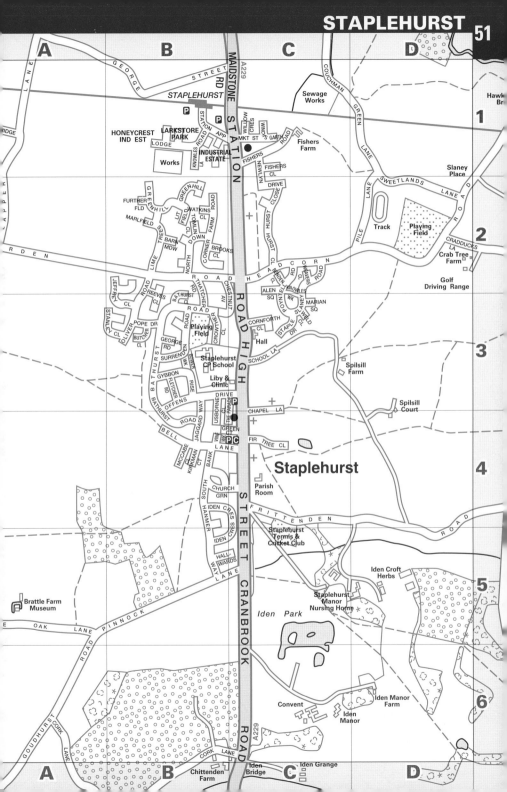

A | B | C | D

1
2
3
4
5
6

STAPLEHURST

MAIDSTONE RD A229

GEORGE STREET

Sewage Works

COUCHMAN GREEN LANE

Hawk Br

HONEYCREST IND EST

LARKSTORE PARK

INDUSTRIAL ESTATE

Works

LODGE

STATION APP

KNOWLES ROAD

LA

MKT ST

WINOR'S

GARTH

LOW TH

CRES

NEWMAN

FISHERS

Fishers Farm

FISHERS CL

FISHERS DRIVE

FISHERS CLOSE

Slaney Place

SWEETLANDS LANE

PILE LANE

Track

Playing Field

CRADDUCKS LA

Crab Tree Farm

Golf Driving Range

FURTHER FLD

MARLFIELD

GREENHILL

GREEN HILL

LIT FIELD

WATKINS CL

DOWNTON CL

FARM ROAD

BARN MDW

LIME TREES

NORTH

CORNER CL

BROOKS CL

JEFFREY CL

REEVES CL

STANLEY CL

OLIVER CL

POPE DR

BUTCHER CL

GEORGE RD

SURRENDEN

BATHURST RD

THATCHER

ROAD

CHESTNUT AV

CROWTHER ROAD

Playing Field

Staplehurst CP School

Hall

CORNFORTH CL

ALEN SQ

POYNTELL RD

KNOWLES RD

STAPLE WK

SLANEY WK

MARIAN SQ

STAPLE DR

WEAVERS RD

CORN ROAD

HEAD CORN ROAD

Spilsill Farm

Spilsill Court

GYBBON

FLETCHER RD

OFFENS

TURNER RISE

Liby & Clinic

USBORNE DRIVE

THE PARK CL

P

CHAPEL LA

BATHURST ROAD

BELL LANE

VINE WK CL

JAGGARD WAY

GREEN

PC

FIR TREE CL

MCCABE CT

KIRKMAN

BANK

VINE LANE

Staplehurst

SOUTH BANK

HANMER

CHURCH GRN

IDEN CRES

IDEN CRES

HALL-WARDS WAY

Parish Room

FRITTENDEN ROAD

Staplehurst Tennis & Cricket Club

Iden Croft Herbs

Brattle Farm Museum

OAK LANE

PINNOCK

GOUDHURST

CORK LANE

ROAD

STREET CRANBROOK ROAD A229

Iden Park

Staplehurst Manor Nursing Home

Iden Manor Farm

Convent

Iden Manor

CORK LANE

Chittenden Farm

Iden Bridge

Iden Grange

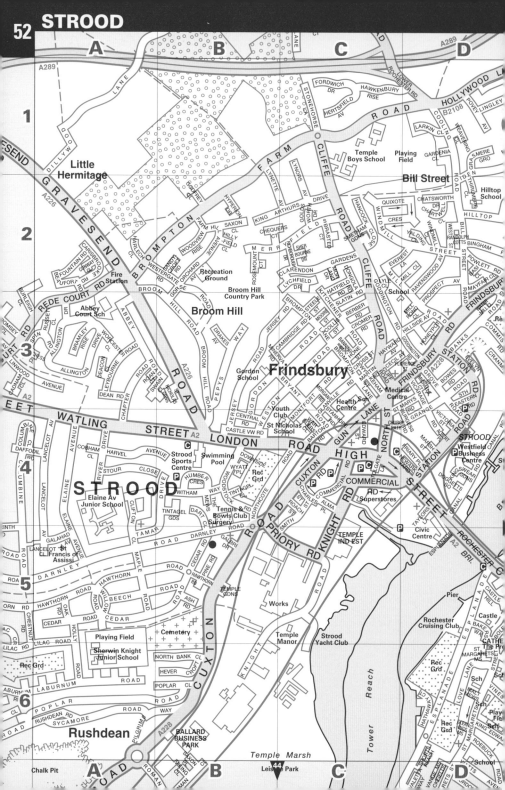

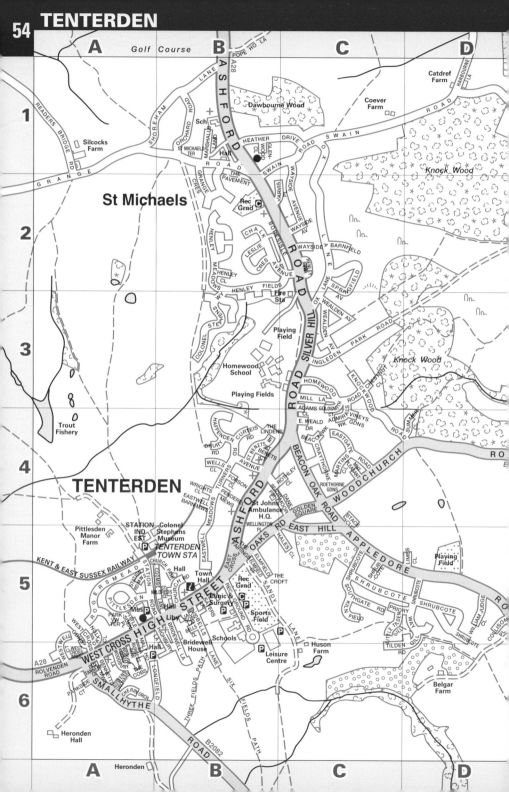

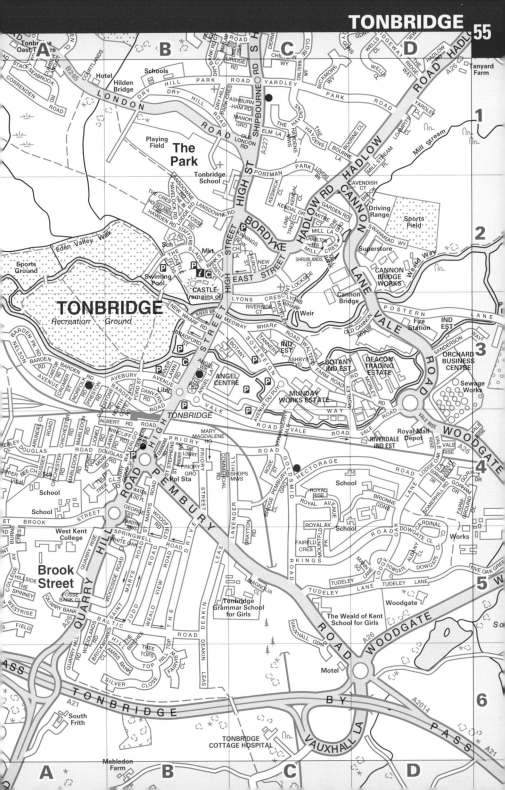

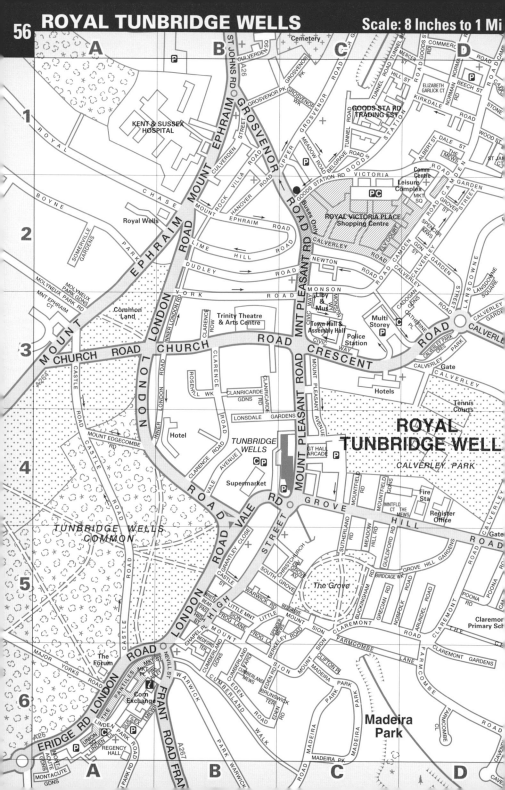

A   B   C   D

1

2

A233 WESTERHAM HILL

Pilgrim House

WAY   PILG

North Downs   Way

AVENUE

The Hill School

Hill Park

LONDON

Betsomhill Farm

PILGRIMS

LANE

Force Green

GREEN

Hartley Wood

Westerham Wood

FORCE

ROAD

BEGGARS   LANE   A233   BEG

3

M25

B2024

CROYDON   ROAD

RYDON   ROAD

Playing Field

Churchill C E Primary School

LONDON   ROAD

HORTONS

ROSSLARE CL

MADAN

THE FLYERS WY

ASH   ROAD   MADAN CL

HARTLEY

ELM RD

OAK RD   ROAD   ROAD

OAK LODGE LA   SANDY LA

RAILWAY   TER   BLOOMFIELD TER

CHURCH   WAY

4

Westerham

CROYDON   LANE

MARWELL   CROFT   FARLEY CROFT   CROFT RD   GRANVILLE ROAD

FARLEY   LANE

Farley Common

Pit

WESTWAYS

THE PADDOCK

BURYS
RD   THE
BRYSTED LA

STH BANK

DELA   GARDE   RD   BARTLETT RD

Fire Sta.

WESTBURY
TER   NEW ST   STREET   GRANGE

SQUERRYES   MEWS

WELLERS   CL

BLACK   EAGLE   CL

Pitts Cottage XIII Century

British Legion Hall

MILL   LA

HIGH   ST

MARKET SQ

LONDON RD

ST MARYS

GRANGE

THE   GREEN
VICARAGE HILL

WESTERHAM   TRADE CENTRE

BUTTERBURY

HOLDOMBE   COSTELLS
MDWS

HORTON   Av
HOLLING WORTH

Hall

War Mem

Quebec Square

Quebec House

George IV Recreation Ground

A25   BRASTED RD   BRAS

HOSEY

R. Darent

LODGE LA

5

6

WESTERHAM   ROAD   HIGH STREET

GOUDLEY STOCK ROAD

Squerryes Court

Cenotaph

Lodge Wood

Spring   Shaw

WATER   LANE

MILL   LA

Glebe House

HILL   B2026

A   B   C   D

Westgate on Sea

Garlinge

Westbrook Bay

St Mildreds Bay

WESTGATE BAY

Ledge Point
Childrens Pool

Garlinge County Primary & Infants School

Football Ground

Dent-De-Lion Castle (remains)

King Ethelbert School

Ursuline Convent School

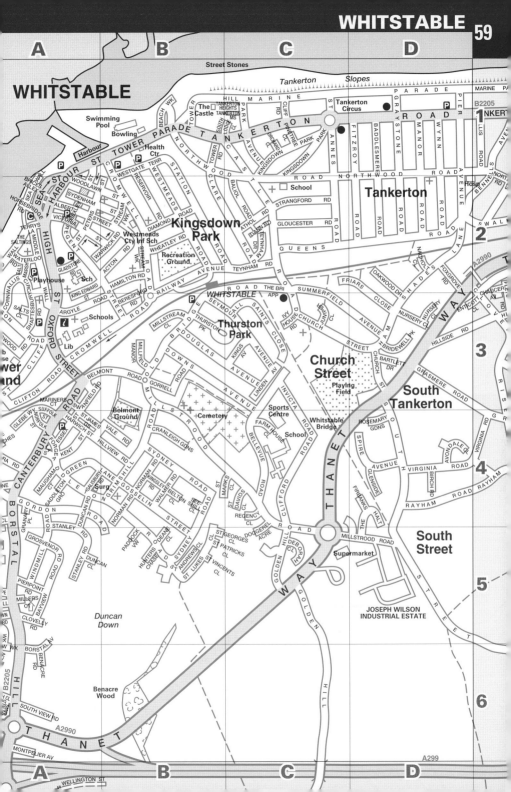

WHITSTABLE

Tankerton Slopes

Street Stones

B2205

1

NKER

MARINE PA

PARADE

PIER

MARINE

Swimming Pool

Bowling

The Castle

TANKERTON HEIGHTS

Tankerton Circus

GRAYSTONE

MANOR

WYNN

ELLIS ROAD

NORTH

AVE

Harbour

Health Ctr

HILL

CLIFF RD

ST ANNES

FITZROY

BADDLESMERE

Hosp

SEA

HARBOUR ST

TOWER

PARADE

TANKERTON

WESTGATE TERR

WESTMEADS

STATION

RESERVOIR

BEACH WK

TOWER

NORTHWOOD

BIRCHING

KINGSDOWN PARK

PINETREE

MARINE

PARK AVENUE

KINGSDOWN

NORTHWOOD

ROAD

ROAD

Tankerton

2

WOODLAWN

SYDENHAM

DIAMOND

ALBERTS

VICTORIA

STREAM

CROMWELL

NORTHWCLARE

BALIOL ROAD

School

STRANGFORD RD

GLOUCESTER RD

QUEENS

ROAD

ROAD

ROAD

SWAL

A2990

HIGH ST

Kingsdown Park

PETERS STREET

WARWICK RD

Westmeads Cty Inf Sch

WHEATLEY RD

ATHOL RD

TEYNHAM DR

TEYNHAM

ROAD

ROAD

ROAD

NICHOLLS

FOXGROVE

LANE

The SALTINGS

REGENT

ST

WATERLOO

Playhouse

Sch

GLADSTONE

ST

KING EDWARD

HAMILTON RD

Recreation Ground

ROAD

ROAD

AVENUE

WHITSTABLE

SUMMERFIELD

THE BRI APP

FRIARS

OAKWOOD DR

HADD

ERICOTT

CHAUCER AV

WALL

CORNWALLIS

CIRCUMFERE

SHAFTESBURY

ARGYLE

Schools

BERESFORD

RAILWAY

AVENUE

SEYMOUR

THURSTON CL

SAINTS CLOSE

IVY RD

HOUSE

CHURCH

NURSERY

NURSERY

BRIDEWELL

HILLSIDE RD

WAY

ENT

WER nd

SALTS CL

Lib

CROMWELL

Millstream CL

ST

PK

Thurston Park

KINGS

AVENUE

LINDEN AV

CHURCH

STREET

BARTLETT DR

GRASMERE ROAD

3

CLIFTON

ROSWELL

MILLFIELD MANOR

GORRELL

DOWNS

B DOUGLAS

INVICTA

Church Street

CHURCH

South Tankerton

RISER

MARINERS CT

BELMONT ROAD

ROAD

MILLSTROOD

AVENUE

Playing Field

ROSEMARY GDNS

VIRGINIA RD

GLEBE WY

SUFFOLK

WINFIELD RD

Belmont Ground

CRANLEIGH GDNS

Cemetery

Sports Centre

Whitstable Bridge

SPIRE

AVENUE

GLENSIDE

VIRGINIA AV

AVONDALE

BIRCH RD

ROAD

4

SUFFOLK

WINFOLK

ST JAMES

HARWICH ST

VALE RD

HILLVIEW RD

SYDNEY

FARM HOUSE

BELLEVUE

School

FIRBANKS HALT

VIRGINIA

RAYHAM ROAD

RAYHAM

CANTERBURY ROAD

FESSEY

KENT

HILL

STREET

NORMAN RD

WALMER

SHEL

MARKS

ST DAVIDS

ROAD

ROAD

THANET

SOUTH

MAUGHAM

SADDLETON

O GREEN

SALISBURY

ELFIN

REGENCY

South Street

5

GRANARY PL

GORDON

DUNCAN RD

HUNTERS CHASE

PADDOCK WY

OCEANE

SYDNEY CL

ANDREWS CL

ST GEORGES CL

ST PATRICKS CL

DOGGEREL ACRE

ST LUKES CL

ST VINCENTS CL

CLIFFORD ROAD

GOLDEN HILL

DEBORAH CL

Supermarket

Millstrood ROAD

STREET

JOSEPH WILSON INDUSTRIAL ESTATE

B2205

PIERPOINT RD

WINDMILL ROAD

GROSVENOR

STANLEY

BAYVIEW

MILLERS

CLOVELLY

BORSTAL AV

BENACRE RD

WK

Duncan Down

WAY

GOLDEN

HILL

6

THANET

HILL

Benacre Wood

BORSTAL

SOUTH VIEW RD

A2990

THANET

A299

MONTPELIER AV

WELLINGTON ST

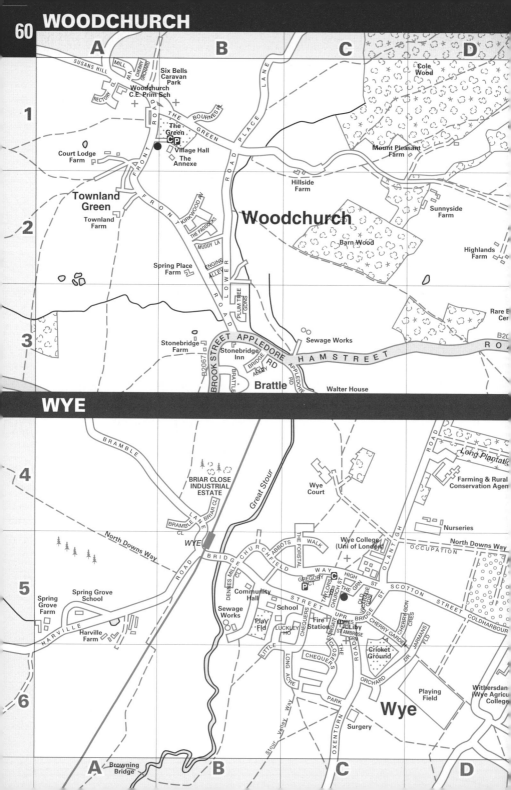

WOODCHURCH

A B C D

1
Susans Hill
Mill
Cherry Orchard
Six Bells Caravan Park
Woodchurch C.E. Prim Sch
Rector Cl
Front Road
The Bourne
The Green
The Green CP
Village Hall
The Annexe
Court Lodge Farm
Place Lane
The Green
Road
Cole Wood
Mount Pleasant Farm

2
Townland Green
Townland Farm
Front Road
Kirwood Wy
The Paddocks
Muddy La
Engine Alley
Spring Place Farm
Lower Road
Woodchurch
Hillside Farm
Barn Wood
Sunnyside Farm
Highlands Farm

3
Stonebridge Farm
Brook Street
Brattle Cl
Plum Tree Gdns
Appledore
Stonebridge Inn
Bridge
Cl Alley
Appledore Rd
Sewage Works
Brattle
HAMSTREET
Walter House
B2067
B20
Rare B Cer
RO

A B C D

4
Bramble
Briar Close Industrial Estate
Bramble Lane
Briar Cl
North Downs Way
WYE
Great Stour
Wye Court
Road
Long Plantatio
Farming & Rural Conservation Agen
Nurseries
North Downs Way
Occupation

5
Spring Grove Farm
Harville
Spring Grove School
Harville Farm
Dennes Mill Cl
Bridge Road
Churchfield
Abbots
The Forstal
Walk
Community Hall
Sewage Works
School
Play Fld
Little
Luckley Ho
Chequers
Street
Gregory Pl
Way
Taylors
Upr Bridge St
Fire Station
High St
Church St
The Green
Wye College (Uni of London)
Olantigh
Scotton Street
Coldharbour
Cherry Garde
Ambrose
Jarmans Fld
Cherry Grdn Cres
The Green

6
Browning Bridge
Long Acre
Chequers
Cosgers
The Slade
Orchard Road
Oxenturn
Park
Stour Valley Way
Cricket Ground
Surgery
Playing Field
Wye
Withersdan (Wye Agricu College

A B C D

Index includes some
es for which there is
ficient space on the
s. These names are
ated by an * and are
wed by the nearest
ning thoroughfare.

ey Cl, Deal CT14 22 A3
ey Cl,
erness ME12 37 D3
ey Ct CT7 58 A4
ey Pl,
tford DA1 21 B1
ey Pl,
ersham ME13 25 D2
ey Rd,
ersham ME13 25 D1
ingham ME8 27 D6
enhithe DA9 29 C2
ey Rd,
ey St ME13 25 D2
eyview Dr ME12 37 B3
ots Hill CT11 43 B4
ots Pl CT1 16 C2
ots Walk TN25 60 B5
ott Rd,
xestone CT20 26 E1
ott Rd,
venoaks TN15 13 B5
otts Cl,
chester ME1 44 B6
anley BR8 53 E3
cia Rd DA1 21 A5
cia Walk BR8 53 B1
n Rd ME7 27 C4
n St ME12 47 D3
n Ct CT17 23 A1
n Rd CT5 59 B2
ms Cl TN30 54 C4
elam Cl CT14 22 A4
elam Rd CT14 22 A4
ington Pl CT11 43 B5
ington Rd,
rgate CT9 36 C2
ington Rd,
tingbourne ME10 48 A3
ington Sq CT9 36 C2
ington St,
rgate CT9 36 C3
ington St,
nsgate CT11 43 A5
iscombe Gdns
e 36 C4
iscombe Rd CT9 36 D4
laide Gdns CT11 43 B4
laide Pl CT1 16 B4
laide Rd ME7 27 A4
sham Way CT9 19 B4
nirals Walk,
atham ME4 18 B1
nirals Walk,
eenhithe DA9 29 B1
nirals Walk,
iterden TN30 54 C4
niralty Cl ME13 25 B2
niralty Ter ME7 18 C1
an Mws CT8 58 C2
an Sq CT8 58 C2
an St CT17 23 C2
nan Rd ME4 18 A5
tree Cl DA12 28 B6
dale Cl CT9 36 D3
hurst La TN13 46 C6
nein Rd DA10 29 D3
n Cl DA1 21 A1
seun Ter ME12 37 A4
any Cl TN9 55 D5
any Dr CT6 32 A1
any Pl CT17 23 C2
any Rd,
lingham ME7 27 B4
any Rd,
chester ME1 44 C5
any Rd,
tingbourne ME10 48 B4
any St ME14 35 C2
any Ter,
atham ME4 18 A4
any Ter,
lingham ME7 27 B4
ert Constain Ct
20 26 C2
ert La CT21 33 B4
ert Murray Cl DA12 28 C3

Albert Pl ME2 52 D4
Albert Rd,
Ashford TN24 12 C3
Albert Rd,
Broadstairs CT10 19 D6
Albert Rd,
Chatham ME4 18 C5
Albert Rd, Deal CT14 22 C2
Albert Rd,
Gillingham ME7 27 A4
Albert Rd, Hythe CT21 33 B4
Albert Rd,
Margate CT9 36 A3
Albert Rd,
Ramsgate CT11 43 C3
Albert Rd,
Rochester ME1 44 C5
Albert Rd,
Swanscombe DA10 29 F3
Albert Rd,
Tonbridge TN9 55 A4
Albert Reed Gdns
ME15 35 A6
Albert St,
Maidstone ME14 35 B1
Albert St,
Ramsgate CT11 43 A5
Albert St,
Tunbridge Wells TN1 56 D1
Albert St,
Whitstable CT5 59 A2
Albion Hill CT11 43 B4
Albion Mews Rd CT20 26 C3
Albion Par DA12 28 D2
Albion Pl,
Canterbury CT1 16 D2
Albion Pl,
Faversham ME13 25 C2
Albion Pl, Hythe CT21 33 D3
Albion Pl,
Maidstone ME15 35 C4
Albion Pl,
Ramsgate CT11 43 B4
Albion Rd,
Birchington CT7 14 D3
Albion Rd,
Broadstairs CT10 15 A2
Albion Rd,
Gravesend DA12 28 C3
Albion Rd,
Margate CT9 19 A3
Albion Rd,
Ramsgate CT11 43 C3
Albion Rd,
Tonbridge TN12 34 C5
Albion St CT10 15 D4
Albion Ter DA12 28 C2
Albion Villas CT20 26 C3
Albion Way TN8 24 B2
Alder Cl ME12 47 B5
Alder Way BR8 53 B1
Alderney Gdns CT10 15 A3
Aldred Rd ME13 25 C3
Alen Sq TN12 51 C2
Alexander Cl ME4 18 B1
Alexander Dr ME13 25 B2
Alexander Rd DA9 29 C2
Alexandra Av ME7 27 B4
Alexandra Cl BR8 53 C2
Alexandra Gdns CT20 26 C3
Alexandra Homes CT9 36 B4
Alexandra Rd,
Birchington CT7 14 D4
Alexandra Rd,
Broadstairs CT10 15 C4
Alexandra Rd,
Chatham ME4 18 D6
Alexandra Rd,
Deal CT14 22 D6
Alexandra Rd,
Margate CT9 36 B4
Alexandra Rd,
Ramsgate CT11 43 A3
Alexandra Rd,
Tonbridge TN9 55 B4
Alexandra Rd,
Whitstable CT5 59 A4
Alexandra St ME14 35 B2
Alexandra Ter CT9 36 C4
Alfred Cl ME4 18 D6
Alfred Rd,
Ashford TN24 12 D6
Alfred Rd,
Birchington CT7 14 B1
Alfred Rd,
Gravesend DA11 28 B5
Alfred Rd,
Margate CT9 19 A4
Alfred Row CT14 22 C1

Alfred Sq CT14 22 C1
Alicia Av CT9 58 D3
Alison Cl CT7 14 E2
Alkali Row CT9 36 C2
Alkerden La,
Greenhithe DA9 29 C3
Alkerden La,
Swanscombe DA10 29 D3
Alkham Rd ME14 35 D3
Allan Av CT9 36 A3
All Saints Cl,
Swanscombe DA10 29 F2
All Saints Cl,
Whitstable CT5 59 C3
All Saints Ind Est
CT9 36 B3
All Saints La CT1 16 B3
All Saints Rd,
Cranbrook TN18 31 C2
All Saints Rd,
Tunbridge Wells TN4 50 D5
All Saints Rise TN4 50 D5
Allanbrooke DA12 28 C3
Allen Av CT8 58 A4
Allen Ct ME12 47 B2
Allen Fld TN23 12 A6
Allen St ME14 35 C2
Allenby Av CT14 22 B3
Allens TN12 34 C5
Allington Dr ME2 52 A3
Allington Dr ME12 52 A3
Allington Rd TN12 40 B3
Allnutt Mill Cl ME15 35 A6
Allotment La TN13 46 D3
Alma Pl,
Ramsgate CT11 43 B3
Alma Pl,
Rochester ME2 52 C4
Alma Rd, Margate CT9 36 C3
Alma Rd,
Ramsgate CT11 43 B3
Alma Rd,
Sheerness ME12 47 D3
Alma Rd,
Swanscombe DA10 29 F2
Almeria Cl CT20 33 A3
Almon Pl ME1 44 D4
Almond Dr BR8 53 B2
Almond Tree Cl ME12 47 B5
Alpha Rd,
Birchington CT7 14 D2
Alpha Rd,
Ramsgate CT11 43 A4
Alsager Rd ME11 41 A3
Alston Cl ME12 37 C2
Amberley Cl TN9 55 A4
Ambrose Hill ME5 27 A6
Ames Rd DA10 29 E3
Amherst Cl CT9 19 C4
Amherst Hill ME7 18 C2
Amherst Rd,
Rochester ME1 44 D6
Amherst Rd,
Sevenoaks TN13 46 C3
Amherst Rd,
Tunbridge Wells TN4 50 C6
Amherst Redoubt ME7 18 C3
Anchor Bsns Pk
ME10 48 D1
Anchor La, Deal CT14 22 C2
Anchor La,
Sheerness ME12 47 B1
Anchor Wharf ME4 18 B2
Andrew Broughton Way
ME14 35 C3
Angel Centre TN9 55 B3
Angel La TN9 55 B3
Angel Walk TN9 55 B3
Angley Rd TN17 20 A5
Angley Walk TN17 20 A5
Anna Pk CT7 14 C1
Anne Cl CT7 14 E2
Anne of Cleves Rd
DA1 21 B2
Anne Roper Cl TN28 38 E3
Annes Rd CT10 15 D1
Annetts Hall TN15 13 C4
Annie Rd ME6 49 B4
Anns Rd CT11 43 B3
Anselm Cl ME10 48 A3
Anvil Cl CT7 14 E2
Apple Cl ME6 49 B5
Apple Ct TN12 40 B4
Apple Orch BR8 53 B3
Applecross Cl ME1 44 B5
Appledore Av ME12 47 C5
Appledore Cl ME1 19 B4
Appledore Rd,
Ashford TN26 60 B3

Appledore Rd,
Tenterden TN30 54 C5
Appleford Dr ME12 37 A2
Applegarth Dr ME1 21 C6
Appletons TN11 17 C6
Approach Rd,
Broadstairs CT10 15 C4
Approach Rd,
Margate CT9 36 D3
Apsley St TN23 12 C4
Archer Way BR8 53 E1
Archery Sq North
CT14 22 C5
Archery Sq South
CT14 22 C5
Archway Rd CT11 43 A4
Arden Dr TN24 12 D3
Arden St ME7 27 A2
Ardenlee Dr ME14 35 D2
Ardent Av CT14 22 C4
Argent Bsns Pk
ME11 41 B3
Argles Cl DA9 29 A2
Argyle Av CT9 58 F2
Argyle Gdns CT9 58 F2
Argyle Rd,
Sevenoaks TN13 46 C6
Argyle Rd,
Tunbridge Wells TN4 50 D1
Argyle Rd,
Whitstable CT5 59 A3
Argyll Dr CT11 43 B1
Ark La CT14 22 C1
Arkley Rd CT6 32 C2
Arklow Sq CT11 43 C3
Arlington TN23 12 A5
Arlington Gdns CT9 19 B6
Arlott Cl ME14 35 B1
Armada Way ME4 18 B5
Armoury Dr DA12 28 C3
Armstrong Rd ME15 35 C6
Arnold Rd,
Gravesend DA12 28 D5
Arnold Rd,
Margate CT9 36 C3
Arnolde Cl ME2 18 A1
Arthur Rd,
Birchington CT7 14 B2
Arthur Rd, Deal CT14 22 A5
Arthur Rd,
Gillingham ME8 42 A2
Arthur Rd, Hythe CT21 33 B5
Arthur Rd,
Margate CT9 36 D2
Arthur Rd,
Rochester ME1 44 D6
Arthur Salmon Cl
ME13 25 B3
Arthur St,
Gravesend DA11 28 A3
Arthur St,
Sittingbourne ME10 48 A3
Arthur St West DA11 28 A3
Artillery Gdns CT11 16 D2
Artillery Rd CT11 43 B3
Artillery Row DA12 28 C3
Artillery St CT1 16 D2
Arundel Av ME10 48 B6
Arundel Cl TN9 55 A4
Arundel Rd,
Dartford DA1 21 A1
Arundel Rd,
Margate CT9 19 A4
Arundel Rd,
Tunbridge Wells TN1 56 D5
Arundel St ME7 35 B1
Ascot Cl TN15 13 C5
Ascot Gdns CT8 58 B3
Ascot Rd DA12 28 B6
Ash Cl,
Edenbridge TN8 24 B5
Ash Cl, Swanley BR8 53 B2
Ash Gro TN29 34 D1
Ash Rd, Dartford DA1 21 B5
Ash Rd,
Rochester ME2 52 B5
Ash Rd,
Sandwich CT13 45 B1
Ash Rd,
Westerham TN16 57 D4
Ash Tree La ME5 27 B6
Ash Trees CT6 32 D3
Ashbee Cl ME6 49 C3
Ashburnham Rd TN10 55 C1
Ashbys Cl TN5 24 C6
Ashbys Yd TN9 55 C3
Ashcombe Dr TN8 24 B2
Ashcroft Rd TN12 40 C5

Ashdown Cres TN28 38 B4
Ashen Tree La CT16 23 C1
Ashenden Cl ME2 52 D1
Ashes La TN11 17 A6
Ashford Rd,
Ashford TN26 30 A4
Ashford Rd,
Faversham ME13 25 C5
Ashford Rd,
Harrietsham ME17 30 A2
Ashford Rd,
Lenham ME17 32 A4
Ashford Rd,
Maidstone ME14 35 C4
Ashford Rd,
New Romney TN28 38 A2
Ashford Rd,
Tenterden TN30 54 B5
Ashgrove TN25 12 A1
Ashleigh Gdns TN27 31 B4
Ashley CT13 46 B4
Ashley Rd TN13 46 B4
Ashurst Rd ME14 35 D2
Aspdin Rd DA11 39 C6
Aspen Cl BR8 53 B1
Astley St ME14 35 C3
Astor Dr CT14 22 B3
Astrid Rd CT14 22 A6
Athelstan Rd,
Chatham ME4 18 B6
Athelstan Rd,
Faversham ME13 25 B3
Athelstan Rd,
Margate CT9 36 D2
Athol Pl ME13 25 A2
Athol Rd CT5 59 C2
Athol Ter CT16 23 E1
Atlantic Cl DA10 29 E2
Atterbury Cl TN16 57 C5
Attlee Dr DA1 21 D2
Atwater Ct ME17 32 D5
Aubretia Walk ME10 48 C3
Audley Av CT9 58 E2
Augusta Cl ME7 27 A1
Augusta Rd CT11 43 C4
Augustine Rd,
Gravesend DA12 28 D3
Augustine Rd,
Sheerness ME12 37 B1
Austen Cl DA9 29 C2
Austen Gdns DA1 21 D1
Austens Orch TN30 54 A6
Austin Cl ME5 27 C6
Austin Rd DA11 28 A4
Avebury Av,
Ramsgate CT11 43 C2
Avebury Av,
Tonbridge TN9 55 B3
Avenue CT11 43 B3
Avenue Gdns CT9 19 B3
Avenue Le Puy TN9 55 C4
Avenue of Remembrance
ME10 48 B3
Avenue Rd,
Herne Bay CT6 32 A1
Avenue Rd,
Ramsgate CT11 43 C2
Avenue Rd,
Sevenoaks TN13 46 C4
Avereng Rd CT19 26 A1
Avery Cl ME15 35 B6
Avington Cl ME15 35 B6
Avon Cl DA12 28 D5
Avondale Cl CT5 59 D4
Avondale Rd ME7 27 B3
Avonmouth Rd DA1 21 B2
Aynsley Cl CT13 45 D1
Azalea Dr BR8 53 C3

Back La,
Faversham ME13 25 D2
Back La,
Sheerness ME12 37 D3
Backfields ME1 44 C4
Baddlesmere Rd CT5 59 D1
Baden Rd ME7 27 B1
Badsell Rd TN12 40 A4
Baffin Cl ME4 18 B6
Baileys Fld TN23 12 A5
Bairds Hill CT10 15 B2
Bairdsley Cl CT10 15 B2
Baker St ME1 44 C5
Bakers Cross TN17 20 C5
Bakers Walk ME1 15 B2
Balcomb Cres CT9 19 B6
Baldwin Rd ME12 37 E3
Balfour Rd CT14 22 A5
Baliol Rd CT5 59 C2
Ballard Bsns Pk ME2 52 B6

Ballard Cl TN12 34 B5
Ballard Way TN12 40 D3
Balliemoor Ct*,
 Argyll Dr CT10 43 B1
Balmer Cl ME8 42 A3
Balmoral Pl CT11 43 C4
Balmoral Rd,
 Gillingham ME7 27 A3
Balmoral Rd,
 Margate CT9 58 E3
Balmoral Ter ME10 48 A3
Baltic Rd TN9 55 A5
Bamford Way CT14 22 C4
Bank St, Ashford TN23 12 C4
Bank St,
 Chatham ME4 18 D5
Bank St,
 Cranbrook TN17 20 B4
Bank St,
 Faversham ME13 25 C3
Bank St,
 Gravesend DA12 28 B2
Bank St,
 Herne Bay CT6 32 C1
Bank St, Hythe CT21 33 B4
Bank St,
 Maidstone ME14 35 B4
Bank St,
 Sevenoaks TN13 46 C6
Bank St,
 Tonbridge TN9 55 B2
Bankfields TN27 31 A4
Banks Rd ME2 52 D3
Bankside,
 Ashford TN26 30 B5
Bankside,
 Gravesend DA11 39 B2
Banky Fields Cl ME8 42 D1
Banner Farm Rd TN2 56 D6
Banning St ME2 52 C3
Bardell Ter ME1 44 D4
Barden Park Rd TN9 55 A3
Barden Rd TN9 55 A3
Barfreston Cl ME15 35 A6
Barham Dr TN17 20 C4
Barker Rd ME16 35 B4
Barkers Ct ME10 48 A3
Barler Pl ME11 41 B1
Barleycorn Dr ME8 42 A4
Barlow Cl ME8 42 A6
Barn Cres CT9 58 E2
Barn Hawe TN8 24 C5
Barn Mdw TN12 51 B2
Barn Platt TN23 12 B6
Barnard Ct ME4 18 C6
Barnes Av CT9 58 E2
Barnes Cl ME13 25 B1
Barnes Walk TN12 34 C5
Barnesende Ct CT13 45 D2
Barnett Fld TN23 12 A6
Barnfield,
 Gravesend DA11 28 A5
Barnfield,
 Tenterden TN30 54 C2
Barnfield Rd ME13 25 C1
Barnsole Rd ME7 27 B3
Baron Cl ME7 27 C1
Barons Ct TN4 50 D6
Barrack Hill CT21 33 A3
Barrack Row DA11 28 B2
Barrel Arch Cl TN12 34 A5
Barretts Rd TN18 31 B1
Barrier Rd ME4 18 B3
Barrington Cres CT7 14 E3
Barrow Gro ME10 48 A3
Barrow Hill TN23 12 B3
Barrow Hill Cotts TN23 12 B3
Barrow Hill Pl TN23 12 B3
Barrow Hill Ter TN23 12 B3
Barrows Cl CT7 14 D3
Bartholomew Cl CT21 33 A2
Bartholomew La CT21 33 A3
Bartholomew St CT21 33 B3
Bartholomew Way
 BR8 53 C2
Bartlett Dr CT5 59 D3
Bartlett Rd,
 Gravesend DA11 28 A4
Bartlett Rd,
 Westerham TN16 57 C5
Bartletts Cl ME12 41 D1
Barton Hill Dr ME12 37 A4
Barton Rd,
 Maidstone ME15 35 C5
Barton Rd,
 Strood ME2 52 C4
Basden Cotts TN18 31 C1
Basi Cl ME2 52 D2
Basing Cl ME15 35 C5
Baskerville TN24 12 C3
Basmere Cl ME14 35 D2
Bassett Cl CT21 33 D2
Bassett Gdns CT21 33 D2
Bassett Rd ME10 48 A3
Bastion Rd CT17 23 B3
Bat & Ball Rd TN14 46 C2

Batchelor St ME4 18 C4
Bath Hard La ME1 44 D4
Bath Pl CT9 36 C2
Bath Rd CT9 36 C2
Bath St DA11 28 B2
Bathurst Cl TN12 51 B3
Bathurst Rd TN12 51 B3
Bay Hill CT15 41 C5
Bay Hill Cl CT15 41 C6
Bay View Rd CT10 15 B6
Bayford Rd ME10 48 D3
Bayham Rd TN13 46 D4
Bayle Ct CT20 26 D3
Bayle St CT20 26 D3
Bayly Rd DA1 21 D3
Bayswater Dr ME8 42 A6
Bayview Rd CT5 59 A5
Beach Av CT7 14 D2
Beach Rd, Dover CT15 41 C6
Beach Rd,
 Westgate-on-Sea CT8 58 C2
Beach Rise CT8 58 D2
Beach St, Deal CT14 22 D1
Beach St,
 Folkestone CT20 26 E3
Beach St,
 Herne Bay CT6 32 B1
Beach St,
 Sheerness ME12 47 C2
Beach Ter ME12 47 C2
Beach Walk CT5 59 B1
Beachy Path TN30 54 B4
Beacon Cl ME8 42 A3
Beacon Hill CT6 32 D1
Beacon Oak Rd TN30 54 C4
Beacon Rd,
 Broadstairs CT10 15 A2
Beacon Rd,
 Chatham ME5 27 A6
Beacon Rd,
 Herne Bay CT6 32 D2
Beacon Rd,
 Maidstone ME17 32 B6
Beacon Walk,
 Herne Bay CT6 32 D1
Beacon Walk,
 Tenterden TN30 54 C4
Beaconsfield Av ME7 27 B3
Beaconsfield Gdns
 CT10 15 B3
Beaconsfield Rd,
 Chatham ME4 18 B6
Beaconsfield Rd,
 Deal CT14 22 C3
Beaconsfield Rd,
 Maidstone ME15 35 A6
Beaconsfield Ter CT21 33 C4
Bean Rd DA9 29 B4
Beaton Cl DA9 29 B1
Beatrice Gdns DA11 39 D5
Beatrice Rd CT9 36 B4
Beatty Av ME7 27 D5
Beauchamp Av CT14 22 A5
Beaufort Ct ME2 18 A2
Beaufort Rd ME2 52 A2
Beaumanor CT6 32 C3
Beaumont Davey Cl
 ME13 25 C4
Beaumont Ter ME13 25 D3
Beaver Rd TN23 12 C6
Becket Ct TN27 31 C5
Becket Mws CT7 14 C2
Beckett St ME13 25 C2
Bedford Ct CT10 15 D2
Bedford Pl ME16 35 A4
Bedford Rd,
 Dartford DA1 21 D4
Bedford Rd,
 Gravesend DA11 28 A5
Bedford Rd,
 Tunbridge Wells TN4 50 C2
Bedford Ter TN1 56 B5
Bedson Walk ME8 42 D1
Beech Av BR8 53 E3
Beech Cl ME13 25 B3
Beech Hurst Cl ME15 35 C5
Beech Rd,
 Dartford DA1 21 B5
Beech Rd,
 Rochester ME2 52 A5
Beech Rd,
 Sevenoaks TN13 56 D1
Beech St TN1 56 D1
Beechcroft Gdns CT11 43 C2
Beechenlea La BR8 53 E4
Beecholme Dr TN24 12 C1
Beechwood Av,
 Chatham ME5 27 B6
Beechwood Av,
 Deal CT14 22 C3
Beechwood Av,
 Sittingbourne ME10 48 A1
Beechwood Ct CT14 22 C3
Beer Cart La CT1 16 B4
Beggars La TN16 57 D3
Belgrave Cl CT11 43 A3

Belgrave Rd,
 Margate CT9 36 B3
Belgrave Rd,
 Tunbridge Wells TN1 56 C1
Belgrove TN1 56 C5
Bell Inn Rd CT21 33 C3
Bell La TN12 51 B4
Bell Rd ME10 48 B5
Belle Vue Rd CT6 32 D1
Bellevue Av CT11 43 B4
Bellevue Rd,
 Ramsgate CT11 43 C4
Bellevue Rd,
 Sheerness ME12 37 C3
Bellevue Rd,
 Whitstable CT5 59 C4
Bellevue St CT20 26 D2
Bellows La TN15 13 A5
Bells Cl TN30 54 B5
Bells La TN30 54 B5
Belmont Rd,
 Broadstairs CT10 15 C4
Belmont Rd,
 Faversham ME13 25 C4
Belmont Rd,
 Gillingham ME7 27 A4
Belmont Rd,
 Ramsgate CT11 43 A3
Belmont Rd,
 Sittingbourne ME10 48 A4
Belmont Rd,
 Westgate-on-Sea CT8 58 C3
Belmont Rd,
 Whitstable CT5 59 A3
Belmont St CT11 43 B3
Belmore Pk TN24 12 B3
Beltinge Rd CT6 32 C1
Belton Cl CT5 59 B4
Beltring Rd TN4 50 C5
Belvedere Cl DA12 28 C4
Belvedere Rd,
 Broadstairs CT10 15 C4
Belvedere Rd,
 Faversham ME13 25 D2
Benacre Rd CT5 59 A6
Bench St CT16 23 C2
Benden Cl TN12 51 C2
Bennett Ho DA11 28 A6
Bennetts Mws TN30 54 A6
Bensted Gro ME13 25 A3
Bentham Hill TN3 50 A2
Bentley St DA12 28 C2
Berber Rd ME2 52 C3
Bere Cl DA9 29 C1
Berengrave La ME8 42 A1
Beresford Gap CT7 14 D1
Beresford Gdns CT9 19 B2
Beresford Rd,
 Gillingham ME7 27 B4
Beresford Rd,
 Gravesend DA11 39 D3
Beresford Rd,
 Ramsgate CT11 43 A4
Beresford Rd,
 Whitstable CT5 59 B3
Berkeley Cres DA1 21 D4
Berkeley Rd,
 Birchington CT7 14 C1
Berkeley Rd,
 Tunbridge Wells TN1 56 B6
Berkley Rd DA12 28 B2
Bernard St DA12 28 C2
Berridge Rd ME12 47 D3
Berry St ME10 48 B3
Berwick Way TN14 46 C1
Best La CT1 16 B3
Best St ME4 18 B4
Bethel Rd TN13 46 D4
Betsham Rd DA10 29 E3
Bettescombe Rd ME8 42 A3
Bevan Pl BR8 53 D3
Bevans Cl DA9 29 C3
Beverley Cl ME8 42 B2
Beverly Cl CT7 14 E2
Bexley St CT5 59 A2
Bickley Rd TN9 55 B4
Bickmore Way TN9 55 C1
Biddenden Rd TN27 31 D6
Bierce Ct CT7 14 C2
Biggin St CT16 23 B1
Bill Street Rd ME2 52 D2
Bilton Sq CT9 36 B2
Bingham Rd ME2 52 D2
Bingley Cl ME6 49 B2
Bingley Rd ME1 18 A4
Binnie Cl CT10 15 B6
Birch Cl TN13 46 C4
Birch Hill Ct CT7 14 E3
Birch Rd,
 Tonbridge TN12 40 C4
Birch Rd,
 Whitstable CT5 59 D4
Birch Tree Way ME15 35 D5
Birchington Cl ME14 35 D3
Birchwood Av TN4 50 B1

Birchwood Park Av
 BR8 53 D2
Birchwood Rd BR8 53 A1
Birchwood Rise CT17 23 A2
Birchwood Ter BR8 53 A1
Birdcage Walk TN1 56 C5
Birds Av CT9 58 E3
Birdwood Av CT14 22 A3
Birling Rd,
 Ashford TN24 12 D4
Birling Rd,
 Snodland ME6 49 B3
Birnam Sq ME16 35 A4
Bishops Av CT10 15 C2
Bishops Way ME15 35 B4
Black Bull Rd CT19 26 C1
Black Eagle Cl TN16 57 B6
Black Griffin La CT1 16 A3
Black Horse Mws TN15 13 B6
Black Mill La TN27 31 A5
Blackberry Way TN12 40 D4
Blackdown Dr TN24 12 C2
Blackfriars St CT1 16 C2
Blackhorse Ct TN27 31 C5
Blackhouse Hill CT21 33 C3
Blackhouse Rise CT21 33 C2
Blackmans Cl DA1 21 A5
Blackthorne Rd ME8 42 D2
Blair Dr TN13 46 C4
Blake Gdns DA1 21 D1
Blandford Gdns ME10 48 A6
Blatcher Cl ME12 37 C4
Blaxland Cl ME13 25 B1
Bleak Rd TN29 34 B2
Blendon Rd ME14 35 D2
Blenheim Cl DA1 21 A3
Blenheim Gro DA12 28 C3
Blenheim Rd,
 Dartford DA1 21 A3
Blenheim Rd,
 Deal CT14 22 C2
Blenheim Rd,
 New Romney TN28 38 D3
Blenheim Rd,
 Sittingbourne ME10 48 D5
Bligh Rd DA11 28 B2
Bloomfield Ter TN16 57 D4
Blue Boar La ME1 44 D3
Blue Line La TN24 12 C3
Bluebell Cl ME7 27 C2
Bluefield Mws CT5 59 A6
Bluett St ME14 35 C2
Bluewater Parkway
 DA9 29 A3
Bluewater Pk Retail Pk
 DA9 29 A3
Blythe Rd ME15 35 D4
Boat House Rd ME12 47 A1
Bodiam Ct ME16 35 A5
Bodle Av DA10 29 E3
Bognor Dr CT6 32 A2
Boley Hill ME1 44 C3
Boleyn Av CT9 58 D2
Boleyn Way DA10 29 E4
Bolton Rd CT19 26 D1
Bolton St CT11 43 A3
Bond Rd,
 Ashford TN23 12 B6
Bond Rd,
 Gillingham ME8 42 A6
Bondfield Cl TN4 50 D2
Bonetta Ct ME12 47 C4
Bonham Dr ME10 48 D2
Bonney Way BR8 53 C2
Booth Rd ME4 18 B6
Bordyke TN9 55 C2
Boresisle TN30 54 B2
Borland Cl DA9 29 A2
Borough Green Rd
 TN15 13 A5
Borough Rd,
 Gillingham ME7 27 B4
Borough Rd,
 Queenborough ME11 41 B2
Borstal Av CT5 59 A4
Borstal Hill CT5 59 A4
Borstal Rd ME1 44 A6
Boscombe Rd CT19 26 B1
Bosville Av TN13 46 B4
Bosville Dr TN13 46 A4
Bosville Rd TN13 46 A4
Botany TN9 55 C3
Botany Cl ME12 47 C3
Botany Ind Est TN9 55 C3
Boughton Av CT10 43 D1
Boulogne Ct CT20 26 E2
Boundary Cl ME12 37 E4
Boundary Rd,
 Chatham ME4 18 A5
Boundary Rd,
 Hythe CT21 33 A4
Boundary Rd,
 Ramsgate CT11 43 A3
Bourne Cl TN9 55 B4
Bourne Enterprise Centre
 TN15 13 B5

Bourne Grange La
 TN11
Bourne La,
 Ashford TN26
Bourne La,
 Tonbridge TN9
Bourne Way BR8
Bournemouth Gdns
 CT19
Bournemouth Rd CT19
Bournes Pl TN26
Bournewood TN26
Bouverie Pl CT20
Bouverie Rd West
 CT20
Bouverie Sq CT20
Bow Arrow La DA1
Bowens Fld TN23
Bower La ME16
Bower Pl ME16
Bower Walk TN12
Bowes Av CT9
Bowes Rd ME2
Bowl Rd TN27
Bowles Lodge TN18
Bowling Green La
 CT14
Bowling Green Ter
 CT17
Bowling St CT13
Bowls Pl TN12
Boxley TN23
Boxley Cl ME12
Boxley Rd ME14
Boyne Pk TN4
Bracken Ct CT10
Brackley Cl ME14
Brackwood Cl ME8
Bradbourne Park Rd
 TN13
Bradbourne Rd TN13
Bradbourne Vale Rd
 TN13
Bradfield Rd TN24
Bradford St TN9
Bradley Dr ME10
Bradstone Av CT14
Bradstone New Rd
 CT20
Bradstone Rd CT20
Bradstow Way CT10
Braeside Av TN13
Braeside CT13
Bramble Cl TN25
Bramble La TN25
Brambledown CT19
Bramblehill Rd ME13
Bramley Cl,
 Gillingham ME8
Bramley Cl,
 Swanley BR8
Bramley Ct TN12
Bramley Dr TN17
Bramley Gdns TN12
Bramley Rd ME6
Bramley Rise ME2
Bramleys TN27
Bramston Rd ME12
Brandon Rd DA1
Brandon St DA11
Brandon Way CT7
Brasenose Av ME7
Brasier Ct ME12
Brassey Av CT10
Brasted Ct ME2
Brasted Rd TN16
Brattle TN26
Breakneck Hill DA9
Brecon Chase ME12
Brecon Rise TN24
Bredgar Cl ME14
Bredhurst Cl ME12
Breedon Av TN4
Bremner Cl BR8
Brenchley Cl ME1
Brenchley Rd,
 Maidstone ME15
Brenchley Rd,
 Sittingbourne ME10
Brendon Dr TN24
Brent Hill ME13
Brent La DA1
Brent Rd ME13
Brentlands Dr DA1
Brents Ind Est ME13
Brewer St, Deal CT14
Brewer St,
 Maidstone ME14
Brewery La TN13
Brewery Rd ME10
Brian Cres TN4
Briar Cl, Ashford TN25
Briar Cl,
 Edenbridge TN8
Briar Cl Ind Est
 TN25

Walk CT10 15 B5
Clo CT9 58 D3
Alley CT5 59 A2
nden Rd TN17 20 C5
makers Bsns Centre
) 48 D1
vorks Cl TN9 55 A6
vell La TN30 54 B5
vell Pk CT5 59 D3
e Cl,
ord TN26 60 B3
e Cl, Hythe CT21 33 A3
e Cl,
ridge TN9 55 C4
e Rd,
ord TN23 12 A4
e Rd,
rsham ME13 25 D2
gham ME7 27 A1
e Rd,
gate CT9 58 E2
e Rd,
ester ME1 44 C6
e Rd,
ness ME12 47 C2
rness ME12 47 C2
side CT14 22 C2
water Rd ME12 47 C4
e Way,
nborough ME11 41 C1
e Way,
rness ME12 47 A6
Rd ME4 18 D6
Ridge TN4 50 B3
lingsea Rd CT13 45 C2
s Pl CT11 43 B3
e Gro CT11 43 C2
es Fld TN9 55 D4
ne Gdns TN9 55 D4
ane Rd ME4 18 C5
nden Cl TN28 38 C2
l Rd DA12 28 D6
e Ct ME12 47 C4
e Rd ME13 25 C3
ns La TN13 46 A4
t St ME7 18 D3
t Rd DA10 29 E3
t St,
erbury CT1 16 D2
t St, Deal CT14 22 D2
t St, Margate CT9 36 B2
t St,
sgate CT11 43 B4
e St,
rness ME12 47 C3
cloth TN17 20 C6
lands Rd TN23 38 C2
lands Cres TN28 38 C2
lley Rd CT9 19 B6
lley Rd CT9 19 B6
rmead Rd CT9 36 D2
stairs Rd CT10 15 A3
view Av ME8 42 A2
lway,
ngham ME8 27 D5
lway,
dstone ME16 35 A4
lway,
rness ME12 47 D2
dway Shopping
tre ME16 35 A4
enhurst Rd CT11 43 C3
hill Rd CT21 33 A2
ley Rd CT9 36 D2
man Rd CT20 26 B2
way TN15 13 C6
dale Rd ME13 25 B5
pton Cl ME4 18 B2
pton Farm Rd
52 A2
pton Hill ME4 18 B2
pton La ME2 52 C3
pton Rd ME7 18 D2
stone Mws CT10 15 A4
stone Rd CT10 15 A5
e Gro DA1 21 D1
e Vw DA12 28 C4
< Ct TN8 24 C3
< La,
dland ME6 49 B5
oridge TN9 55 D2
< Rd,
sford ME20 49 A6
< Rd,
rsham ME13 25 D1
< Rd,
nley BR8 53 B2
k St,
ford TN26 60 B3
k St,
dland ME6 49 D3
< Ter ME7 27 B2
ke Av CT9 58 F3
ke Rd TN24 12 C3

Brookfield Ct,
Ashford TN23 12 A6
Brookfield Ct,
Tunbridge Wells TN4 50 C2
Brookfield Ind Pk
TN23 12 A4
Brookfield Rd TN23 12 A6
Brookfields TN11 17 B5
Brooklands,
Ashford TN27 31 B4
Brooklands,
Dartford DA1 21 B5
Brooklyn Pad ME7 27 B2
Brooklyn Villas TN12 34 A5
Brooks Cl TN12 34 A5
Brooks Pl ME14 35 C3
Brooks Way TN29 34 B3
Brookside TN17 20 C5
Broom Hill Rd ME2 52 A2
Broomfield Rd,
Faversham ME13 25 C1
Broomfield Rd,
Sevenoaks TN13 46 A3
Broomfield Rd,
Swanscombe DA10 29 E2
Broomhill Park Rd TN4 50 B3
Broomhill Rd TN3 50 A5
Broomwaters TN11 17 B4
Brown St ME8 42 D2
Browning Rd DA1 21 D1
Brownings TN8 24 B2
Bruce Cl CT14 22 B2
Brunswick Rd CT7 14 D4
Brunswick Sq CT6 32 B1
Brunswick St,
Maidstone ME15 35 B5
Brunswick St,
Ramsgate CT11 43 B4
Brunswick St East
ME15 35 C4
Brunswick Ter TN1 56 D3
Brunswick Walk DA12 28 D3
Bryant Rd ME7 27 B2
Bryant St ME4 18 C5
Buckham Thorns Rd
TN16 57 C5
Buckhurst Av TN13 46 C6
Buckhurst La TN13 46 C6
Buckingham Rd,
Broadstairs CT10 15 D4
Buckingham Rd,
Gillingham ME7 27 B3
Buckingham Rd,
Gravesend DA11 39 C3
Buckingham Rd,
Margate CT9 36 B4
Buckingham Rd,
Tunbridge Wells TN1 56 C5
Buckland Hill ME16 35 A3
Buckland Pl ME16 35 A3
Buckland Rd ME16 35 A2
Buckthorn Cl CT14 22 C1
Buenos Ayres CT9 36 A3
Bull La ME1 44 C3
Buller Rd ME4 18 B6
Bullers Av CT6 32 A2
Bullfields ME6 49 C3
Bullfinch Cl TN12 40 C5
Bullion Cl TN12 40 B4
Bullivant Cl DA9 29 A2
Bulwark Rd CT14 22 D1
Bulwark St West CT17 23 B4
Bunkley Mdw TN26 30 B6
Burch Av CT13 45 C3
Burdens TN27 31 C5
Burgate CT1 16 C3
Burgate La CT1 16 D4
Burgess Rd ME2 52 C4
Burgess Row TN30 54 A6
Burgoyne Ct ME14 35 B1
Burleigh Rd TN27 17 B3
Burley Rd ME10 48 A3
Burlington Gdns CT9 58 F2
Burnaby Rd DA1 39 D3
Burnham Cres DA1 21 A1
Burnham Rd DA1 21 A1
Burnham Trading Est
DA1 21 A1
Burns Cres TN9 55 A5
Burns Rd ME7 27 A1
Burnt Oak Ter ME7 27 A2
Burritt Mws ME1 44 D5
Burritt St ME1 44 D5
Burrow Rd CT9 26 F1
Burrstock Way ME8 42 D1
Busbridge Rd ME6 49 A4
Bushfield Walk DA10 29 E3
Butcher Cl TN12 51 B3
Butcher Walk DA10 29 E3
Butchery La CT1 16 C4
Buttercup Cl TN12 40 C5
Butterfly Av DA1 21 C6
Buttermere Cl ME7 27 D3
Bybrook Ct TN24 12 D2
Bybrook Rd TN24 12 D1
Bychurch Pl ME15 35 C5

Bycliffe Mws DA11 28 A3
Bycliffe Ter DA11 28 A3
Byron Av CT9 36 C3
Byron Rd ME7 27 A5
Bysing Wood Rd ME13 25 A1
Bythorne Ct ME8 42 D1

Cadogan Gdns TN1 56 C3
Caernarvon Gdns
CT10 15 C3
Caernarvon Rd ME15 35 B6
Cairns Cl DA1 21 B1
Caistor Rd TN9 55 A3
Calcroft Av DA9 29 C2
Caldecote Cl ME8 42 D1
Caldew Gro ME10 48 D4
Caledon Ter CT1 16 C6
Caledonian Ct ME8 42 A2
Calehill Cl ME14 35 D5
Callis Court Rd CT10 15 B2
Calverley Park Cres
TN1 56 D3
Calverley Park Gdns
TN1 56 D3
Calverley Pk TN1 56 D3
Calverley Rd TN1 56 C2
Calverley St TN1 56 D2
Cambourne Av CT8 58 B3
Cambrian Gro DA11 28 B3
Cambridge Cl CT7 14 E3
Cambridge Gdns,
Folkestone CT20 26 C2
Cambridge Gdns,
Tunbridge Wells TN2 56 D5
Cambridge Rd,
Deal CT14 22 C5
Cambridge Rd,
Dover CT17 23 C3
Cambridge Rd,
Faversham ME13 25 B3
Cambridge Rd,
Sittingbourne ME10 48 D4
Cambridge Rd,
Strood ME2 52 C3
Cambridge Ter,
Chatham ME4 18 B4
Cambridge Ter,
Folkestone CT20 26 E2
Camden Cl DA11 39 C4
Camden Cres CT16 23 C2
Camden Ct TN1 56 D3
Camden Hill TN1 56 D5
Camden Rd,
Broadstairs CT10 19 D6
Camden Rd,
Gillingham ME7 27 B1
Camden Rd,
Ramsgate CT11 43 B4
Camden Rd,
Sevenoaks TN13 46 C3
Camden Rd,
Tunbridge Wells TN1 56 C2
Camden Sq CT11 43 B4
Camden St ME14 35 C2
Camelia Cl CT9 58 F2
Campbell Rd,
Deal CT14 22 C5
Campbell Rd,
Maidstone ME15 35 B5
Campbell Rd,
Tunbridge Wells TN4 50 C5
Cample Shon Rd ME8 42 A5
Canada Rd CT14 22 C4
Canada Ter ME14 35 B1
Canadian Av ME7 27 C4
Canal Basin CT16 23 D2
Canal Rd,
Gravesend DA12 28 C2
Canal Rd, Strood ME2 52 D4
Canal Rd Ind Pk
DA12 28 D2
Canning St ME14 35 B1
Cannon Bridge Works
TN9 55 D2
Cannon La TN9 55 C2
Cannon Rd CT11 43 A4
Cannon St, Deal CT14 22 C1
Cannon St, Dover CT16 23 C2
Cannon St,
New Romney TN28 38 C3
Cannon St,
Romney Marsh TN29 34 B2
Cannon Walk DA12 28 C3
Cannonbury Rd CT13 45 A5
Cannongate Av CT21 33 C3
Cannongate Cl CT21 33 D3
Cannongate Gdns
CT21 33 D3
Cannongate Rd CT21 33 D2
Canon Cl ME1 44 C6
Canons Gate Rd CT16 23 D1
Canterbury La CT1 16 C4
Canterbury Rd,
Ashford TN24 12 C3
Canterbury Rd,
Birchington CT7 14 C4

Canterbury Rd,
Faversham ME13 25 D4
Canterbury Rd,
Gravesend DA12 28 C5
Canterbury Rd,
Herne Bay CT6 32 C2
Canterbury Rd,
Margate CT9 36 A3
Canterbury Rd,
Sittingbourne ME10 48 D3
Canterbury Rd,
Westgate-on-Sea CT8 58 A3
Canterbury Rd,
Whitstable CT5 59 A4
Canterbury St ME7 27 A3
Canute Rd,
Birchington CT7 14 A2
Canute Rd,
Faversham ME13 25 C4
Capel Rd,
Faversham ME13 25 B3
Capel Rd,
Sittingbourne ME10 48 A4
Capstan Mws DA11 39 D3
Capstan Row CT14 22 D1
Cardinal Cl,
Sheerness ME12 37 D3
Cardinal Cl,
Tonbridge TN9 55 D5
Carey Cl TN28 38 C4
Carisbrooke Rd ME2 52 A2
Carleton Rd DA1 21 D4
Carlton Av,
Broadstairs CT10 15 C2
Carlton Av,
Gillingham ME7 27 B4
Carlton Av,
Ramsgate CT11 43 A4
Carlton Av,
Sheerness ME12 47 C4
Carlton Rd TN23 12 A4
Carlton Rd East CT8 58 B2
Carlton Rd West CT8 58 A3
Carlton Rise CT8 58 A2
Caroline Cres CT10 15 A2
Caroline Sq CT9 36 C2
Carp Cl ME4 18 C4
Carpenters Cl ME1 18 A6
Carpenters La TN11 17 B5
Carriage Mws CT9 58 F2
Carrick Dr TN13 46 B4
Carriers Rd TN17 20 C4
Carrington Cl ME7 27 C2
Carrington Rd DA1 21 D3
Carroways Pl CT9 36 C2
Carsington Gdns DA11 21 B6
Carters Wood TN26 30 B5
Carton Cl ME1 44 D6
Carville Av TN4 50 C2
Caspian Way DA10 29 E2
Castalia Cotts CT14 22 C5
Castle Av,
Broadstairs CT10 15 C2
Castle Av, Hythe CT21 33 B3
Castle Av,
Rochester ME1 44 C6
Castle Cres CT13 33 B2
Castle Flds TN9 55 B2
Castle Hill ME1 44 C3
Castle Hill Av CT20 26 A2
Castle Hill Pass CT20 26 B2
Castle Hill Rd CT16 23 D1
Castle Rd,
Chatham ME4 18 C6
Castle Rd, Hythe CT21 33 B1
Castle Rd,
Sittingbourne ME10 48 D3
Castle Rd,
Swanscombe DA10 29 F3
Castle Rd,
Tunbridge Wells TN4 56 A3
Castle Rd,
Whitstable CT5 59 C1
Castle Rd Bsns Precinct
ME10 48 D1
Castle Rd Technology
Centre ME10 48 D1
Castle Row CT1 16 B5
Castle St,
Canterbury CT1 16 A5
Castle St, Dover CT16 23 C2
Castle St,
Greenhithe DA9 29 A2
Castle St,
Queenborough ME11 41 B1
Castle St,
Southborough TN4 50 C1
Castle St,
Swanscombe DA10 29 F3
Castle St,
Tonbridge TN9 55 B2
Castle Ter TN11 17 B6
Castle View Rd ME2 52 A2

Castle Vw Bsns Centre
ME1 44 D3
Castleacres Ind Est
ME10 48 D1
Castlemaine Av ME7 27 C2
Castlemere Av ME11 41 B1
Castlemount Rd CT16 23 C1
Catherine Pl TN1 56 D3
Catherine St ME1 44 D6
Catherine Way CT10 15 B2
Cattle Market CT13 45 D2
Causton Rd TN17 20 B4
Cavalry Ct CT14 22 C5
Cave Hill ME15 35 A6
Cavenagh Rd CT15 41 D5
Cavendish Av,
Gillingham ME7 27 C2
Cavendish Av,
Sevenoaks TN13 46 A3
Cavendish Ct,
Herne Bay CT6 32 C1
Cavendish Dr TN9 55 D2
Cavendish Dr TN2 56 D6
Cavendish Rd,
Herne Bay CT6 32 C2
Cavendish Rd,
Rochester ME1 44 D6
Cavendish St CT11 43 B4
Caversham Cl ME8 42 C1
Cavour Rd,
Faversham ME13 25 C3
Cavour Rd,
Sheerness ME12 47 D3
Caxton Cl TN30 54 A6
Caxton La TN11 17 B5
Caxton Rd CT9 58 F3
Cecil Av,
Sheerness ME12 47 C4
Cecil Av, Strood ME2 52 C3
Cecil Ct, Ashford TN24 12 C3
Cecil Ct,
Herne Bay CT6 32 D2
Cecil Pk CT6 32 C2
Cecil Rd,
Gravesend DA11 28 A4
Cecil Rd,
Rochester ME1 44 C5
Cecil Sq CT9 36 B2
Cecil St CT9 36 C2
Cecilia Gro CT10 15 A2
Cecilia Rd CT11 43 B2
Cedar Cl,
Birchington CT7 14 E3
Cedar Cl,
Broadstairs CT10 15 B1
Cedar Cl, Margate CT9 19 B4
Cedar Cl,
Sittingbourne ME10 48 D4
Cedar Cl, Swanley BR8 53 A2
Cedar Ct TN8 50 C6
Cedar Dr TN8 24 B4
Cedar Rd,
Dartford DA1 21 B5
Cedar Rd, Strood ME2 52 A5
Cedar St*,
Burgess Row TN30 54 A6
Cedar Ter Rd TN13 46 C3
Cedric Rd CT8 58 B2
Celtic Rd CT14 22 A5
Cemetery La,
Ashford TN24 12 D2
Cemetery La,
Tonbridge TN11 17 C4
Cemetery Rd ME6 49 B2
Centenary Cl TN27 17 B2
Central Av,
Gravesend DA12 28 B5
Central Av,
Sittingbourne ME10 48 B3
Central Bsns Pk
ME2 18 A1
Central Par CT6 32 A1
Central Park Gdns ME4 18 A6
Central Rd,
Dartford DA1 21 C1
Central Rd,
Ramsgate CT11 43 A2
Central Rd,
Strood ME2 52 B8
Century Rd ME8 42 A2
Century Walk CT14 22 C2
Chada Av ME7 27 B5
Chadwick Cl DA11 39 D6
Chaffinch Way TN12 40 C5
Chalk Av TN30 54 B2
Chalk Hill Rd ME4 18 C5
Chalk Pit Hill ME4 18 C5
Chalk Rd ME11 41 B1
Chalkwell Rd ME10 48 A3
Challenger Cl TN12 40 B6
Chamberlain Rd ME4 18 D6
Chambers Cl DA9 29 A2
Chancellor Way TN13 46 B3
Chancery Cl DA1 21 D4
Chancery La ME15 35 C4
Chandos Rd CT10 15 C4

Chandos Sq CT10 15 D4
Channel View Rd CT17 23 B4
Channel Vw CT20 26 E2
Chantlers Hill TN12 40 C6
Chantry Ct CT1 16 C2
Chantry Pl TN12 34 B5
Chantry Rd TN12 34 B5
Chapel Ct DA10 29 E3
Chapel Hill Cl CT9 36 D6
Chapel La,
Dover CT16 23 C2
Chapel La,
St Margarets at Cliffe
CT15 41 B4
Chapel La,
Tonbridge TN12 51 C4
Chapel Pl,
Birchington CT7 14 E3
Chapel Pl, Dover CT17 23 C2
Chapel Pl,
Ramsgate CT11 43 A4
Chapel Pl,
Tunbridge Wells TN1 56 B6
Chapel Place La CT11 43 A4
Chapel Rd ME6 49 C3
Chapel St, Deal CT14 22 D2
Chapel St,
Faversham ME13 25 D3
Chapel St,
Herne Bay CT6 32 C1
Chapel St, Hythe CT21 33 B4
Chapel St,
Minster ME12 37 E3
Chapel St,
Sheerness ME12 47 B2
Chaplin Dr TN27 31 C5
Chapman Ho CT14 22 B5
Chappell Way ME10 48 A1
Chapter Rd ME2 52 A4
Charing Cres CT8 58 A3
Charing Hill TN27 17 C2
Charles Cl ME6 49 C3
Charles Ho CT14 22 B5
Charles Rd, Deal CT14 22 B4
Charles Rd,
Ramsgate CT11 43 B2
Charles St,
Chatham ME4 18 A5
Charles St,
Greenhithe DA9 29 A1
Charles St,
Herne Bay CT6 32 C1
Charles St,
Maidstone ME16 35 A5
Charles St,
Sheerness ME12 47 B2
Charles St,
Strood ME2 52 C4
Charles St,
Tunbridge Wells TN4 50 C3
Charlesworth Dr CT7 14 E3
Charlotte Sq CT9 36 C3
Charlotte St,
Folkestone CT20 26 D2
Charlotte St,
Sittingbourne ME10 48 A2
Charlton Ter TN9 55 C2
Charnock BR8 53 C3
Chart Cl ME13 25 B3
Chart Rd TN23 12 A3
Charter House Dr TN13 46 B4
Charter St,
Chatham ME4 18 B6
Charter St,
Gillingham ME7 27 A1
Chartway TN13 46 C5
Chartwell Cl ME2 52 D2
Chater Ct CT14 22 C4
Chatham Hill,
Chatham ME5 18 D5
Chatham Hill,
Gillingham ME7 27 A5
Chatham Hill Rd TN14 46 C2
Chatham Pl CT11 43 A3
Chatham Rd ME14 35 A1
Chatham St CT11 43 A3
Chatsworth Dr ME2 52 D2
Chatsworth Rd,
Dartford DA1 21 A1
Chatsworth Rd,
Gillingham ME7 27 A2
Chattenden Ct ME14 35 C1
Chaucer Pk DA1 21 C4
Chaucer Rd,
Broadstairs CT10 15 B5
Chaucer Rd,
Gillingham ME7 27 A5
Chaucer Rd,
Gravesend DA11 39 C6
Chaucer Rd,
Sittingbourne ME10 48 A4
Cheddar Cl TN24 12 C2
Cheeselands TN27 13 B2
Chegworth Gdns
ME10 48 A6
Chelmar Rd ME4 18 C5

Chequers Centre
ME15 35 C4
Chequers Ct ME2 52 B2
Chequers Pk TN25 60 C6
Chequers Rd ME12 37 F3
Cheriton Gdns CT20 26 B2
Cheriton Pl, Deal CT14 22 C4
Cheriton Pl,
Folkestone CT20 26 C3
Cheriton Rd,
Deal CT14 22 C4
Cheriton Rd,
Folkestone CT19 26 A2
Cherry Amber Cl ME8 42 B2
Cherry Av BR8 53 B3
Cherry Cl,
Ashford TN26 30 B6
Cherry Cl,
Maidstone ME17 32 B5
Cherry Cl,
Sittingbourne ME10 48 A1
Cherry Garden Cres
TN25 60 C5
Cherry Garden La
TN25 60 C5
Cherry Gdns,
Herne Bay CT6 32 B3
Cherry Gdns,
New Romney TN28 38 E3
Cherry Orch,
Ashford TN26 60 A1
Cherry Orch,
Tenterden TN30 54 A6
Cherry Tree Cl ME12 47 B5
Cherry Tree Rd ME8 42 B5
Cherrywood Rise TN25 12 A2
Chesfield Cl TN11 17 C5
Chesham Dr ME8 42 A4
Chester Rd,
Gillingham ME7 27 B6
Chester Rd,
Westgate-on-Sea CT8 58 C2
Chestnut Av,
Greenhithe DA9 29 A4
Chestnut Av,
Tonbridge TN12 51 B2
Chestnut Av,
Tunbridge Wells TN4 50 D3
Chestnut Cl,
Edenbridge TN8 24 B4
Chestnut Cl,
Tenterden TN30 54 C3
Chestnut Cl,
Tunbridge Wells TN4 50 D6
Chestnut La TN13 46 B4
Cheviot Rd DA1 21 B4
Cheviot Ho DA11 39 C2
Cheviot Way TN24 12 C2
Chicago Av ME7 27 C3
Chichester Cl,
Ashford TN23 12 B5
Chichester Cl,
Gillingham ME8 42 C2
Chichester Dr TN13 46 A6
Chichester Rd TN9 55 A4
Chiddingfold Cl ME12 37 D3
Chiffinch Gdns DA11 39 D6
Childs Cres DA10 29 D3
Chilham Av CT8 58 A3
Chilham Cl,
Chatham ME4 18 A5
Chilham Cl,
Sheerness ME12 47 C5
Chillington St ME14 35 B1
Chilston Cl TN4 50 D6
Chilston Rd,
Maidstone ME17 32 C5
Chilston Rd,
Tunbridge Wells TN4 50 D6
Chiltern End TN24 12 B3
Chiltern Rd DA11 39 B6
Chiltern Way TN9 55 C1
Chilternhurst TN8 24 A3
Chilton Av ME10 48 C3
Chilton Ct ME8 42 A1
Chippendayle Dr
ME17 30 B2
Christ Church Rd CT20 26 B3
Christchurch Av TN1 56 C5
Christchurch Cres
DA12 28 C3
Christchurch Ct CT17 23 B2
Christchurch Rd,
Ashford TN23 12 B5
Christchurch Rd,
Gravesend DA12 28 C4
Christmas St ME7 27 C1
Chulkhurst TN27 13 B2
Church App TN28 20 B4
Church Cotts TN17 20 B4
Church Cres ME17 30 D2
Church Fld,
Dartford DA2 21 B6
Church Fld,
Edenbridge TN8 24 C5

Church Fld,
Snodland ME6 49 D1
Church Flds CT9 36 C3
Church Grn,
Staplehurst TN12 51 B4
Church Grn,
Tonbridge TN12 34 B5
Church Hill,
Chatham ME5 27 A6
Church Hill,
Dartford DA2 21 B6
Church Hill,
Hythe CT21 33 B3
Church Hill,
Ramsgate CT11 43 B4
Church La, Rosemary La,
Canterbury CT1 16 A5
Church La, The Borough,
Canterbury CT1 16 C2
Church La,
Chatham ME4 18 B1
Church La, Deal CT14 22 A3
Church La,
Maidstone ME17 30 C2
Church La,
New Romney TN28 38 B3
Church La,
Tonbridge TN9 55 C2
Church Mdws CT14 22 A2
Church Mws ME8 42 B2
Church Path,
Chatham ME7 18 D2
Church Path,
Deal CT14 22 A4
Church Path,
Gillingham ME7 27 B2
Church Path,
Gravesend DA11 39 C2
Church Path,
Strood ME2 52 C4
Church Path,
Tenterden TN30 54 A5
Church Rd,
Ashford TN23 12 C4
Church Rd,
Broadstairs CT10 15 D4
Church Rd,
Faversham ME13 25 D2
Church Rd,
Harrietsham ME17 30 C2
Church Rd,
Hythe CT21 33 B3
Church Rd,
Maidstone ME15 35 A6
Church Rd,
Margate CT9 36 C3
Church Rd,
New Romney TN28 38 A4
Church Rd,
Ramsgate CT11 43 B4
Church Rd,
Romney Marsh TN29 34 C2
Church Rd,
Sittingbourne ME10 48 D3
Church Rd,
Southborough TN4 50 B1
Church Rd,
Swanscombe DA10 29 F2
Church Rd,
Tenterden TN30 54 B5
Church Rd,
Tonbridge TN12 40 C2
Church Rd,
Tunbridge Wells TN1 56 A3
Church St Marys CT13 45 D1
Church Sq,
Broadstairs CT10 15 D4
Church Sq,
Maidstone ME17 32 D6
Church St,
Ashford TN25 60 C5
Church St,
Broadstairs CT10 15 A3
Church St,
Canterbury CT1 16 D4
Church St,
Chatham ME4 18 C4
Church St, Dover CT16 23 C2
Church St,
Edenbridge TN8 24 C5
Church St,
Faversham ME13 25 D2
Church St,
Folkestone CT20 26 D3
Church St,
Gillingham ME7 27 C2
Church St,
Gravesend DA11 28 B2
Church St,
Hadlow TN11 17 C6
Church St,
Maidstone ME15 35 A6
Church St,
Maidstone ME14 35 B3
Church St,
Margate CT9 36 C3

Church St,
Rochester ME1 44 D4
Church St, Charlotte St,
Sittingbourne ME10 48 A2
Church St, Dover St,
Sittingbourne ME10 48 A3
Church St,
Tonbridge TN9 55 C2
Church St,
Whitstable CT5 59 C3
Church Ter,
Chatham ME5 27 A6
Church Ter,
Sheerness ME12 37 D3
Church Vw,
Ashford TN27 13 B2
Church Vw,
Swanley BR8 53 B2
Church Walk,
Ashford TN27 31 B5
Church Walk,
Cranbrook TN18 31 C2
Church Walk,
Dartford DA2 21 B6
Church Walk,
Gravesend DA12 28 D4
Church Walk,
Northfleet DA11 39 B2
Churchfield Pl CT9 36 C3
Churchfield Way
TN25 60 B5
Churchfields CT10 15 B1
Churchill Av CT14 22 B6
Churchill Cl CT15 41 B5
Churchill Ct,
Hythe CT21 33 A4
Churchill Ct,
Westerham TN16 57 D4
Churchill Rd,
Gravesend DA11 28 A4
Churchill Rd,
Sheerness ME12 37 E3
Churchill Way ME13 25 B1
Cinque Ports Av CT21 33 A5
Citadel Cres CT17 23 A4
Citadel Rd CT17 23 A4
City Way ME1 44 D5
Civic Way TN1 56 C3
Claire Ct CT10 15 C3
Clanricarde Gdns TN1 56 B3
Clanricarde Rd TN1 56 B3
Clanwilliam Rd CT14 22 D3
Clapper La TN12 51 A2
Clare Rd CT5 59 B1
Claremont Gdns TN2 56 D6
Claremont Pl CT1 16 A6
Claremont Rd,
Deal CT14 22 B3
Claremont Rd,
Folkestone CT20 26 B2
Claremont Rd,
Maidstone ME14 35 D3
Claremont Rd,
Tunbridge Wells TN1 56 C5
Claremont Way ME4 18 B4
Clarence Av,
Margate CT9 19 C3
Clarence Av,
Rochester ME1 44 D5
Clarence Pl, Deal CT14 22 C1
Clarence Pl,
Dover CT17 23 C4
Clarence Pl,
Gravesend DA12 28 B3
Clarence Rd,
Chatham ME4 18 D6
Clarence Rd,
Deal CT14 22 D6
Clarence Rd,
Herne Bay CT6 32 A2
Clarence Rd,
Sheerness ME12 47 D2
Clarence Rd,
Tunbridge Wells TN1 56 B3
Clarence Row,
Gravesend DA12 28 B3
Clarence Row,
Sheerness ME12 47 D2
Clarence Row,
Tunbridge Wells TN1 56 B3
Clarence St,
Folkestone CT20 26 D2
Clarence St,
Herne Bay CT6 32 B1
Clarendon Cl ME10 48 B6
Clarendon Gdns,
Ramsgate CT11 43 A4
Clarendon Gdns,
Rochester ME2 52 C2
Clarendon Mws,
Broadstairs CT10 15 B4
Clarendon Mws,
New Romney TN28 38 C1
Clarendon Pl CT17 23 A3
Clarendon Rd,
Broadstairs CT10 15 C4

Clarendon Rd,
Dover CT17
Clarendon Rd,
Gravesend DA12
Clarendon Rd,
Margate CT9
Clarendon Rd,
Sevenoaks TN13
Clarendon St CT17
Claridge Mws CT21
Clavadal Rd TN12
Clearmount Dr TN27
Cleave Rd ME7
Cleaver La CT11
Clerks Fld TN27
Cleveland Ho DA11
Cleveland Rd ME7
Cliff Cl CT21
Cliff Fld CT8
Cliff Gdns ME12
Cliff Prom CT10
Cliff Rd,
Birchington CT7
Cliff Rd,
Broadstairs CT10
Cliff Rd, Hythe CT21
Cliff Rd, Strood ME2
Cliff Rd,
Whitstable CT5
Cliff St CT11
Cliff Ter CT9
Cliffe Av CT9
Cliffe Rd ME2
Clifford Gdns CT14
Clifford Rd CT5
Cliffside Dr CT10
Clifton Cl,
Maidstone ME14
Clifton Cl,
Rochester ME2
Clifton Cres CT20
Clifton Gdns CT9
Clifton Gro CT11
Clifton Marine Par
DA11
Clifton Mws CT9
Clifton Pl,
Margate CT9
Clifton Pl,
Tunbridge Wells TN2
Clifton Rd,
Folkestone CT20
Clifton Rd,
Gillingham ME7
Clifton Rd,
Gravesend DA11
Clifton Rd,
Margate CT9
Clifton Rd,
Whitstable CT5
Clifton St CT9
Cliftonville Av CT9
Clipper Cl ME2
Clipper Ct ME2
Clive Rd,
Gravesend DA11
Clive Rd,
Rochester ME1
Clock Tower Mws ME6
Clockhouse La CT14
Cloth Hall Gdns TN27
Clovelly Dr ME12
Clovelly Rd CT5
Clover Ct ME10
Clover St ME4
Clover Walk TN8
Clover Way TN12
Coast Rd TN28
Coastguard Cotts CT21
Coats Av ME12
Cobay Cl CT21
Cobb Walk ME13
Cobbets Way TN8
Cobblers Bridge Rd
CT6
Cobbs Cl TN12
Cobbs Mws CT20
Cobbs Pas CT21
Cobbs Pl CT9
Cobbs Wood Ind Est
TN23
Cobden Pl CT1
Cobden Rd,
Chatham ME4
Cobden Rd,
Hythe CT21
Cobden Rd,
Sevenoaks TN13
Cobham Av ME10
Cobham Chase ME13
Cobham Cl,
Maidstone ME16
Cobham Cl,
Rochester ME2
Cobham Rise ME7
Cobham St DA11

m Ter DA9 29 B3
a TN26 30 B6
eed La TN28 38 A3
gton Rd CT11 43 A4
e Rd TN12 40 B4
m Rd CT10 43 D1
arbour La TN25 60 D5
arbour Rd DA11 39 D5
er ME17 32 B6
an Stairs CT7 14 D1
ans CITN29 34 C2
ans Stairs Rd 14 D1
d ME1 44 C3
e CI CT6 32 D3
e Av,
gham ME7 18 D4
e stone ME15 35 B5
e Av,
ridge TN9 55 A5
e Cotts ME15 35 B5
e CtTN23 12 C4
e PI DA9 29 C1
e Rd,
ham ME4 18 C1
e Rd, Deal CT14 22 C1
esend DA11 39 A1
e Rd,
stone ME15 35 B5
e Rd,
ate CT9 36 B5
e Rd,
sgate CT11 43 A2
e Rd,
gbourne ME10 48 A4
e Walk ME15 35 B5
gwood CT10 15 A4
gwood CI CT8 58 A4
gwood Ho DA9 29 C2
gwood Rd CT5 59 A3
St ME2 52 C3
on PITN30 54 D5
y Rd DA1 21 C3
el Stephens Way
els Way TN4 50 D1
r Rd DA11 39 C5
erce Way TN8 24 B3
ercial PI DA12 28 C2
ercial Rd,
ock Wood TN12 40 B4
ercial Rd,
od ME2 52 C4
ercial Rd,
ridge TN9 55 B4
issioners Rd 52 D3
nodore Rd ME14 35 D2
non Rd TN11 17 B4
nonwealth CI
D 48 D4
ord CITN12 40 B3
uit St ME13 25 D2
r Way BR8 53 A1
ton Av TN4 50 B6
ton CI ME7 27 D2
ton Rd ME7 27 A3
aught Gdns CT9 36 C4
aught Rd,
ham ME4 18 D6
aught Rd,
estone CT20 26 C2
aught Rd,
gate CT9 36 C4
aught Rd,
gbourne ME10 48 A4
aughtWayTN4 50 B6
ort CI ME14 35 D3
able Rd,
ington CT7 14 D1
able Rd,
esend DA11 39 D6
ables Rd CT16 23 D1
ancia Ct CT20 26 B2
itution Hill,
ham ME5 18 D5
itution Hill,
esend DA12 28 C4
itution Hill,
dland ME6 49 B2
itution Hill Rd 50 B2
itution Rd ME5 18 D5
ent CI CT15 41 C5
ay CI, 14 B2
ington CT7 14 B2
ay CI,
ester ME2 52 A2
ay Mws ME7 18 C2
erd RdTN15 13 A6
ham Hill ME1 44 B6
s La ME10 48 B1
ng Rd ME2 52 D1

Coolinge Rd CT20 26 B2
Coomb Fld TN8 24 B5
Coombe Av TN14 46 C1
Coombe CI ME6 49 C4
Coombe La TN30 54 A5
Coombe Rd,
Gravesend DA12 28 C5
Coombe Rd,
Maidstone ME15 35 B6
Cooper Rd ME6 49 B5
Copenhagen Rd ME7 27 A4
Copland Av ME12 37 C4
Copper Beech CI
DA12 28 D3
Copper Beech Vw TN9 55 A4
Copper La TN12 34 C6
Copperfields TN29 34 B2
Copperwood TN24 12 D2
Coppin St CT14 22 D1
Copthall Av TN18 31 B2
Copthall Gdns CT20 26 C2
Cordelia Cres ME1 44 A6
Cork La TN12 51 A6
Corkwell St ME4 18 A5
Corner Farm RdTN12 51 B2
Cornford Rd CT7 14 E3
Cornforth CITN12 51 C3
Cornhill CT11 43 A5
Cornwall Av CT11 43 A4
Cornwall Gdns CT9 19 B3
Cornwall Rd,
Deal CT14 22 C5
Cornwall Rd,
Gillingham ME7 27 A2
Cornwall Rd,
Rochester ME1 44 C5
Cornwallis Av ME7 27 D4
Cornwallis Circle CT5 59 A3
Cornwallis Gdns CT10 15 C2
Cornwell Av DA12 28 C6
Corona Ter ME6 49 B5
Coronation CI CT10 15 A1
Coronation Cres,
Margate CT9 58 E3
Coronation Cres,
Queenborough ME11 41 A1
Coronation Par CT19 26 F2
Coronation Rd,
Chatham ME5 27 A6
Coronation Rd,
Ramsgate CT11 43 A4
Coronation Sq TN29 34 B2
Corporation Rd ME7 27 B2
Corporation St ME1 44 C2
Corral CI ME5 27 B6
Correnden RdTN10 55 A1
Cortland CI ME10 48 A1
Corunna CI CT21 33 A3
Cossack St ME1 44 C5
Cossington Rd CT11 16 D5
Costells Mdws TN16 57 D5
Cotswold CITN24 12 C2
Cotswold Rd DA11 39 D6
Cottage Rd,
Chatham ME4 18 B2
Cottage Rd,
Ramsgate CT11 43 B4
Cottage Row CT13 45 D1
Cottall Av ME4 18 B6
Cotton Hill Walk TN26 30 B6
Couchman Green La
TN12 51 C1
Coulman St ME7 27 B3
Coulter Ho DA9 29 C2
Coulton Av DA11 39 D3
Council Rd DA11 39 B2
County Rd ME14 35 B3
Court App CT20 26 B3
Court Cres BR8 53 C4
Court Hall ME11 41 A1
Court La TN11 17 C6
Court Lane PITN11 17 C6
Court Lodge La ME17 30 C1
Court Lodge Rd ME7 27 D2
Court Rd CT14 22 A6
Court St ME13 25 D2
Courtenay Rd ME15 35 A6
Courthope TN12 40 C4
Courtlands,
Herne Bay CT6 32 D3
Courtlands,
Tonbridge TN10 55 A1
Courtlands Way CT8 58 C2
Courtwood DrTN13 46 A4
Coventry Gdns CT14 22 C4
Covey Hall Rd ME6 49 C2
Cowdray Rd CT14 22 A5
Cowdray Sq CT14 22 A5
Cowgate Hill CT17 23 C2
Cowley Av DA9 29 A2
Cowley Rise CT9 19 B6
Cowper Rd, Deal CT14 22 B3
Cowper Rd,
Gillingham ME7 27 A5
Cowper Rd,
Margate CT9 36 C3

Cowper Rd,
Sittingbourne ME10 48 D3
Coxs CI ME6 49 B2
Cozenton CI ME8 42 A1
Cradducks La TN12 51 D2
Cragie Walk ME8 42 A6
Cramptons RdTN14 46 C1
Cranbourne CI CT11 43 C2
Cranbrook Dr ME10 48 A6
Cranbrook Rd,
Cranbrook TN18 31 B1
Cranbrook Rd,
Tonbridge TN12 51 C5
Crane House Gdns
TN18 31 B1
Crane La TN17 20 C5
Cranford CI ME8 42 A1
Cranford Rd DA1 21 B4
Cranham Sq TN12 51 A6
Cranleigh Dr BR8 53 C4
Cranleigh Gdns CT5 59 B4
Cranmere Ct ME2 52 D3
Crates Yd TN4 50 C6
Craven CI CT9 58 F3
Crawford Gdns CT9 19 A3
Crawford Rd CT10 15 B3
Crawshay CITN13 46 A3
Crayford CI ME14 35 D2
Craylands La DA10 29 C2
Craylands Sq DA10 29 D2
CraythorneTN30 54 C4
Craythorne CITN28 38 C2
Craythorne La TN28 38 B3
Cremer PI ME13 25 B2
Cremers Rd ME10 48 D2
Crendon PkTN4 50 C6
Crescent Gdns BR8 53 A1
Crescent Rd,
Birchington CT7 14 D2
Crescent Rd,
Faversham ME13 25 D2
Crescent Rd,
Margate CT9 36 A3
Crescent Rd,
Ramsgate CT11 43 A4
Crescent Rd,
Tunbridge WellsTN1 56 C3
Crescent St ME10 48 B3
Cress Way ME13 25 B3
Cressey Ct ME4 18 A6
Cressfield TN23 12 A5
Crest Ind Est TN12 34 B4
Crete Hall Rd DA11 39 C2
Cricketers CI ME17 30 B2
Crinan Ct*,
Argyll Dr CT10 43 B1
Cripps La CT15 41 B5
Crispin CI ME13 25 D1
Croft CtTN8 24 C5
Croft Gdns ME17 32 C6
Croft La TN8 24 C5
Croft Rd, Ashford TN24 12 D4
Croft Rd,
Westerham TN16 57 B5
Crofton Rd CT8 58 C4
Cromer Rd ME4 52 C3
Cromer StTN9 55 A3
Crompton Gdns ME15 35 C4
Cromwell Rd,
Maidstone ME14 35 C4
Cromwell Rd,
Whitstable CT5 59 B1
Cromwell Ter ME4 18 C5
Crooked La DA12 28 B2
Crosley Rd ME7 27 B6
Cross La,
Faversham ME13 25 C3
Cross La,
Sittingbourne ME10 48 B1
Cross La East DA12 28 B5
Cross La West DA11 28 B5
Cross Rd,
Birchington CT7 14 E2
Cross Rd, Deal CT14 22 A6
Cross St,
Chatham ME4 18 C4
Cross St,
Gillingham ME7 27 A2
Cross St,
Gravesend DA12 28 C2
Cross St,
Herne Bay CT6 32 A3
Cross St,
Maidstone ME14 35 B1
Cross St, Strood ME2 52 C3
Cross Way ME1 44 C6
Crossways ME10 48 B6
Crossways Blvd DA9 29 A1
Crouch House Cotts
TN8 24 A4
Crouch House RdTN8 24 A2
Crouch La TN15 13 C5
Crow Hill,
Broadstairs CT10 15 C3
Crow Hill,
Sevenoaks TN15 13 C5

Crow Hill Rd,
Margate CT9 58 E3
Crow Hill Rd,
Sevenoaks TN15 13 C5
Crow La ME1 44 C4
Crowhurst RdTN15 13 B6
Crown CtTN17 20 B4
Crown Quay La ME10 48 C3
Crown Rd,
Edenbridge TN8 24 D2
Crown Rd,
Sittingbourne ME10 48 A1
Crown St ME7 27 A2
Crownfields TN13 46 B6
Crowther CITN12 51 B3
Croydon RdTN16 57 A4
Crundwell RdTN4 50 B2
Crusader Ct DA1 21 D1
Crystal Bsns Centre
CT13 45 F1
Cudham Gdns CT9 19 D3
Cullet Dr ME11 41 A2
Culverden Av TN4 50 C5
Culverden Down TN4 50 B6
Culverden Park RdTN4 50 C6
Culverden PkTN4 50 C6
Culverden SqTN4 56 B1
Culverden StTN1 56 B1
Cumber Ld Rd CT11 43 A4
Cumberland Av,
Broadstairs CT10 15 C3
Cumberland Av,
Gravesend DA12 28 C3
Cumberland CtTN10 55 A1
Cumberland Dr DA1 21 D4
Cumberland Gdns TN1 56 B6
Cumberland Mws TN1 56 B6
Cumberland Rd,
Gillingham ME7 27 A1
Cumberland Rd,
Margate CT9 19 A3
Cumberland WalkTN1 56 B6
Cumberland YdTN1 56 B6
Cunningham CITN4 50 D4
Cunningham Cres CT7 14 C2
Cunningham RdTN4 50 D4
Currie RdTN4 50 D6
Curteis RdTN30 54 B4
Curtis Way ME13 25 C2
Curzon CI CT14 22 C5
Curzon Rd,
Chatham ME4 18 B5
Curzon Rd,
Maidstone ME14 35 C1
Cutbush CI ME17 30 B2
Cutbush St ME14 35 D3
Cuthbert Rd CT8 58 B2
Cutmore St DA11 28 B3
Cutty Sark Ct DA9 29 A2
Cuxton Rd ME2 52 B6
Cyclamen Rd BR8 53 B3
Cygnet Gdns DA11 28 A5
Cylinder Rd CT21 33 A2
Cypress Ct ME7 27 D2

Daglish RdTN28 38 C3
Dagmar Rd ME4 18 D6
Dahlia Dr BR8 53 E2
Dalby Rd CT9 36 D2
Dalby Sq CT9 36 D2
Dale Ct CT11 43 C2
Dale Rd,
Rochester ME1 44 C6
Dale Rd, Swanley BR8 53 A2
Dale St, Chatham ME4 18 A6
Dale St,
Tunbridge WellsTN1 56 D1
Dalewood ME10 48 D5
Dallinger Rd CT7 14 C1
Dalmaney CI CT10 15 D3
Dalmeny Av CT9 19 C4
Dalton St ME7 27 A2
Damson Ct BR8 53 B3
Dan Dr ME13 25 A1
Dane Cres CT11 43 B2
Dane End Rd CT8 58 A2
Dane Gdns CT9 19 B6
Dane Hill CT9 36 C2
Dane Hill Row CT9 36 C2
Dane Mt CT9 19 B6
Dane Park Rd,
Margate CT9 36 D2
Dane Park Rd,
Ramsgate CT11 43 B2
Dane Pk CT9 36 D3
Dane Rd,
Birchington CT7 14 A2
Dane Rd,
Margate CT9 36 C2
Dane Rd,
Ramsgate CT11 43 B3
Dane Valley Rd CT9 19 A5
Danedale Av ME12 37 F3
Danemoor TN30 54 C4
Danes CI DA11 39 B6
Danes Hill ME7 27 D2

Danes Mead Ter CT9 36 C2
Danvers RdTN9 55 B3
Darby PI CT20 26 C2
Darby Rd CT20 26 C2
Darcy SqTN28 38 E4
Darenth Gdns TN16 57 D5
Darenth Rd DA1 21 C3
Dark Hill ME13 25 C2
Dark La CT21 33 A2
Darland Av ME7 27 C6
Darlington Dr ME12 37 A4
Darlington St CT20 26 C2
Darnley CI CT10 15 B5
Darnley Rd,
Gravesend DA11 28 A4
Darnley Rd,
Strood ME2 52 A5
Darnley St DA11 28 B3
Darracott CI CT14 22 B3
Darren Gdns CT10 15 B6
Dart CI ME2 52 B4
Dartford Rd,
Dartford DA1 21 A3
Dartford Rd,
Sevenoaks TN13 46 C5
Darwin Rd CT7 14 C2
Dashwood Rd DA11 28 A5
Davenport Av ME7 27 B2
David Av CT9 19 C3
Davids CI CT10 15 C5
Davie CI ME12 47 C5
Davington Hill ME13 25 C2
Davis Av, Deal CT14 22 A4
Davis Av,
Gravesend DA11 39 D4
Davis CITN13 46 C2
Dawes St ME7 27 A3
Dawks MdwTN27 31 B5
Dawson Rd CT19 26 D1
De Burgh St CT17 23 A1
De Mere CI ME8 42 A5
De Warren Ho DA11 39 C2
Deacon CI ME8 52 A3
Deacon CtTN4 50 C6
Deacon Trading Est
TN9 55 D3
Deakin Leas TN9 55 B5
Deal Castle Rd CT14 22 D3
Deal Rd CT13 45 D4
Dean Rd,
Rochester ME2 52 A3
Dean Rd,
Sittingbourne ME10 48 A1
Deane CI CT5 59 B5
Deanwood Dr ME8 42 A5
Deborah CI CT5 59 C5
Deedes CI CT21 33 C3
Delagarde RdTN16 57 C5
Delamark Rd ME12 47 D2
Delamere Gdns ME6 49 C2
Delamere Rd ME6 49 C2
Delane Rd CT14 22 A3
Delce Rd ME1 44 D4
Delf St CT13 45 D1
Delfside CT13 45 D2
Dence CI CT6 32 D1
Dence Pk CT6 32 D2
Dencorra WayTN23 12 A5
Dene Holm Rd DA11 39 C6
Dene Lodge CITN15 13 A5
Dene Rd DA1 21 C4
Dene Walk CT9 36 C5
Dengemarsh RdTN29 34 C3
Denington CtTN4 50 C1
Denmark Rd CT11 43 B3
Dennes La TN29 34 B1
Dennes Mill CITN25 60 B5
Dennis Rd DA11 28 B6
Dental St CT21 33 B3
Dent-de-Lion CI CT8 58 D3
Dent-de-Lion Rd,
Margate CT9 58 E3
Dent-de-Lion Rd,
Westgate-on-Sea CT8 58 B2
Denton Way CT9 19 B4
Derby CI ME10 48 A1
Dering Rd CT6 32 B2
Derwent DrTN4 50 B6
D'Este Av CT11 43 C4
Detling Av CT10 43 C1
Detling CI ME12 47 C5
Detling Rd DA11 39 D4
Devon Av CT14 22 C5
Devon CI ME8 42 B1
Devon Gdns CT7 14 C3
Devon Rd CT9 19 B6
Devonshire Gdns CT9 19 B3
Devonshire Rd,
Gillingham ME7 27 A1
Devonshire Rd,
Gravesend DA12 28 B4
Dial CI,
Gillingham ME7 27 D2
Dial CI,
Greenhithe DA9 29 D2
Dial Rd ME7 27 D2

Diamond Ct ME12 47 C4
Diamond Rd CT5 59 B2
Diana Gdns CT14 22 A3
Dibden Rd CT14 22 D1
Dickens Rd,
  Broadstairs CT10 15 D3
Dickens Rd,
  Rochester ME1 44 C6
Dickens Way TN18 31 C2
Dickley La ME17 32 A4
Dickson Ct ME10 48 D3
Dickson Rd CT17 23 A1
Dieu Stone La CT16 23 C1
Dignals Cl ME8 42 B1
Dillywood La ME2 52 A1
Dimmock Cl TN12 40 D3
Dixon Cl ME15 35 B5
Dobwells TN17 20 C5
Dock Rd ME4 18 B3
Doddington Ct ME16 35 A3
Does Alley ME10 48 B3
Doggerel Acre CT5 59 C5
Doggets Ct TN8 24 B6
Doggetts Sq ME2 52 D4
Dola Av CT14 22 B2
Dolphin Dr ME8 42 A6
Dolphin La CT16 23 C2
Dolphin Pk ME10 48 D2
Dolphin Pl CT16 23 C2
Dolphin Rd ME10 48 D2
Dolphin St,
  Deal CT14 22 D1
Dolphin St,
  Herne Bay CT6 32 B1
Dombey Cl ME1 44 C6
Domneva Rd CT8 58 B2
Dongola Rd ME2 52 C2
Doon Brae TN4 50 C1
Dorcas Gdns CT10 15 C2
Dorchester Cl DA1 21 C4
Dorchester Rd DA12 28 D6
Doric Av TN4 50 B2
Doric Cl TN4 50 B2
Dorothy Av TN17 20 C6
Dorset CT14 22 B6
Dorset Ct CT14 22 C6
Dorset Gdns,
  Birchington CT7 14 C3
Dorset Gdns,
  Deal CT14 22 B6
Dorset Pl ME13 25 C3
Dorset Rd ME12 47 B4
Dorset Rd Ind Est
ME12 47 B4
Dorset St TN13 46 C6
Dossett Ct CT14 22 A6
Douglas Alms Houses
ME17 32 C5
Douglas Av,
  Hythe CT21 33 C3
Douglas Av,
  Whitstable CT5 59 B3
Douglas Cl CT10 15 A3
Douglas Rd, Deal CT14 22 A5
Douglas Rd,
  Herne Bay CT6 32 C3
Douglas Rd,
  Lenham ME17 32 C5
Douglas Rd,
  Maidstone ME16 35 A5
Douglas Rd,
  Tonbridge TN9 55 A4
Douglas Ter CT14 22 C3
Dour St CT16 23 B1
Douro Pl CT16 23 D2
Doust Way ME1 18 A4
Dovedale Ct,
  Ashford TN24 12 B3
Dovedale Ct,
  Birchington CT7 14 E3
Dover Pl TN23 12 C5
Dover Rd, Deal CT14 22 C6
Dover Rd, Dover CT15 41 A4
Dover Rd,
  Folkestone CT20 26 D2
Dover Rd,
  Gravesend DA11 39 C2
Dover Rd,
  Sandwich CT13 45 C4
Dover Rd East DA11 39 D3
Dover St,
  Canterbury CT1 16 D4
Dover St,
  Sittingbourne ME10 48 B3
Dowding Walk DA11 39 D6
Dowell Mws CT14 22 C5
Dowgate Cl TN9 55 D5
Dowling Cl ME6 49 A3
Downland Rd TN24 12 B3
Downlands ME17 30 D2
Downs Av,
  Dartford DA1 21 D4
Downs Av,
  Whitstable CT5 59 B3
Downs Cl,
  Charing TN27 17 B2

Downs Cl,
  Headcorn TN27 31 D5
Downs Pk CT6 32 D2
Downs Rd CT14 22 B6
Downs Way TN27 17 B2
Downside, Dover CT15 41 C5
Downside,
  Strood ME2 52 B4
Downsview Cl BR8 53 D2
Dr Hopes Rd TN17 20 C5
Drake Av ME12 37 D4
Drakes Av ME2 52 B3
Draper St TN4 50 C1
Drapers Av CT9 36 C4
Drapers Cl CT9 36 D5
Dray Ct TN11 17 B6
Drayton Rd TN9 55 C5
Dreadnought Av ME12 37 B4
Drew La CT14 22 C4
Drop Redoubt Rd CT17 23 B3
Droveway Gdns CT15 41 C5
Drum La TN24 12 C4
Drury Rd TN30 54 B4
Dry Bank Ct TN10 55 B1
Dry Bank Rd TN10 55 B1
Dry Hill Park Cres TN10 55 B1
Dry Hill Park Rd TN10 55 B1
Dry Hill Rd TN10 55 B1
Dryland Rd,
  Sevenoaks TN15 13 B6
Dryland Rd,
  Snodland ME6 49 B3
Drywall ME10 48 D1
Duck La CT1 16 C2
Dudley Av CT8 58 B2
Dudley Rd,
  Folkestone CT19 26 E1
Dudley Rd,
  Gravesend DA11 39 D3
Dudley Rd,
  Tunbridge Wells TN1 56 B2
Duke St, Deal CT14 22 C1
Duke St, Margate CT9 36 B2
Dukes Mdw TN26 30 B5
Dumergue Av ME11 41 B1
Dumpton Gap Rd
CT10 15 C6
Dumpton La CT11 43 B2
Dumpton Park Dr,
  Broadstairs CT10 15 C6
Dumpton Park Dr,
  Ramsgate CT11 43 C3
Dumpton Park Rd CT11 43 B2
Dumpton Pk CT11 43 B1
Duncan Cl CT5 59 A5
Duncan Dr CT7 14 C2
Duncan Rd,
  Gillingham ME7 27 A3
Duncan Rd,
  Ramsgate CT11 43 A4
Duncan Rd,
  Whitstable CT5 59 B4
Dunera Dr ME14 35 B1
Dungeness Rd TN29 34 C2
Dunkery Rise TN24 12 B2
Dunkin Rd DA1 21 D1
Dunlop Ct TN18 31 C1
Dunnings La ME1 44 C4
Dunoon Ct*,
  Argyll Dr CT10 43 B1
Dunstan Av CT8 58 A4
Dunstan Gro TN4 50 D6
Dunstan Rd TN4 50 D5
Durban Rd CT9 36 D4
Durham Cl CT17 23 B2
Durham Hill CT17 23 B2
Durling Ct ME8 42 D1
Durrant Way DA10 29 E4
Dyke Rd CT19 26 E2
Dymchurch Rd,
  Hythe CT21 33 A4
Dymchurch Rd,
  New Romney TN28 38 C2

East Hill,
  Tenterden TN30 54 C5
East Hill Dr DA1 21 C4
East Kent Av DA11 39 B2
East La ME12 47 B2
East Lodge Rd TN23 12 A3
East Mill DA11 28 A2
East Milton Rd DA12 28 D3
East Rd ME4 18 B1
East Roman Ditch
CT16 23 E1
East Row ME1 44 C4
East St, Ashford TN23 12 B4
East St, Chatham ME4 18 C5
East St, Dover CT17 23 A1
East St,
  Faversham ME13 25 D3
East St,
  Folkestone CT19 26 E2
East St,
  Gillingham ME7 27 B2
East St,
  Herne Bay CT6 32 C1
East St, Hythe CT21 33 C3
East St,
  Maidstone ME17 30 B2
East St,
  Sittingbourne ME10 48 C3
East St,
  Snodland ME6 49 D3
East St, Tonbridge TN9 55 C2
East Ter DA12 28 C2
East Weald Dr TN30 54 C4
Eastbrook Pl CT16 23 C1
Eastchurch Rd CT9 19 D3
Eastern Av,
  Ashford TN23 12 B4
Eastern Av,
  Queenborough ME11 41 B2
Eastern Esp,
  Broadstairs CT10 15 D2
Eastern Esp,
  Margate CT9 19 A2
Eastern Rd,
  Gillingham ME7 27 D2
Eastern Rd,
  Romney Marsh TN29 34 C2
Eastfield Rd CT7 14 D3
Eastfields CT19 26 D1
Eastgate ME1 44 D3
Eastgate Ct ME1 44 D4
Eastgate Rd TN30 54 C4
Eastgate Terr ME1 44 C4
Eastlands Est TN12 40 B2
Eastling Rd ME13 25 A6
Eastmead Av TN23 12 C6
Eastwell Barn Mws
TN30 54 B4
Eastwell Cl,
  Sheerness ME12 37 D4
Eastwell Cl,
  Tonbridge TN12 40 B3
Eastwell Mdws TN30 54 B5
Eastwood Rd ME10 48 A2
Eaton Hill CT9 36 B3
Eaton Rd CT9 36 B3
Eaves Ct ME10 48 D1
Ebbsfleet Ind Est
DA11 39 A1
Ebbsfleet Walk DA11 39 A2
Eccleston Rd ME15 35 A5
Echo Sq DA12 28 C5
Echo Walk ME12 37 E4
Eddington Bsns Pk
CT6 32 B3
Eddington La CT6 32 A3
Eden Ct TN18 31 B1
Eden Pl DA12 28 B3
Eden Rd TN1 56 B6
Edenbridge Dr ME12 47 C5
Edenbridge Trading
Centre TN8 24 C6
Edenfield CT7 14 E3
Edgar Cl BR8 53 D2
Edgar Ho CT14 22 B5
Edgar Rd CT9 36 D1
Edge End Rd CT10 15 B4
Edgeler Ct ME6 49 B4
Edinburgh Rd,
  Ashford TN24 12 C4
Edinburgh Rd,
  Chatham ME4 18 C5
Edinburgh Rd,
  Gillingham ME7 27 A3
Edinburgh Rd,
  Margate CT9 36 B3
Edith Rd,
  Faversham ME13 25 C4
Edith Rd,
  Westgate-on-Sea CT8 58 C2
Edmanson Av CT9 58 D2
Edred Rd CT17 23 A1
Edward Dr CT7 14 F2
Edward Rd ME11 41 B1
Edward St,
  Chatham ME4 18 C5

Edward St,
  Strood ME2 52 C4
Edward St,
  Tunbridge Wells TN4 50 C2
Edwards Gdns BR8 53 B3
Edwards Rd CT16 23 C1
Edwin St DA12 28 B3
Edwina Av ME12 37 B3
Effingham Cres CT17 23 B1
Effingham St,
  Dover CT17 23 B1
Effingham St,
  Ramsgate CT11 43 B4
Egbert Rd,
  Birchington CT7 14 B2
Egbert Rd,
  Faversham ME13 25 C4
Egbert Rd,
  Westgate-on-Sea CT8 58 C2
Egdean Walk TN13 46 C4
Eglinton Rd DA10 29 F3
Elaine Av ME2 52 A4
Eldon St ME4 18 C4
Eldon Way TN12 40 B2
Eldon Way Ind Est
TN12 40 B2
Elfrida Cl CT9 19 C5
Elham Way CT10 15 C6
Elizabeth Ct,
  Broadstairs CT10 15 D1
Elizabeth Ct,
  Gravesend DA11 28 A2
Elizabeth Garlick Ct
TN1 56 D1
Elizabeth Gdns CT21 33 B4
Elizabeth Huggins Cotts
DA11 28 B5
Elizabeth Rd CT11 43 C4
Elizabeth St CT17 23 B4
Elizabeth Way CT6 32 D3
Ellen Av CT11 43 B1
Ellerslie DA12 28 D3
Ellesmere Mws TN28 38 C1
Ellington Av CT9 58 E3
Ellington Rd CT11 43 A4
Elliott St DA12 28 D3
Elliotts Pl ME13 25 D3
Ellis Cl DA9 53 B8
Ellis Dr TN28 38 C1
Ellis Way DA1 21 D6
Elm Cl DA1 21 A5
Elm Cotts TN8 24 B2
Elm Dr BR8 53 B1
Elm Gdns CT21 33 D3
Elm Gro,
  Maidstone ME15 35 C5
Elm Gro,
  Westgate-on-Sea CT8 58 B3
Elm La,
  Sheerness ME12 37 D4
Elm La,
  Tonbridge TN10 55 C1
Elm Pass CT21 33 B3
Elm Rd, Dartford DA1 21 A5
Elm Rd,
  Gillingham ME7 27 C2
Elm Rd,
  Gravesend DA12 28 C6
Elm Rd,
  Tunbridge Wells TN4 50 C2
  Westerham TN16 57 D4
Elmfield TN30 54 B5
Elmfield Cl DA11 28 B4
Elmfield CT10 54 B5
Elmhurst Gdns ME4 18 A5
Elmley Way CT9 36 C6
Elms Av CT11 43 A4
Elmstead Pl CT20 26 E2
Elmstone Gdns CT9 19 D4
Elmstone Rd,
  Gillingham ME8 42 A3
Elmstone Rd,
  Ramsgate CT11 43 C4
Elmwood Cl CT10 15 B1
Elwick La TN23 12 C4
Elwick Rd TN23 12 C4
Ely Ct TN1 56 C2
Emily Jackson Cl TN13 46 B5
Empire Ter CT9 36 B5
Engine Alley TN26 60 B2
Engineers Ct TN23 12 B4
Enterprise Way TN8 24 B3
Enticott Cl CT5 59 D3
Epple Bay Av CT7 14 E1
Epple Bay Rd CT7 14 D2
Epple Cottages St CT7 14 F2
Epple Rd CT7 14 E1
Epps Rd ME10 48 A3
Erica Ct BR8 53 C3
Eridge Rd TN4 56 A6
Ernest Rd ME4 18 C5
Esplanade,
  Dover CT17 23 C3
Esplanade,
  Rochester ME1 52 D5

Esplanade,
  Sheerness ME12 47
Esplanade,
  Strood ME2
Esplanade,
  Westgate-on-Sea CT8
Essex Gdns CT7
Essex Rd,
  Dartford DA1
Essex Rd,
  Gravesend DA11
Essex Rd,
  Westgate-on-Sea CT8
Essex St CT5
Estuary Rd ME12
Ethel Rd CT10
Ethelbert Cres CT9
Ethelbert Gdns CT9
Ethelbert Rd,
  Birchington CT7
Ethelbert Rd,
  Dover CT17
Ethelbert Rd,
  Faversham ME13
Ethelbert Rd,
  Margate CT9
Ethelbert Rd,
  Ramsgate CT11
Ethelbert Rd,
  Rochester ME1
Ethelbert Sq CT8
Ethelbert Ter,
  Margate CT9
Ethelbert Ter,
  Westgate-on-Sea CT8
Ethelred Ct ME13
Ethelred Rd CT8
Eton Way DA1
Eureka Leisure Pk
TN24
Eurogate Bsns Pk
TN24
Eurolink Ind Est
ME10
Eurolink Way ME10
Eva Rd ME7
Evans Cl DA9
Evelyn Cl ME2
Everard Way ME13
Everest La ME2
Everest Pl BR8
Evesham Rd DA12
Ewins Cl TN12
Exchange St CT14
Exeter Rd DA12
Exmoor Rise TN24
Exmouth Rd ME7
Eynsford Rd DA9

Factory Rd DA11
Fair St CT10
Fairacre CT10
Fairbourne La ME17
Fairfield Cl TN28
Fairfield Cres TN9
Fairfield Ct TN15
Fairfield Pk CT10
Fairfield Rd,
  Broadstairs CT10
Fairfield Rd,
  New Romney TN28
Fairfield Rd,
  Ramsgate CT11
Fairfield Rd,
  Sevenoaks TN15
Fairfield Ter TN26
Fairlawn Cl TN4
Fairlight Cl TN4
Fairlight Rd CT21
Fairmead Rd TN8
Fairmeadow ME14
Fairview TN18
Fairview Cl TN9
Fairview Gdns CT14
Fairview Rd ME10
Fairwood Ind Est
TN23
Falcon Cl DA1
Falcon Ct ME10
Falcon Gdns ME12
Falcon Mws DA11
Fallowfield ME10
Farleigh Hill ME15
Farley Cft TN16
Farley La TN16
Farley Nursery TN16
Farley Rd CT9
Farlow Cl DA11
Farm Av BR8
Farm Cres ME10
Farm Hill Av ME2
Farm House Cl CT5
Farm La CT16
Farm Rd,
  Ashford TN26
Farm Rd,
  Sevenoaks TN14

combe Cl TN2 56 D6
combe La TN2 56 C5
combe Rd TN2 56 D6
croft DA11 28 A5
dale Av ME1 44 A6
er Cl CT21 33 D2
ground Cl TN9 55 D4
stead Dr TN8 24 C3
aby Dr TN13 46 A6
ham Cl ME8 42 D2
ol Rd DA1 21 D1
r Rd CT7 14 E3
er Cl TN23 12 A1
er St CT14 22 D1
ing Cl DA1 21 C1
rsham ME13 25 D3
rsham Rd ME17 32 D5
rsham Reach
3 25 D1
es Av DA1 21 C6
ey Cl ME14 35 A1
el Cl ME1 44 B5
ulhet Way CT6 32 C1
on Ct CT14 22 A2
dale TN13 46 C3
dale Ct CT7 14 D3
dale Rd,
ngham ME7 27 B3
dale Rd,
vesend DA12 28 B5
hurst Cres TN4 50 C1
ea Av CT6 32 A2
eigh Ter ME10 48 A5
er Cl ME8 42 A6
Vw ME11 41 A3
ers Cl DA9 29 B1
Dr TN8 24 C3
ing St ME13 25 C2
ways TN18 31 C2
works Rd ME7 18 C1
Av CT9 19 B2
ee Rd CT10 15 B1
Mws CT14 22 C4
ay Cl ME8 42 A5
Line Ind Est
2 44 D1
y Cl ME13 25 B2
oury Rd CT11 43 B3
nagh Dr ME14 35 C1
ee Cl TN12 51 C4
ank Gdns CT9 36 B5
anks CT5 59 D4
oft Way TN8 24 B3
horne Cl ME7 27 C2
Av, Chatham ME4 27 A6
Av,
ingham ME7 27 C6
Av,
vesend DA11 39 D4
Av, Margate CT9 19 A2
Av,
eenborough ME11 41 A2
Av,
eerness ME12 47 D3
er Cl CT21 33 C4
er St,
idstone ME14 35 B2
er St,
dwich CT13 45 D2
ermens Hill DA11 39 B1
ers Cl TN12 51 C1
ers Oak TN14 46 D2
ers Rd TN12 51 C1
nary Av CT9 58 E2
oy Av CT9 19 A4
oy Rd CT5 59 D1
Bells La ME1 44 D4
Oak La TN12 51 A5
Wents BR8 53 E1
mans Ct ME7 18 C2
more Pl TN4 50 D1
Av ME12 47 C4
Rd DA11 39 B6
twood Av CT6 32 A2
twood Cl ME12 37 B4
cher Rd TN12 51 B3
d La ME13 25 C2
a Rd CT11 43 B3
ence Rd ME16 35 A5
ence St ME2 52 C3
n Dr ME1 44 B5
ver Rise ME14 35 B1
d Cl TN4 50 C4
ng Horse La CT16 23 C2
y St ME14 35 C2
estone CT20 26 D4
estone Rd CT17 23 A2
y Rd CT20 26 E1
d Rd,
kestone CT19 26 C1
d Rd,
idstone ME17 32 C5
d St ME1 44 D4
es Rd ME13 25 C4
e Green La TN16 57 C3
Rd DA11 39 B1
Ford Way TN23 12 A5
Fordoun Rd CT10 15 B3
Fordwich Dr ME2 52 C1
Fordwich Gro CT10 15 A1
Fordwich Pl CT13 45 C2
Foreland Av CT9 19 C3
Foreland Ct CT15 41 C6
Foreland Heights CT10 15 D1
Foreland Rd CT15 41 C6
Forelands Sq CT14 22 B6
Foremans Walk TN27 31 B5
Forest Hill ME15 35 B6
Forest Rd TN12 40 C4
Foresters Way CT20 26 C2
Forge Cft TN8 24 C5
Forge Cl ME13 25 D4
Forge La,
Ashford TN23 12 B4
Forge La,
Gillingham ME7 27 B2
Forge La,
Headcorn TN27 31 B4
Forge La,
Whitstable CT5 59 A4
Forge Mdw ME17 30 B2
Forge Mdws TN27 31 B5
Forge Rd,
Sittingbourne ME10 48 A1
Forge Rd,
Tunbridge Wells TN4 50 C3
Forge Way TN12 40 C3
Forson Cl TN30 54 B4
Fort Cres CT9 36 C1
Fort Hill CT9 36 B2
Fort Pitt Hill ME1 18 A4
Fort Pitt St ME4 18 A5
Fort Prom CT9 36 C1
Fort Rd,
Broadstairs CT10 15 D4
Fort Rd, Hythe CT21 33 A4
Fort Rd, Margate CT9 36 C2
Fort St ME1 44 D5
Fortrye Cl DA11 39 D5
Fortuna Ct CT11 43 A3
Fosse Bank Cl TN9 55 A5
Fosse Rd TN9 55 B2
Fostall Rd ME13 25 C1
Fosten La TN27 13 A2
Foster Clark Est ME15 35 D5
Foster St ME15 35 B4
Foster Way CT14 22 B3
Fosters Av CT10 15 A1
Fougeres Way TN24 12 B2
Foundry La ME7 27 D1
Fountain Rd ME2 52 A2
Fountain St ME10 48 B3
Four Elms Rd TN8 24 C3
Fourth Av ME7 27 C4
Fox Lea TN15 13 B5
Fox St ME7 27 A2
Foxglove Cl TN8 24 C3
Foxglove Rise ME14 35 A1
Foxgrove Rd CT5 59 D2
Foxley Rd ME11 41 A1
Foxwood Gro DA11 39 D4
Foys Pass CT21 33 C3
Frampton Rd CT21 33 A4
Frances Gdns CT11 43 C3
Francis Rd,
Ashford TN23 12 B6
Francis Rd,
Broadstairs CT10 15 C1
Francis Rd,
Dartford DA1 21 A2
Franklin Rd ME7 27 B3
Frant Fld TN8 24 C5
Frant Rd TN2 56 B6
Freda Cl CT10 43 C1
Frederick Rd,
Deal CT14 22 A5
Frederick Rd,
Gillingham ME7 27 A4
Frederick St ME10 48 A3
Freelands Rd ME6 49 A3
Freemens Way CT14 22 B5
Freesia Cl ME7 27 C2
Freight La TN17 20 B6
Frensham Cl ME10 48 D3
Freshfield La CT21 33 A2
Friars Cl CT5 59 C2
Friary Pl ME2 52 D4
Friendly Cl CT9 19 C4
Friends Av CT9 19 C5
Frindsbury Rd ME2 52 D3
Frittenden Rd TN12 51 C4
Frobisher Way DA9 29 B1
Frog La TN1 56 B5
Frogmore Walk ME17 32 B5
Front Brents ME13 25 D2
Front Rd TN26 60 A2
Frythe Cl TN17 20 C5
Frythe Cres TN17 20 C5
Frythe Walk TN17 20 C5
Frythe Way TN17 20 C6
Fuggles Cl TN12 40 B4
Fulham Av CT9 58 F3
Fullers Dr CT9 36 C3
Fullers Hill TN16 57 C5
Fulsam Pl CT9 36 A3
Fulston Pl ME10 48 C4
Fulwich Rd DA1 21 C3
Furrells Rd ME1 44 D4
Further Fld TN12 51 B2

Gabriels Hill ME15 35 B4
Gads Hill ME7 27 D1
Gagetown Ter ME14 35 B1
Gainsborough Av CT9 19 C5
Gainsborough Cl ME8 42 A4
Gainsborough Dr
DA11 39 C6
Gainsborough Rd CT7 14 D2
Galahad Av ME2 52 A5
Galbri Dr ME2 52 B5
Galley Hill Rd DA10 29 F2
Galley Hill Trading Est
DA10 29 E2
Galliard St CT13 45 D2
Galloways Rd TN29 34 B3
Gallwey Av CT7 14 B2
Galway Rd ME12 47 D3
Gann Rd CT5 59 C2
Gaol La CT16 23 C2
Garden Rd,
Sevenoaks TN13 46 D2
Garden Rd,
Tonbridge TN9 55 C2
Garden Rd,
Tunbridge Wells TN1 56 D2
Garden St,
Gillingham ME7 18 C2
Garden St,
Tunbridge Wells TN1 56 D2
Gardenia Cl ME2 52 D1
Gardens ME12 47 D4
Gardiner St ME7 27 A2
Gardyne Mws TN9 55 B4
Garfield Rd,
Gillingham ME7 27 B2
Garfield Rd,
Margate CT9 36 A3
Garlinge Rd TN4 50 C2
Garrard Av CT9 58 F2
Garrison Rd ME12 47 B1
Garrolds Cl BR8 53 C2
Gas House Rd ME1 44 C2
Gas Pass CT1 16 A5
Gas Rd ME10 48 B1
Gas St CT1 16 A5
Gasson Rd DA10 29 F3
Gassons Rd ME6 49 A3
Gasworks La TN23 12 B4
Gatefield La ME13 25 D3
Gatekeeper Chase
ME8 42 B2
Gatwick Rd DA12 28 B6
Gaunts Cl CT14 22 A4
Gaze Hill Av ME10 48 D4
Gdn St TN1 56 D2
George Hill Rd CT10 19 D4
George La,
Folkestone CT20 26 D3
George La,
New Romney TN28 38 B3
George Pk CT9 58 F2
George Rd TN12 51 B3
George St,
Ashford TN23 12 C5
George St,
Maidstone ME15 35 C5
George St,
Ramsgate CT11 43 B4
George St,
Sittingbourne ME10 48 D3
George St,
Staplehurst TN12 51 B1
George St,
Tonbridge TN9 55 B4
George V Av CT9 36 A4
George Wood Cl
TN29 34 C2
Georges Lees CT13 45 D2
Georgian Cl ME11 41 B3
Gerald Av ME4 18 B6
Gerrards Dr ME10 48 B5
Gibbs Hill TN27 31 C5
Gibraltar Av ME7 18 C1
Gibraltar Hill ME4 18 B4
Gibson St ME10 48 A3
Gilbert Cl DA10 29 D3
Gilbert Rd CT11 43 A3
Gilbert Ter ME14 35 B1
Giles Gdns CT9 36 C4
Gilford Rd CT14 22 C3
Gilham Gro CT14 22 A4
Gill Cres DA11 28 A6
Gillett Rd TN29 34 C1
Gillingham Grn ME7 27 C2
Gillingham Rd ME7 27 A4
Gills Cotts ME1 18 A4
Ginsbury Cl ME2 18 A2
Giraud Dr ME13 25 B1
Gladstone Rd,
Broadstairs CT10 15 B5
Gladstone Rd,
Chatham ME4 18 A6
Gladstone Rd,
Dartford DA1 21 C3
Gladstone Rd,
Deal CT14 22 C5
Gladstone Rd,
Maidstone ME14 35 B1
Gladstone Rd,
Margate CT9 36 C4
Gladstone Rd,
Tonbridge TN9 55 A4
Gladstone Rd,
Whitstable CT5 59 A2
Glanville Rd,
Gillingham ME7 27 B3
Glanville Rd,
Strood ME2 52 C4
Gleanings Mws ME1 44 C4
Glebe Cl CT15 41 B5
Glebe Gdns,
Maidstone ME17 32 D6
Glebe Gdns,
Margate CT9 58 E3
Glebe La ME10 48 D5
Glebe Rd,
Gillingham ME7 27 C5
Glebe Rd,
Margate CT9 58 E3
Glebe Way CT5 59 A4
Glebelands TN27 13 B2
Glen Vw DA12 28 C4
Glencoe Rd,
Chatham ME4 18 B6
Glencoe Rd,
Margate CT9 36 D3
Glendale BR8 53 D4
Glendale Rd ME12 37 C2
Glenside CT5 59 D4
Glenwood Cl TN30 54 B1
Glenwood Dr ME12 37 C3
Glistening Glade ME8 42 A4
Globe La ME4 18 B3
Gloucester Av,
Broadstairs CT10 15 A5
Gloucester Av,
Margate CT9 19 C3
Gloucester Cl ME8 42 C2
Gloucester Mws TN28 38 C1
Gloucester Pl CT20 26 C3
Gloucester Rd CT5 59 C2
Glovers Cres ME10 48 B4
Glovers Mill ME1 44 D5
Glynne Cl ME8 42 A5
Goblands Farm Ind Est
TN11 17 D6
Goddards Cl TN17 20 A5
Godden Rd ME6 49 B3
Goddings Dr ME1 44 B6
Goddington La ME17 30 A1
Goddington Rd ME2 52 C2
Godfrey Cl ME2 52 B2
Godfrey Walk TN23 12 C6
Godinton Rd,
Ashford TN23 12 A3
Godinton Rd,
Ashford TN23 12 B4
Godinton Rd,
Ashford TN23 12 C4
Godinton Way TN23 12 B4
Godinton Way Ind Est
TN23 12 B4
Godwin Rd,
Dover CT16 23 D1
Godwin Rd,
Margate CT9 19 A3
Godwyne Cl CT16 23 C1
Godwyne Rd CT16 23 C1
Golden Acre La CT8 58 A3
Golden Cl CT8 58 A3
Golden Hill CT5 59 C5
Golden Sq TN30 54 C4
Golden St CT14 22 D1
Goldfinch Cl,
Faversham ME13 25 C1
Goldfinch Cl,
Tonbridge TN12 40 C5
Golding Rd TN13 46 C2
Goldings TN12 40 B5
Goldsel Rd BR8 53 B4
Goldsmid Rd TN9 55 C4
Goldsmith Ct TN30 54 C4
Goldsmith Rd ME8 42 A6
Goldsworth Dr ME2 52 C2
Goldthorne Cl ME14 35 D3
Golf Rd CT14 22 C1
Golford Rd TN17 20 D5
Goodall Cl ME8 42 A5
Goodfellow Way CT16 23 B1
Goodnestone Rd
ME10 48 D3
Goods Station Rd TN1 56 C2
Goods Station Rd
Trading Est TN1 56 C1
Goodwin Cl TN8 24 A4
Goodwin Rd CT15 41 C6
Gooseneck La TN27 31 B5
Gordon Av ME11 41 B1
Gordon Gro CT8 58 B2
Gordon Henry Ho
TN8 24 C4
Gordon Pl DA12 28 C2
Gordon Prom East
DA12 28 D2
Gordon Rd,
Canterbury CT1 16 A5
Gordon Rd,
Gillingham ME4 18 C1
Gordon Rd,
Chatham ME4 18 C6
Gordon Rd,
Dartford DA1 21 B4
Gordon Rd,
Gillingham ME7 27 B3
Gordon Rd,
Gravesend DA11 39 D3
Gordon Rd,
Herne Bay CT6 32 C2
Gordon Rd,
Margate CT9 36 D2
Gordon Rd,
Ramsgate CT11 43 A2
Gordon Rd,
Sevenoaks TN13 46 B5
Gordon Rd,
Strood ME2 52 B4
Gordon Rd,
Whitstable CT5 59 A4
Gordon Sq CT7 14 C2
Gordon Ter ME1 44 C4
Gore Court Rd ME10 48 A5
Gore End Cl CT7 14 C2
Gorham Cl ME6 49 B3
Gorham Dr TN9 55 D4
Gorrell Rd CT5 59 B3
Gorse Mead TN23 12 A6
Gorse Rd ME2 52 B3
Gorst St ME7 27 A3
Gosfield Rd CT6 32 C2
Gosselin St CT5 59 B4
Goudhurst Cl ME16 35 A3
Goudhurst Rd,
Cranbrook TN17 20 A1
Goudhurst Rd,
Marden TN12 34 A6
Goudhurst Rd,
Tonbridge TN12 51 A6
Gouge Av DA11 39 D4
Grace Ct CT20 26 D2
Grace Hill CT20 26 C2
Grace Rd ME12 47 B3
Grace Walk CT14 22 A3
Grafton Rd ME10 48 B3
Grafton Way ME10 48 C3
Grampion Cl TN24 12 C3
Granary TN12 40 D4
Granary Cl ME8 42 B1
Granary Pl CT5 59 A5
Granby Rd DA11 39 C2
Grand Par TN28 38 F4
Grange Cl,
Edenbridge TN8 24 C4
Grange Cl,
Westerham TN16 57 C5
Grange Cres TN30 54 B1
Grange Ct CT20 26 B3
Grange Hill ME5 18 D5
Grange Rd,
Broadstairs CT10 15 A1
Grange Rd, Deal CT14 22 B3
Grange Rd,
Gillingham ME7 27 C2
Grange Rd,
Gravesend DA11 28 A3
Grange Rd,
Hythe CT21 33 A1
Grange Rd,
Ramsgate CT11 43 A5
Grange Rd,
Sevenoaks TN15 13 D5
Grange Rd,
Strood ME2 52 D4
Grange Rd,
Tenterden TN30 54 A2
Grange Way,
Broadstairs CT10 15 A6
Grange Way,
Rochester ME1 44 C6
Grant Cl CT10 15 A2
Grantham Av CT14 22 A3
Grantley Cl TN1 56 B5
Granville Av CT10 15 C5
Granville Cl ME13 25 C2
Granville Pl ME12 47 D3
Granville Rd,
Broadstairs CT10 15 C5
Granville Rd,
Deal CT14 22 C6
Granville Rd,
Dover CT15 41 C5

Granville Rd, Gillingham ME7 27 C3
Granville Rd, Gravesend DA11 28 A4
Granville Rd, Maidstone ME14 35 B1
Granville Rd, Sevenoaks TN13 46 B5
Granville Rd, Sheerness ME12 47 C3
Granville Rd, Westerham TN16 57 B5
Granville St CT14 22 C3
Grasmere Gro ME2 52 D1
Grasmere Rd CT5 59 D3
Gravel Walk, Ashford TN23 12 B3
Gravel Walk, Rochester ME1 44 D4
Gravesend Rd ME2 52 A2
Graylen Cl CT14 22 B1
Grayshott Cl ME10 48 C4
Graystone Rd CT5 59 D1
Great Basin Rd ME12 47 B2
Great Elms TN11 17 B5
Great Hall Arcade TN1 56 C4
Great Lines ME7 18 C3
Great Mead TN8 24 B3
Great Queen St DA1 21 C3
Greatness La TN14 46 C2
Greatness Rd TN14 46 D2
Grecian Rd TN1 56 C5
Grecian St ME14 35 C2
Green Court Rd BR8 53 B4
Green Ct TN12 51 B4
Green La, Broadstairs CT10 15 A3
Green La, Hythe CT21 33 A3
Green La, Margate CT9 19 D5
Green La, Tonbridge TN12 40 C5
Green La, Whitstable CT5 59 A4
Green Manor Way DA11 29 F1
Green Rd CT7 14 C2
Green St ME7 27 A3
Green Way TN29 34 B3
Greenacre Cl BR8 53 C4
Greenbanks DA1 21 B6
Greenfield TN8 24 C4
Greenfield Rd ME7 27 B2
Greenhill TN12 51 B2
Greenhithe, Greenhithe DA9 29 A2
Greenhithe, Maidstone ME15 35 B5
Greenlands TN15 13 D5
Greenly Way TN28 38 C3
Greenside, Maidstone ME15 35 C4
Greenside, Swanley BR8 53 B2
Greenview Walk ME7 27 D4
Greenway, Cranbrook TN17 20 A5
Greenway, Faversham ME13 25 B2
Greenways ME10 48 D4
Greenwood Way TN13 46 A5
Gregory Cl ME8 42 A6
Gregory Ct TN25 60 C5
Grenham Bay Av CT7 14 B2
Grenham Rd CT7 14 C2
Grenville Gdns CT7 14 C2
Grenville Way CT10 15 A4
Gresham Av CT9 58 E2
Gresham Cl ME8 42 B1
Greshams Way TN8 24 A4
Griffin St CT14 22 C1
Grigg La TN27 31 C5
Griggs Way TN15 13 C5
Grimshill Rd CT5 59 B4
Grimthorpe Av CT5 59 A5
Grisbrook Farm Cl TN29 34 C2
Groom Way ME17 32 D6
Grosvenor Av ME4 18 A5
Grosvenor Cres DA1 21 A2
Grosvenor Gdns CT9 36 C3
Grosvenor Pk TN1 56 B1
Grosvenor Rd, Broadstairs CT10 15 B4
Grosvenor Rd, Tunbridge Wells TN1 56 B1
Grosvenor Rd, Whitstable CT5 59 A5
Grosvenor Walk TN1 56 C1
Grotto Gdns CT9 36 D2
Grotto Hill CT9 36 C2
Grotto Rd CT9 36 D2
Grove Av TN1 56 C5
Grove Cl ME13 25 A3
Grove Hill Gdns TN1 56 D5
Grove Hill Rd TN1 56 C4
Grove Pl ME13 25 A3
Grove Rd, Chatham ME4 18 D6
Grove Rd, Deal CT14 22 C5
Grove Rd, Folkestone CT20 26 D1
Grove Rd, Gillingham ME7 27 D2
Grove Rd, Gravesend DA11 39 A1
Grove Rd, Ramsgate CT11 43 A4
Grove Rd, Sevenoaks TN14 46 D2
Grove Rd, Strood ME2 52 D3
Grove Ter CT1 16 A6
Grovelands ME17 32 D5
Grover St TN1 56 D2
Grundys Hill CT11 43 B4
Guardian Ind Est TN12 34 B4
Guildcourt La CT13 45 D1
Guildford Av CT8 58 B3
Guildford Ct CT14 22 D6
Guildford Lawn CT11 43 A4
Guildford Rd TN1 56 C5
Guildhall St, Canterbury CT1 16 C3
Guildhall St, Folkestone CT20 26 C2
Gun La ME2 52 C4
Gundulph Rd ME1 18 A4
Gunn Rd DA10 29 E3
Guston Rd ME14 35 D2
Guy Cl CT10 15 C1
Gwynn Rd DA11 39 C5
Gybbon Rise TN12 51 B3

Hackfield TN23 12 A5
Hadleigh Gdns CT6 32 D1
Hadley Ct TN4 50 C5
Hadlow Pk TN11 17 C5
Hadlow Rd, Maidstone ME14 35 D2
Hadlow Rd, Tonbridge TN9 55 C2
Haffenden Cl TN12 34 B5
Haffenden Mdw TN27 17 B2
Haffenden Rd TN30 54 B4
Hafod Pass CT21 33 C3
Haig Av, Chatham ME4 18 C6
Haig Av, Gillingham ME7 27 C4
Haig Gdns DA12 28 C3
Hailstone Cl TN11 17 B6
Haldane Gdns DA11 39 B4
Hales Cl TN30 54 B5
Halfmile Ride CT9 36 B6
Hall Cl ME10 48 B1
Hall Rd, Dartford DA1 21 C1
Hall Rd, Gravesend DA11 39 B6
Halland Ct TN8 24 B5
Hallford Way DA1 21 A2
Halliday Dr CT14 22 C5
Hallwards TN12 51 B5
Halstatt Rd CT14 22 A6
Halstow Way TN23 12 A6
Ham La ME17 32 B5
Ham Rd ME13 25 C1
Ham Shades La CT5 59 D3
Hamerton Rd DA11 39 A1
Hamilton Ct TN4 50 D6
Hamilton Rd, Deal CT14 22 B4
Hamilton Rd, Gillingham ME7 27 B1
Hamilton Rd, Whitstable CT5 59 B2
Hammonds TN18 31 C1
Hammonds Sq ME6 49 C3
Hamond Hill ME4 18 A4
Hampton Rd ME14 35 D1
Hamstreet Rd, Ashford TN26 60 C3
Hamstreet Rd, Hamstreet TN26 30 C6
Hancock Cl ME2 52 C2
Hancocks Fld CT14 22 A3
Hanmer Way TN12 51 B4
Hanover Cl, Ashford TN23 12 A4
Hanover Cl, Deal CT14 22 D6
Hanover Cl, Margate CT9 19 D3
Hanover Cl, Sittingbourne ME10 48 B4
Hanover Rd TN1 56 B2
Hanover Sq CT6 32 C1
Hanover St CT6 32 B1
Hanway ME8 27 D6
Harbledown Gdns CT9 19 D2
Harbour Approach Rd CT20 26 E3
Harbour Par CT11 43 B4
Harbour St, Broadstairs CT10 15 D4
Harbour St, Folkestone CT20 26 E2
Harbour St, Ramsgate CT11 43 B4
Harbour St, Whitstable CT5 59 A2
Harbour Way CT20 26 E2
Harbourne La TN30 54 D1
Harcourt Gdns ME8 42 A6
Harden Rd, Gravesend DA11 28 A5
Harden Rd, Romney Marsh TN29 34 C2
Hardinge Rd TN24 12 C3
Hardres Rd CT11 43 B3
Hardres St CT11 43 B4
Hards Town ME4 18 C4
Hardy Av DA11 39 D5
Hardy St ME14 35 B2
Hare St ME4 18 D5
Harebrook CT11 43 C2
Harkness Ct ME10 48 D3
Harlech Cl ME2 52 A2
Harmer Ct TN4 50 C2
Harmer Rd DA10 29 F3
Harmer St DA12 28 C2
Harmsworth Gdns CT10 15 C2
Harnet St CT13 45 D1
Harold Av, Gillingham ME7 27 C4
Harold Av, Westgate-on-Sea CT8 58 C2
Harold Ct ME13 25 C4
Harold Pass CT16 23 D1
Harold Rd, Birchington CT7 14 B1
Harold Rd, Margate CT9 19 A3
Harold Rd, Sittingbourne ME10 48 D3
Harold St, Dover CT16 23 C1
Harold St, Queenborough ME11 41 B2
Harolds Rd CT16 23 D1
Harper Rd TN23 12 A6
Harps Av ME12 37 C3
Harpswood La CT21 33 A2
Harrier Dr ME10 48 C4
Harriet Dr ME1 44 B6
Harris Rd ME12 47 D3
Harrison Dr ME17 30 C2
Harrison Rd, Ramsgate CT11 43 A5
Harrison Rd, Sevenoaks TN15 13 B6
Harrison Way TN13 46 B3
Harrow Cl TN8 24 C3
Harrow Dene CT10 15 A3
Harrowby Gdns DA11 39 D5
Hart Dyke Cres BR8 53 B2
Hart Dyke Rd BR8 53 B2
Hart St ME16 35 A5
Hart Street Commercial Centre ME16 35 A5
Hartfield Pl DA11 39 C3
Hartington St ME4 18 C5
Hartley Rd, Cranbrook TN17 20 A6
Hartley Rd, Westerham TN16 57 D4
Hartlip Cl ME12 47 C6
Hartnokes TN18 31 C1
Hartsdown Rd CT9 36 A3
Hartshill Rd DA11 28 A5
Hartslands Rd TN13 46 D4
Harvel Av ME2 52 A4
Harvesters Cl ME8 42 A4
Harvey Av CT14 22 C5
Harvey Dr ME10 48 C5
Harvey Pl CT20 26 E2
Harvey Rd ME8 42 A2
Harvey St CT20 26 D2
Harville Rd TN25 60 A6
Harwich St CT5 59 A4
Harwick Dr TN28 38 C2
Harwood Rd ME8 42 D1
Hasted Cl DA9 29 C3
Hastings Av CT9 19 A4
Hastings Pl CT13 45 D2
Hastings Rd ME15 35 C4
Hatch Rd ME17 32 B6
Hatch St ME13 25 C2
Hatfield Rd, Margate CT9 36 A3
Hatfield Rd, Ramsgate CT11 43 A4
Hatfield Rd, Rochester ME2 52 C3
Hathaway Ct ME1 44 B4
Hatherall Rd ME14 35 C2
Hatton Cl DA11 39 D6
Havelock Rd, Deal CT14 22 B5
Havelock Rd, Tonbridge TN9 55 B2
Havelock St CT1 16 D3
Haven Cl BR8 53 D2
Haventhorpe TN24 12 C3
Havock La ME14 35 B3
Hawden Rd TN9 55 B2
Hawkenbury Rise ME2 52 C1
Hawkesbury St CT17 23 B4
Hawkhurst Cl CT7 14 E2
Hawkhurst Way CT10 15 C6
Hawkins Cl ME7 18 C2
Hawks La CT1 16 B4
Hawkwood Cl ME1 44 D4
Hawley Rd DA1 21 B6
Hawley Sq CT9 36 C2
Hawley St CT9 36 C2
Hawthorn Av ME12 47 B5
Hawthorn Cl, Edenbridge TN8 24 B4
Hawthorn Cl, Ramsgate CT11 43 A1
Hawthorn Rd, Dartford DA1 21 A5
Hawthorn Rd, Sittingbourne ME10 48 A2
Hawthorn Rd, Strood ME2 52 A5
Haydens Mws TN9 55 C1
Hayle Rd ME15 35 B5
Haymen St ME4 18 A5
Haynes Rd DA11 28 A6
Hays Rd ME6 49 A4
Haysel ME10 48 C5
Haywain Cl TN12 40 C5
Hayward Av ME2 52 C3
Hayward Dr DA1 21 C6
Haywards Cl, Deal CT14 22 A4
Haywards Cl, New Romney TN28 38 C3
Hazebrouck Rd ME13 25 A2
Hazel End BR8 53 C4
Hazel Gro ME12 37 B1
Hazel Rd DA1 21 B6
Hazelwood Mdw CT13 45 D3
Hazlemere Dr ME7 27 D3
Headcorn Gdns CT9 19 D3
Headcorn Rd, Maidstone ME17 32 C6
Headcorn Rd, Tonbridge TN12 51 C2
Headley Ct TN8 24 C4
Heard Way ME10 48 D2
Heartenoak Rd TN18 31 C1
Heath Cl BR8 53 C2
Heath Ct CT15 41 B5
Heath Gdns DA1 21 A4
Heath La DA1 21 A4
Heath St DA1 21 B4
Heather Bank TN12 40 D4
Heather Cl, Margate CT9 36 A4
Heather Cl, Sittingbourne ME10 48 C3
Heather Dr, Maidstone ME15 35 C6
Heather Dr, Tenterden TN30 54 B1
Heather End BR8 53 B4
Heathfield Cl ME14 35 D1
Heathfield Rd, Ashford TN24 12 C3
Heathfield Rd, Maidstone ME14 35 D1
Heathfield Ter BR8 53 B1
Heathorn St ME14 35 C2
Heathview TN4 50 B1
Heathwood Dr CT11 43 B1
Heathwood Gdns BR8 53 A1
Hectorage Rd TN9 55 C4
Hedge Place Rd DA9 29 A3
Hedley St ME14 35 C3
Heights Ter CT17 23 A3
Helena Av CT9 36 C4
Hellyar Ct ME1 44 D5
Hendley Dr TN17 20 B4
Hendy Rd ME6 49 D2
Hengist Av CT9 19 A4
Hengist Rd, Birchington CT7 14 A2
Hengist Rd, Deal CT14 22 C1
Hengist Rd, Westgate-on-Sea CT8 58 A2
Henley Cl, Gillingham ME8 42 A2
Henley Cl, Tenterden TN30 54 B2
Henley Flds TN30 54 B3
Henley Mdws TN30 54 B2
Henley Rd TN12 40 C3
Henley Vw TN30 54 C2
Henry Ct CT1 16 B6
Henry St, Chatham ME4 18 D5
Henry St, Gillingham ME8 42 C1
Henshill La TN18 31 A3
Herald Walk DA1
Herbert Rd, Chatham ME4
Herbert Rd, Gillingham ME8
Herbert Rd, Swanscombe DA10
Hereford Gdns CT7
Hereson Rd CT11
Hereward Av CT7
Heritage Gdns CT16
Herman Ter ME4
Hermitage Cl CT21
Herne Av CT6
Herneville Gdns CT6
Heron Cl TN8
Heron Dr ME12
Herschell Rd CT7
Herschell Rd East CT14
Herschell Rd West CT14
Herschell Sq CT14
Hertford Pl CT11
Hertford Rd CT9
Hertford St CT11
Hertsfield Av ME2
Hever Cft ME2
Hever Gdns ME16
Hever Rd TN8
Hewett Pl BR8
Hewitt Cl ME7
Hewitt Rd CT16
Hibbs Cl BR8
Hibernia St CT11
Higgins La ME4
High Dewar Rd ME8
High Elms ME8
High Firs BR8
High Halden Rd TN27
High St, Ashford TN24
High St, Ashford TN25
High St, Biddenden TN27
High St, Borough Green TN15
High St, Broadstairs CT10
High St, Broadstairs CT10
High St, Canterbury CT1
High St, Canterbury CT1
High St, Catham ME7
High St, Chatham ME4
High St, Cranbrook TN17
High St, Dartford DA1
High St, Deal CT14
High St, Dover CT17
High St, Edenbridge TN8
High St, Garlinge CT9
High St, Gillingham ME7
High St, Gravesend DA11
High St, Greenhithe DA9
High St, Hadlow TN11
High St, Hawkhurst TN18
High St, Headcorn TN27
High St, Herne Bay CT6
High St, Hythe CT21
High St, Lenham ME17
High St, Maidstone ME14
High St, Marden TN12
High St, Margate CT9
High St, Minster ME12
High St, New Romney TN28
High St, Northfleet DA11
High St, Queenborough ME11
High St, Rainham ME8
High St, Ramsgate CT11
High St, Rochester ME1
High St, Rochester ME2
High St, Rochester ME1
High St, Romney Marsh TN29
High St, Sandwich CT13
High St, Sevenoaks TN13
High St, Sheerness ME12

St, [...]
erness ME12 47 D2
St, [...]
gbourne ME10 48 B1
St, [...]
gbourne ME10 48 B3
St, [...]
land ME6 49 C2
St, [...]
argarets at Cliffe 41 B4
St, [...]
lehurst TN12 51 C3
St, Swanley BR8 53 D3
St, [...]
nscombe DA10 29 F2
St, [...]
erden TN30 54 A5
St, Tonbridge TN9 55 B4
St, [...]
ridge Wells TN1 56 B5
St, [...]
terham TN16 57 B6
St, [...]
tstable CT5 59 A2
Street Chatham 18 A4
Street Rochester 18 A4
bury La TN30 54 B5
ield Cl,
brook TN18 31 B2
ield Cl,
e CT21 33 A2
ield Gdns CT9 36 A4
ield Rd DA1 21 B4
ield Rd South 21 B3
ields Rd TN8 21 B4
gate Hill TN18 24 B1
ands Hill BR8 31 B3
sted Rd ME10 53 E1
iew Rd ME7 48 B4
 May Av BR8 37 D3
 Rd ME4 53 C2
rs Cl TN8 18 C5
rs La TN8 24 B1
rsham Cl CT10 24 B1
res ME17 15 A2
rest TN13 32 D5
d DA2 46 A3
t TN1 21 B6
p TN9 56 C1
p Rd CT6 55 B5
iew TN12 32 D1
iew Cl TN15 12 D3
w TN15 13 B5
y Av DA11 13 B5
y Rd ME14 39 D6
ow La TN23 35 B1
ow Rd,
ford TN23 12 A5
ow Rd,
sgate CT11 12 A6
est,
enhithe DA9 43 A2
est,
bridge Wells TN4 29 A2
est Dr DA9 50 D3
est Rd,
tham ME4 29 B2
est Rd,
nbridge TN8 18 B6
e CT21 24 B1
 Cl CT10 33 A3
arth TN4 15 B2
gdon Av TN13 50 D2
gdon Rise TN13 46 C2
ter ME4 46 D2
de TN9 18 B5
de Av,
vesend DA12 55 A5
de Av,
enborough ME11 28 D5
de Av,
hester ME2 41 A3
de Ct BR8 52 D3
de Dr DA12 53 E3
de Rd,
tham ME4 28 D5
de Rd,
enoaks TN13 18 C4
de Rd,
erness ME12 46 D4
de Rd,
tstable CT5 37 B2
de St CT21 59 D3
p Gdns DA1 33 B3
p Rd,
hester ME2 21 D2
p Rd,
erness ME12 52 D2
37 A4

Hillview Rd CT5 59 A4
Hillfield Cl ME2 52 B2
Hillfield Rd TN23 12 A6
Hillfields Rise TN23 12 A5
Hilton Cl ME13 25 D4
Hilton Rd TN23 12 A3
Hinchliffe Way CT9 19 C5
Hitchen Hatch La TN13 46 B4
Hither Fld TN27 17 B3
Hive La DA11 39 B2
Hockenden La BR8 53 A1
Hockeredge Gdns CT8 58 D2
Hodges Gap CT9 19 B2
Hodgson Cres ME6 49 C2
Hog La DA11 39 C6
Hogs Cnr CT13 45 E2
Holborough Rd ME6 49 C2
Holcombe Cl TN16 57 C5
Holcombe Rd,
 Chatham ME4 18 B6
Holcombe Rd,
 Rochester ME1 44 C6
Holden Corner TN4 50 B2
Holden Park Rd TN4 50 C3
Holden Rd TN4 50 B2
Holding St ME8 42 B2
Holford St TN9 55 B3
Holland Cl ME12 47 C3
Holland Rd ME14 35 C2
Hollicondane Rd CT11 43 A3
Hollington Pl TN24 12 C3
Hollingworth Way
 TN16 57 D5
Hollow La ME6 49 A4
Holly Bush La TN13 46 C3
Holly Cl,
 Gillingham ME7 27 C2
Holly Cl, Hythe CT21 33 C3
Holly Cotts TN8 24 A4
Holly Gdns,
 Maidstone ME14 35 D1
Holly Gdns,
 Margate CT9 19 C4
Holly La CT9 19 B3
Holly Rd, Dartford DA1 21 A4
Holly Rd,
 Ramsgate CT11 43 B2
Holly Rd,
 Rochester ME2 52 A5
Hollybush Cl TN13 46 D4
Hollybush Cl TN13 46 D5
Hollybush Rd DA12 28 C5
Hollytree Av BR8 53 C2
Hollywood La ME2 52 D1
Holm Oak Gdns CT10 15 B4
Holmesdale Rd TN13 46 D4
Holmleigh Av DA1 21 A1
Holmside ME7 27 C6
Holton Cl CT7 14 E4
Holtye Cres ME15 35 C6
Holyoake Ter TN13 46 B5
Holyrood Dr ME12 37 A4
Home Gdns DA1 21 B3
Home Mead Cl DA12 28 B3
Home Vw ME10 48 D3
Homefield Av CT14 22 B2
Homefield Cl BR8 53 D2
Homestead Ct CT14 22 A4
Homestead Rd TN8 24 B1
Homewood Av ME10 48 A4
Homewood Rd TN30 54 C3
Honduras Ter ME14 35 C1
Hone St ME2 52 C3
Honeybee Glade ME8 42 A5
Honeycrest Ind Est
 TN12 51 B1
Honeypot Cl ME2 52 D3
Honeysuckle Cl CT9 36 A5
Honeysuckle Rd CT11 43 C3
Honfleur Rd CT13 45 C2
Honywood Rd ME17 32 B6
Hook La, Ashford TN27 17 A2
Hook La,
 Maidstone ME17 30 A2
Hook Rd ME6 49 B2
Hookfields DA11 39 D6
Hoopers Pl ME1 44 C4
Hoopers Rd ME1 44 C4
Hop Pocket La TN12 40 C2
Hope Av TN11 17 B5
Hope La TN28 38 A1
Hope Rd, Deal CT14 22 C3
Hope Rd,
 Swanscombe DA10 29 F2
Hope St,
 Chatham ME4 18 C5
Hope St,
 Maidstone ME14 35 B2
Hope St,
 Sheerness ME12 47 C3
Hope Ter TN4 50 C6
Hopgarden CT18 24 C3
Hopsons Pl ME12 37 D4
Hopwood Gdns TN4 50 D5
Hornbeam Cl,
 Ashford TN23 12 A3

Hornbeam Cl,
 Tonbridge TN12 40 B5
Horsa Rd CT7 14 A2
Horse Wash La ME1 44 C2
Horsebridge Rd CT5 59 A2
Horsford Walk ME13 25 B1
Horsley Rd ME1 44 C5
Horton Pl TN16 57 D4
Hortons Way TN16 57 C5
Hoser Gdns CT7 14 E2
Hosey Hill TN16 57 D5
Hospital La,
 Canterbury CT1 16 B4
Hospital La,
 Rochester ME1 18 A4
Hospital Rd TN13 46 C2
Hotel Rd, Dover CT15 41 D5
Hotel Rd,
 Gillingham ME8 27 D6
Hothfield Rd ME8 42 B1
Houselands Rd TN9 55 B2
Howard Av,
 Rochester ME1 44 C6
Howard Av,
 Sittingbourne ME10 48 A1
Howard Cl ME12 37 D2
Howard Rd CT10 15 B5
Howland Rd TN12 34 B5
Hubert Pas CT16 23 D2
Hubert Way CT10 15 A2
Hugh Pl ME13 25 D2
Hugin Av CT10 15 A1
Hulkes La ME1 18 A4
Humber Cres ME2 52 B4
Humber Rd DA1 21 B2
Hundreds Cl CT8 58 A3
Hunsdon Dr TN13 46 C4
Hunters Chase CT5 59 B5
Hunters Walk CT14 22 A2
Hunting Gate CT7 14 C2
Huntingdon Cl TN17 20 C5
Huntley Av DA11 39 B2
Huntleys Pk TN4 50 B6
Hunts Farm Cl TN15 13 C5
Huntsman La ME14 35 D3
Hurst Cl TN12 51 C2
Hurst Pl ME8 42 B2
Hutsons Ct TN8 31 B1
Hyde Ct CT17 23 A2
Hydes Orch TN27 31 C5
Hyndford Cres DA9 29 C2
Hyperion Dr ME2 52 B2
Hythe Cl TN4 50 C2
Hythe Pl CT13 45 D3
Hythe Rd ME10 48 A1
Hythe St DA1 21 B3
Hyton Dr CT14 22 A2

Iden Cres TN12 51 B4
Iden Rd ME2 52 D1
Imber Ct TN17 20 C5
Imbert Cl TN28 38 C4
Impala Gdns TN4 50 D5
Imperial Av ME12 37 D3
Imperial Bsns Pk
 DA11 28 A2
Imperial Rd ME7 27 A5
Imperial Retail Pk
 DA11 28 A2
Industrial Distribution
 Centre ME6 49 B4
Ingle Cl CT7 14 E2
Ingle Rd ME4 18 B6
Ingledene Park Rd TN30 54 C3
Ingles La CT20 26 C2
Ingles Mws CT20 26 B3
Ingles Rd CT20 26 B3
Inglewood BR8 53 C1
Ingoldsby Rd CT17 14 B2
Ingram Rd,
 Dartford DA1 21 B5
Ingram Rd,
 Gillingham ME7 27 C2
Ingress Gdns DA9 29 D2
Ingress Park Av DA9 29 C1
Inner London Rd TN1 56 B4
Institute Rd,
 Chatham ME4 18 C5
Institute Rd,
 Faversham ME13 25 A3
Instone Rd DA1 21 B4
Inverness Ter CT10 15 C5
Invicta Rd,
 Margate CT9 19 B5
Invicta Rd,
 Sheerness ME12 47 D3
Invicta Rd,
 Whitstable CT5 59 C4
Irchester St CT11 43 C4
Iron Bar La CT1 16 C5
Irvine Dr CT9 19 C5
Irving Walk DA10 29 E4
Irving Way BR8 53 B1
Island Wall CT5 59 A2
Ivanhoe Rd,
 Herne Bay CT6 32 D3

Ivanhoe Rd,
 Westgate-on-Sea CT8 58 B2
Ivens Way ME17 30 B2
Ivory Cl ME13 25 A1
Ivy Bower Cl DA9 29 B2
Ivy Cl DA12 28 D6
Ivy House Rd CT5 59 C3
Ivy La, Canterbury CT1 16 D4
Ivy La, Ramsgate CT11 43 A5
Ivy Pl, Deal CT14 22 C1
Ivy Pl, Canterbury CT1 16 A6
Ivy St ME8 42 B2
Ivy Villas DA9 29 A2

Jaarlen Rd TN29 34 A3
Jackson Cl DA9 29 A2
Jacksons La TN30 54 B5
Jacob Cl CT9 36 B5
Jaggard Way TN12 51 B4
James Cl TN11 17 C5
James Hall Gdns
 CT14 22 B5
James St,
 Ashford TN23 12 B4
James St,
 Chatham ME4 18 B4
James St,
 Gillingham ME7 27 A2
James St,
 Maidstone ME14 35 C2
James St,
 Ramsgate CT11 43 A5
James St,
 Rochester ME1 44 D4
James Whatman Way
 ME14 35 B2
Jarmans Fld TN25 60 D6
Jarvis Pl TN30 54 B2
Jasper Av ME1 44 D6
Jefferson Cl TN23 12 A5
Jeffery St ME7 27 A2
Jeffrey Cl TN12 51 B2
Jeffrey St ME14 35 C3
Jellicoe Av DA12 28 C6
Jellicoe Av West DA12 28 C6
Jemmett Rd TN23 12 B6
Jempsons TN17 20 B4
Jenkins Dale ME4 18 B5
Jenner Rd ME1 44 C5
Jennifer Gdns CT9 19 C6
Jersey Rd ME2 52 B4
Jesmond St TN19 26 C1
Jessamine Ter BR8 53 A1
Jetty Rd ME12 47 A2
Jewell Gro TN12 34 C5
Jewry La CT1 16 B3
Jeyes Rd ME7 27 A4
Jezreels Rd ME7 27 B6
Jockey La TN17 20 C4
John St,
 Broadstairs CT10 15 D4
John St,
 Maidstone ME14 35 B1
John St,
 Rochester ME1 44 C4
John St,
 Tunbridge Wells TN4 50 C6
Johns Grn CT13 45 B4
Johnson Av ME4 18 D1
Johnson Cl DA11 39 C6
Johnson Rd ME13 25 B1
Johnson Rd ME10 48 A3
Johnson Way ME12 37 B3
Johnsons Way DA9 29 C3
Joiners Ct ME4 18 D6
Jointon Rd CT20 26 B3
Joseph Wilson Ind Est
 CT5 59 D5
Joy La CT5 59 A4
Joy Rd DA12 28 C4
Joyce Cl TN17 20 B5
Joyce Green La DA1 21 D1
Joyce Green Walk DA1 21 D1
Jubilee Cl DA9 29 C2
Jubilee Dr CT14 22 C5
Jubilee Rd CT13 45 C2
Jubilee St ME10 48 A2
Jubilee Ter ME7 27 A2
Jubilee Way CT16 23 F1
Judd Cl,
 Faversham ME13 25 A3
Judd Rd,
 Tonbridge TN9 55 B5
Julian Rd CT19 26 A2
Julie Cl CT10 15 B1
Junction Rd,
 Dartford DA1 21 B3
Junction Rd,
 Gillingham ME7 27 B4
Juniper Cl CT5 59 C3
Juniper Walk BR8 53 C1
Jurys Gap Rd TN29 34 A3

Katherine Rd CT14 24 C6
Keary Rd DA10 29 F4
Keating Cl ME1 44 B5

Keel Gdns TN4 50 B3
Keeley Mws ME7 27 C5
Kelly Dr ME7 27 A1
Kelvedon Rd CT14 22 C6
Kempes Pl TN25 60 C5
Kemsley Cl DA9 29 B3
Kendal Cl TN9 55 C2
Kendal Dr TN9 55 C2
Kendal Pk TN4 50 C6
Kendal Rise CT10 15 B3
Kenilworth Cl CT15 41 C5
Kenilworth Dr ME8 42 A4
Kennedy Cl ME13 25 D1
Kennedy Dr CT14 22 B6
Kennedy Gdns TN13 46 D3
Kennet Dr CT14 22 A6
Kent Av,
 Sheerness ME12 37 B2
Kent Av,
 Sittingbourne ME10 48 A4
Kent Cl TN12 40 C3
Kent Gdns CT7 14 C2
Kent Ho TN18 31 C1
Kent Kraft Ind Est
 DA11 29 F1
Kent Pl CT11 14 C2
Kent Rd, Dartford DA1 21 B3
Kent Rd,
 Gravesend DA11 28 A4
Kent Rd, Margate CT9 19 B5
Kent Rd,
 Sheerness ME12 47 B2
Kent Rd,
 Snodland ME6 49 C4
Kent Rd,
 Tunbridge Wells TN4 50 C5
Kent St,
 Sheerness ME12 47 B2
Kent St,
 Whitstable CT5 59 A4
Kentish Ct ME16 35 A4
Kenward Ct TN11 17 B6
Kenwyn Rd DA1 21 B2
Kenya Ter ME14 35 B1
Keston Cl ME8 27 D6
Kestrel Cl,
 Edenbridge TN8 24 C3
Kestrel Cl,
 Sittingbourne ME10 48 C4
Keswick Cl TN4 50 B3
Kettlewell Ct BR8 53 D2
Keyes Av ME4 18 B6
Keyes Rd DA1 21 D1
Keyworth Cl TN12 40 B3
Khalsa Av DA12 28 C3
Khartoum Pl DA12 28 C2
Khartoun Rd ME7 27 A4
Khyber Rd ME4 18 D1
Kibbles La TN4 50 B2
Kilbride Ct*,
 Argyll Dr CT13 43 B1
Kiln Cl ME10 48 C4
Kiln Ct ME13 25 A2
Kiln Fld TN30 54 C5
Kiln Way TN12 40 C5
Kilndow Gdns CT9 19 D3
Kimberley Rd ME7 27 A5
Kincraig Dr TN13 46 B4
King Arthurs Dr ME2 52 B2
King Edward Av,
 Broadstairs CT10 15 C4
King Edward Av,
 Dartford DA1 21 A3
King Edward Rd,
 Birchington CT7 14 C4
King Edward Rd,
 Chatham ME4 18 B6
King Edward Rd,
 Gillingham ME7 27 D2
King Edward Rd,
 Greenhithe DA9 29 A2
King Edward Rd,
 Maidstone ME15 35 B6
King Edward St CT5 59 A4
King Fisher Walk CT10 15 A3
King St,
 Canterbury CT1 16 C3
King St, Chatham ME4 18 C4
King St, Deal CT14 22 C5
King St, Dover CT16 23 C2
King St,
 Gillingham ME7 27 A2
King St,
 Gravesend DA12 28 B2
King St,
 Maidstone ME14 35 B3
King St, Margate CT9 36 B2
King St,
 Ramsgate CT11 43 B4
King St,
 Rochester ME1 44 C4
King St,
 Sandwich CT13 45 D2

King St, Sheerness ME12 47 B2
King St, Sittingbourne ME10 48 B1
King St, Walmer CT14 22 D2
King William Rd ME7 27 A1
Kingfisher Cl CT9 58 E3
Kingfisher Ct CT6 32 A3
Kings Av, Ashford TN23 12 B4
Kings Av, Birchington CT7 14 A2
Kings Av, Broadstairs CT10 15 C3
Kings Av, Rochester ME1 44 C5
Kings Av, Whitstable CT5 59 C3
Kings Bastion ME7 18 C3
Kings Dr DA12 28 B6
Kings Head Alley ME12 47 B2
Kings Head La CT21 33 C3
Kings Mill Cl ME10 48 A1
Kings Orch ME1 44 C3
Kings Rd, Ashford TN27 31 B5
Kings Rd, Birchington CT7 14 D4
Kings Rd, Faversham ME13 25 C3
Kings Rd, Herne Bay CT6 32 B2
Kings Rd, Ramsgate CT11 43 A3
Kings Rd, Sheerness ME12 37 D3
Kings Rd, Tonbridge TN9 55 C5
Kings Row ME15 35 C6
Kings Walk ME14 35 C3
Kingsbridge Ct CT20 26 E2
Kingsdale Ct DA10 29 E2
Kingsdown Cl ME16 35 A3
Kingsdown Pk CT5 59 C1
Kingsdown Rd, Deal CT14 22 D6
Kingsdown Rd, Dover CT15 41 B4
Kingsland Gro TN27 31 C5
Kingsley Rd, Maidstone ME15 35 C4
Kingsley Rd, Whitstable CT5 59 B4
Kingsmead Rd CT1 16 D1
Kingsnorth Gdns CT20 26 A2
Kingsnorth Rd ME13 25 C4
Kingsridge Gdns DA1 21 A3
Kingston Av CT9 58 F3
Kingston Ct DA11 39 A1
Kingswear Gdns ME2 52 D4
Kingswood TN24 12 D1
Kingswood Av, Chatham ME4 18 B6
Kingswood Av, Swanley BR8 53 D3
Kingswood Cl DA1 21 A2
Kingswood Rd ME7 27 B3
Kinnings Row TN9 55 C2
Kipling Rd TN23 12 B4
Kippington Cl TN13 46 A5
Kippington Rd TN13 46 A4
Kirby Cl TN17 20 C5
Kirbys La CT2 16 A2
Kirk Ct TN13 46 B4
Kirkdale Rd TN1 56 D1
Kirkman Ct TN12 51 B4
Kirkwood Av TN26 60 B2
Kitchener Av DA12 28 C6
Kitchener Rd ME2 52 C2
Klondyke Ind Est ME11 41 A2
Knaves Acre TN27 31 C5
Knight Av ME7 27 B2
Knight Rd ME2 52 B6
Knightrider Ct ME15 35 C4
Knightrider St, Maidstone ME15 35 B4
Knightrider St, Sandwich CT13 45 E2
Knights Av CT10 15 C2
Knights Manor Way DA1 21 C2
Knights Rd CT16 23 D1
Knights Templars CT17 23 A3
Knights Way TN27 31 C5
Knightsbridge Cl TN4 50 B6
Knockhall Chase DA9 29 B2
Knockhall Rd DA9 29 C3
Knockwood Rd TN30 54 C3
Knold Pk CT9 36 B5
Knole Rd TN13 46 D4
Knole Way TN13 46 C6
Knott Ct ME14 35 B1
Knotts La, Canterbury CT1 16 C2
Knotts La, Dover CT15 41 B4
Knotts Pl TN13 46 B5
Knowle Rd ME14 35 C1
Knowles Gdns TN27 31 C5
Knowles La TN12 51 B1
Knowles Walk TN12 51 C2

La Tene CT14 22 A6
Laburnum Av, Dartford DA1 21 A5
Laburnum Av, Sandwich CT13 45 C2
Laburnum Av, Swanley BR8 53 B3
Laburnum Gro DA11 39 C3
Laburnum Pl ME10 48 A2
Laburnum Rd ME2 52 A6
Ladds La ME6 49 C1
Ladds Way BR8 53 B3
Ladies Walk CT21 33 C4
Lady Woottons Grn CT1 16 D3
Ladys Gift Rd TN4 50 B3
Ladywell CT16 23 B1
Lagonda Way DA1 21 A1
Lake View Rd TN13 46 A3
Lakelands ME17 30 C2
Lakeside ME6 49 B5
Lakeside Ct ME2 18 A1
Lakeside Pk ME2 18 A1
Lakeview Cl ME6 49 C5
Laking Av CT10 15 C1
Laleham Gdns CT9 19 B4
Laleham Rd CT9 19 B4
Laleham Walk CT9 19 A5
Lambarde Dr TN13 46 B3
Lambarde Rd TN13 46 A3
Lambert Ho CT14 22 B5
Lambert Mws ME6 49 C2
Lambs Bank TN9 55 A6
Lambs Walk CT5 59 A6
Laming Rd CT7 14 E3
Lammas Dr ME10 48 A1
Lammas Gate ME13 25 D1
Lamorna Av DA12 28 D5
Lamplighters Cl DA1 21 C3
Lancaster Cl TN26 30 B5
Lancaster Ct DA12 28 C6
Lancaster Gdns CT7 14 C3
Lancaster Rd CT17 23 B2
Lancelot Av ME2 52 A4
Lancelot Cl CT14 22 A5
Landale Gdns DA1 21 A4
Landbury Walk TN25 12 A2
Landseer Av DA11 39 C6
Lane Av DA9 29 C2
Lane End CT6 32 A1
Lanes Av DA11 28 A6
Langdon Cl CT15 41 B5
Langdon Rd ME1 44 C5
Langham Cl CT9 58 E2
Langhorne Gdns CT20 26 B4
Langley Gdns CT9 19 D2
Langport Rd TN28 38 D3
Langton Cl ME14 35 D3
Lansbury Cres DA1 21 D2
Lansdown Rd CT1 16 C6
Lansdowne Rd, Chatham ME4 18 A6
Lansdowne Rd, Sevenoaks TN13 46 D3
Lansdowne Rd, Tonbridge TN9 55 B2
Lansdowne Rd, Tunbridge Wells TN1 56 D3
Lansdowne Sq TN1 56 D2
Lanthorne Rd CT10 15 B1
Lapwing Cl ME12 37 C4
Larch Gro TN12 40 C4
Larch Rd DA1 21 B5
Larch Ter ME12 47 B5
Larch Walk BR8 53 B1
Larkfield Av, Gillingham ME7 27 C4
Larkfield Av, Sittingbourne ME10 48 A1
Larkfield Trading Est ME20 49 D6
Larkfields DA11 39 D6
Larkin Cl ME2 52 D1
Larksfield Rd ME13 25 C1
Larkstore Pk TN12 51 B1
Laser Quay ME2 44 D2
Latimer Pl ME7 27 A1
Laureate Cl CT9 19 B4
Laurel Av DA12 28 C5
Laurel Bk TN4 50 D4
Laurel Cl DA1 21 A5
Laurel Rd ME7 27 A1
Laurel Walk ME8 42 A4
Laureston Pl CT16 23 D1
Lauriston Mt CT10 15 B3
Lausanne Rd CT9 36 C3
Lavender Cl CT9 36 A4
Lavender Ct ME10 48 C4
Lavender Hill, Swanley BR8 53 B2
Lavender Hill, Tonbridge TN9 55 C5
Lavinia Rd DA1 21 C3
Lawford Gdns DA1 21 A2
Lawn Cl, Chatham ME4 18 D6
Lawn Cl, Swanley BR8 53 A1
Lawn Rd, Broadstairs CT10 15 C3
Lawn Rd, Gravesend DA11 39 B1
Lawn Rd, Tonbridge TN9 55 B4
Lawrance Sq DA11 28 A6
Lawrence Hill Rd DA1 21 A2
Lawrence St ME7 27 A3
Lawson Gdns DA1 21 B1
Lawson Rd DA1 21 A1
Laxton Gdns TN12 40 B3
Laxton Way ME10 48 A1
Layfield Rd ME7 27 C1
Le Temple Rd TN12 40 D3
Lea Cl CT21 33 A2
Leacon Rd TN23 12 A4
Learoyd Rd TN28 38 C4
Leas Rd CT14 22 B4
Leather Cl TN8 24 B6
Leathermarket TN8 24 C5
Leatt Cl CT10 15 A4
Lee Rd ME6 49 B2
Leechcroft Av BR8 53 D3
Leet Cl ME7 27 C2
Leewood Pl BR8 53 B3
Leicester Av CT9 19 C3
Leigh Ct ME12 37 A4
Leigh Rd DA11 28 B5
Leighton Cl TN4 50 C4
Leighville Dr CT6 32 A2
Leitch Row ME7 18 C1
Leith Park Rd DA12 28 B4
Leivers Rd CT14 22 A5
Lendon Rd TN15 13 B6
Lenfield Av ME14 35 D3
Lenham Cl CT10 15 B6
Lenham Gdns CT9 58 E3
Lenham Rd TN27 31 B4
Lennard Ct CT20 26 E1
Lennard Rd CT20 26 E1
Lennox Av DA11 28 A2
Lennox Rd DA11 28 A2
Lennox Rd East DA11 28 A3
Lennox Row ME4 18 C1
Leonard Av DA10 29 E4
Leonard Rd ME4 18 D6
Leonards Av CT11 43 B2
Leopold Rd, Chatham ME4 18 C5
Leopold Rd, Ramsgate CT11 43 B2
Leopold St CT11 43 B4
Lesley Cl BR8 53 B2
Lesley Pl ME16 35 A3
Leslie Av CT9 58 E3
Leslie Cres TN30 54 B2
Leslie Rd, Birchington CT7 14 D2
Leslie Rd, Gillingham ME7 27 B1
Leslie Smith Dr ME13 25 C2
Lester Rd ME4 18 C5
Lewis Cl ME13 25 A2
Lewis Cres CT9 19 A2
Lewis Rd DA10 29 E3
Leybourn Rd CT10 15 C6
Leybourne Dr CT9 58 E3
Leybourne Rd ME2 52 A3
Leybourne Way ME20 49 A6
Leyburne Rd CT16 23 C1
Leyhill Cl BR8 53 C4
Libya Ter ME14 35 B1
Lightermans Mws DA11 39 D3
Lighthouse Rd CT15 41 C6
Lila Pl BR8 53 C3
Lilac Gdns BR8 53 B3
Lilac Rd ME2 52 A6
Lillian Rd CT11 43 B2
Lime Av DA11 39 C3
Lime Cl TN12 34 B5
Lime Gro ME10 48 C3
Lime Hill Rd TN1 56 B2
Lime Kiln Rd CT1 16 B6
Lime Rd BR8 53 B2
Lime Tree Av DA9 29 A4
Lime Tree Cl TN9 55 C2
Lime Tree Walk TN13 46 C6
Lime Trees TN12 51 B2
Limekiln St CT17 23 B4
Limes Cl TN30 54 D5
Limetree Ter ME17 32 D4
Lincoln Gdns CT7 14 C3
Lincoln Rd ME7 27 B1
Linden Av, Broadstairs CT10 15 C3
Linden Av, Dartford DA1 21 A5
Linden Av, Herne Bay CT6 32 A3
Linden Av, Whitstable CT5 59 C3
Linden Chase CT2 16 A2
Linden Chase Rd TN13 46 B3
Linden Cl, Sittingbourne ME10 48 A4
Linden Cl, Tonbridge TN12 40 C4
Linden Cl, Tunbridge Wells TN4 56 A6
Linden Cl, Westgate-on-Sea CT8 58 C3
Linden Dr ME12 47 B5
Linden Gro CT2 16 A2
Linden Park Rd TN4 56 A6
Linden Rd, Gillingham ME7 27 B3
Linden Rd, Westgate-on-Sea CT8 58 C3
Lindenthorpe Rd CT10 15 B2
Lindfield Cotts ME13 25 A3
Lindisfarne Gdns ME16 35 A5
Lindridge La TN12 51 A1
Lines Ter ME4 18 C4
Lingfield Rd, Edenbridge TN8 24 A6
Lingfield Rd, Gravesend DA12 28 B5
Lingfield Rd, Sevenoaks TN15 13 C5
Lingley Dr ME2 52 D1
Linington Rd CT7 14 E3
Link La CT1 16 C4
Links Way TN28 38 E3
Linksfield Rd CT8 58 A4
Linley Rd CT10 15 A1
Linnet Av TN12 40 C5
Lion Fld ME13 25 A3
Lion Yd ME13 25 A3
Lionel Rd TN9 55 A4
Lions Rd TN28 38 B4
Lister Cl CT14 22 B3
Lister Rd CT9 36 D4
Listmas Rd ME4 18 D5
Little Chequers TN25 60 B6
Little Court Rd TN13 46 A4
Little Fld TN12 51 B2
Little Glovers ME10 48 B4
Little Knoll TN23 12 A6
Little Mount Sion TN1 56 B5
Little Queen St DA1 21 C3
Little Tilden Gill TN30 54 C5
Littlebrook Cl TN23 12 B3
Littlebrook Manor Way DA1 21 D2
Littlestone Rd TN28 38 D3
Littlewood TN13 46 D2
Liverpool Lawn CT11 43 B5
Liverpool Rd CT14 22 C6
Livingstone Circus ME7 27 B3
Livingstone Rd, Broadstairs CT10 15 A2
Livingstone Rd, Gillingham ME7 27 B3
Lloyd Rd CT10 15 C3
Loam Ct DA1 21 B5
Loampits Cl TN9 55 D1
Lobelia Cl ME7 27 C2
Lock St, Chatham ME7 18 D3
Lock St, Gillingham ME7 27 A3
Lockington Gr ME1 44 C4
Lockside TN9 55 C2
Loder Cl ME17 32 B5
Lodge Av DA1 21 A3
Lodge La TN16 57 C5
Lodge Oak Rd TN9 55 D5
Lodge Rd, Staplehurst TN12 51 B1
Lodge Rd, Tonbridge TN9 55 B2
London Rd, Deal CT14 22 A4
London Rd, Dover CT17 23 A1
London Rd, Faversham ME13 25 B4
London Rd, Gravesend DA11 39 C2
London Rd, Greenhithe DA9 29 A2
London Rd, Maidstone ME16 35 A3
London Rd, Rochester ME2 52 B4
London Rd, Sevenoaks TN13 46 A4
London Rd, Sevenoaks TN13 46 C5
London Rd, Sittingbourne ME10 48 A3
London Rd, Southborough TN4
London Rd, Swanley BR8
London Rd, Swanley BR8 5
London Rd, Tonbridge TN10 5
London Rd, Tunbridge Wells TN1 5
London Rd, Westerham TN16 5
London Rd Trading Est ME10 4
London St CT20 2
Lonewood Way TN11
Long Mill La TN15 1
Long Port CT1 1
Long Reach Cl CT5 5
Long Steps CT15 4
Longfellow Rd, Chatham ME4 1
Longfellow Rd, Gillingham ME7 2
Longfield TN30 5
Longford Cl ME8 4
Longford Ter CT20 2
Longford Way CT20 2
Longhill Av ME5
Longley Rd, Gillingham ME8 4
Longley Rd, Rochester ME1 4
Longmarket CT1 1
Longridge ME10 4
Longs Acre TN25 6
Lonsdale Av CT9 1
Lonsdale Dr ME8 4
Lonsdale Gdns TN1 5
Lookers La CT21 3
Loop Court Mws CT13 4
Loop St CT13 4
Loose Rd ME15 3
Lord St DA12 2
Lord Warden Sq CT17 2
Lorenden Pk TN18 3
Louisville Av ME7 2
Love La, Canterbury CT1 1
Love La, Gravesend DA12 2
Love La, Margate CT9 3
Love La, Rochester ME1 4
Love La, Sheerness ME12 3
Lovell Rd ME12 3
Lovers Walk TN9 5
Low Cl DA9 2
Lower Blackhouse Hill CT21 3
Lower Boxley Rd ME14 3
Lower Bridge St CT1 1
Lower Cft BR8 5
Lower Denmark Rd TN23 1
Lower Northdown Av CT9 1
Lower Rd, Ashford TN26 6
Lower Rd, Faversham ME13 2
Lower Rd, Gravesend DA11 2
Lower Rd, Maidstone ME15 3
Lower Rochester Rd ME2 5
Lower Sandgate Rd CT20 2
Lower Stone St ME15 3
Lower Tovil ME15 3
Lower Woodlands Rd ME7 2
Lowfield St DA1 2
Lucas Rd ME6 4
Lucerne St ME14 3
Lucilina Dr TN8 2
Luckhurst Gdns CT9 1
Luckley Ho TN25 6
Lucknow Rd TN12 4
Lucks La TN12 4
Lucks Way TN12 3
Lucys Hill CT21 3
Lucys Walk CT21 3
Lullingstone Av BR8 5
Lumsden Ter ME4 1
Lunsford La ME20 4
Luton Av CT10 1
Luton Ct CT10 1
Luton High St ME5 2
Luton Rd, Chatham ME4 1
Luton Rd, Gillingham ME4 2

Way ME8	42 A6
ield Dr ME2	52 C2
Rd TN28	38 A3
Rd CT14	22 A6
CI CT21	33 A4
Rd CT7	14 C2
CI ME2	52 C2
Pk TN13	46 C3
nge Way CT9	19 B4
ngton CI CT8	58 B3
ngton Rd CT8	58 B3
en Way BR8	53 A3
hurst Av CT9	19 A3
hurst Gro ME10	48 A5
hurst Rd, adstairs CT10	15 C2
hurst Rd, nsgate CT11	43 C3
tte Av ME2	52 B1
ate Ct CT9	19 D3
rs Av ME2	52 C1
outh Dr ME12	37 D2
n Rd, vesend DA11	28 B4
n Rd, Hythe CT21	33 B4
n Rd South DA11	28 A4
s Cres TN9	55 C3
s Wharf TN9	55 C3
edon CI TN28	38 B3
edon Rd TN9	55 A4
Donald CT TN12	40 C4
Donald Rd ME7	27 B2
e La End Est TN24	12 D3
e La TN24	12 D4
millan Gdns DA1	21 D1
an CI TN16	57 D4
an Rd TN16	57 D4
den CI DA10	29 E3
dison Av DA1	21 C5
eira Ct CT20	26 A4
eira Pk TN2	56 C6
eira Rd, rgate CT9	36 D2
eira Rd, v Romney TN28	38 F4
eira Walk CT11	43 B4
son Way TN13	46 A3
azine Rd TN24	12 B3
dala Rd CT10	15 A2
dalen Ct CT10	15 C2
ness Rd CT14	22 A4
nolia Av CT9	19 C3
nolia Rd TN9	55 C5
pie Ct ME12	37 B3
pie Grn TN8	24 C3
pie Hall Rd ME4	18 C5
witch CI ME1	44 A5
la Rd ME4	18 D6

dstone Ind Centre 16   35 A3

Istone Rd, ford TN24	12 A1
Istone Rd, ford TN27	31 A4
Istone Rd, aring TN27	17 A1
Istone Rd, atham ME4	18 B6
Istone Rd, ingham ME8	42 A3
Istone Rd, llow TN11	17 C6
Istone Rd, dstone ME17	32 C5
Istone Rd, rden TN12	34 B5
Istone Rd, dock Wood TN12	40 B4
Istone Rd, chester ME1	44 C6
Istone Rd, enoaks TN15	13 B5
Istone Rd, anley BR8	53 A1
Istone Rd, bridge TN12	40 A2
n Gate Rd ME4	18 B2
Istone Rd, nbridge TN8	24 B1
Istone Rd, eenborough ME11	41 B1
erness ME12	47 B2
Rd, Swanley BR8	53 E1
son Dieu PI CT16	23 B1
son Dieu Rd CT16	23 B1
land CT16	25 B1
r Yorks Rd TN9	56 A6
enade Av ME13	25 D4
ham Dr CT9	36 B3
ard CI DA1	21 D2
ard Ct ME12	37 A3
ard Way TN8	24 C3
ing Rd ME6	49 B5

Malt Ho La TN30	54 A5
Malt Mws ME1	44 C3
Malta Ter ME14	35 B1
Malthouse CI ME17	32 C6
Malthouse Hill CT21	33 B3
Maltings CI TN11	17 B6
Malvern Ho DA11	39 C2
Malvern Rd, Ashford TN24	12 C2
Malvern Rd, Dover CT17	23 A2
Malvern Rd, Gillingham ME7	27 B6
Malvina Av DA12	28 C5
Mann Sq TN9	55 D5
Manor Av CT14	22 A4
Manor CI, Deal CT14	22 A4
Manor CI, Queenborough ME11	41 A3
Manor Dr CT7	14 D3
Manor Gro, Sittingbourne ME10	48 A4
Manor Gro, Tonbridge TN10	55 C1
Manor House Gdns TN8	24 B5
Manor La ME1	44 A6
Manor Rd, Broadstairs CT10	15 B4
Manor Rd, Chatham ME4	18 B4
Manor Rd, Deal CT14	22 A4
Manor Rd, Edenbridge TN8	24 B5
Manor Rd, Folkestone CT20	26 B3
Manor Rd, Gravesend DA12	28 B2
Manor Rd, Queenborough ME11	41 A3
Manor Rd, Romney Marsh TN29	34 C3
Manor Rd, Swanscombe DA10	29 D3
Manor Rd, Tunbridge Wells TN4	50 B2
Manor Rd, Whitstable CT5	59 D1
Manor St ME7	18 C2
Manor Way, Ashford TN23	12 A3
Manor Way, Swanscombe DA10	29 E1
Manse Par ME7	53 E4
Manse Way BR8	53 E3
Mansell Dr ME1	44 A6
Mansion House CI TN27	13 C1
Mansion Row ME7	18 C2
Manston Rd CT9	36 B6
Manwood CI ME10	48 B5
Manwood Rd CT13	45 E2
Maple Av ME7	27 C3
Maple CI BR8	53 C1
Maple Rd, Dartford DA1	21 A5
Maple Rd, Rochester ME2	52 A5
Maple St ME12	47 D4
Maplins CI ME8	42 B2
Marathon Pad ME7	27 B4
Marcet Rd DA1	21 A2
Marconi Rd DA11	39 C6
Mardale CI ME8	42 C2
Marden Rd, Rochester ME2	52 D1
Marden Rd, Tonbridge TN12	51 A2
Mardol Rd TN24	12 D1
Margaret St CT20	26 D2
Margate CI ME7	27 C2
Margate Rd CT11	43 A2
Marian Av ME12	37 A3
Marian Sq TN12	51 C3
Marilyn Cres CT7	14 F2
Marina Dr, Dartford DA1	21 D4
Marina Dr, Sheerness ME12	37 B3
Marina Esp CT11	43 C4
Marina Rd CT11	43 C4
Marine Cres CT20	26 D3
Marine Ct CT16	23 D2
Marine Dr CT9	36 B2
Marine Gap CT5	59 A2
Marine Gdns CT9	36 B2
Marine Par, Dover CT16	23 D2
Marine Par, Folkestone CT20	26 D4
Marine Par, Hythe CT21	33 C5
Marine Par, New Romney TN28	38 F4
Marine Par, Whitstable CT5	59 C1

Marine Parade Mws CT20	26 D3
Marine Prom CT20	26 D4
Marine Rd CT14	22 D4
Marine Ter, Folkestone CT20	26 E3
Marine Ter, Margate CT9	36 B3
Marine Walk St CT21	33 B3
Mariners Ct, Greenhithe DA9	29 A1
Mariners Ct, Whitstable CT5	59 A3
Mariners Way DA11	39 D3
Maritime CI DA9	29 B2
Maritime Gate DA11	39 D3
Mark Way BR8	53 E4
Market Bldgs ME14	35 B3
Market Hill CT21	33 B3
Market PI, Ashford TN27	17 B2
Market PI, Dartford DA1	21 C3
Market PI, Faversham ME13	25 D2
Market PI, Folkestone CT20	26 D2
Market PI, Sevenoaks TN13	46 C6
Market PI, Tunbridge Wells TN2	56 A6
Market Sq, Dover CT16	23 C2
Market Sq, Tunbridge Wells TN1	56 B5
Market Sq, Westerham TN16	57 C5
Market St, Dartford DA1	21 B3
Market St, Deal CT14	22 D2
Market St, Dover CT16	23 C2
Market St, Faversham ME13	25 D3
Market St, Herne Bay CT6	32 B1
Market St, Maidstone ME14	35 B3
Market St, Margate CT9	36 B2
Market St, Sandwich CT13	45 D1
Market St, Tonbridge TN12	51 C1
Market St, Tunbridge Wells TN2	56 A6
Market Way TN16	57 D5
Marl Hill TN4	50 B2
Marlborough CI, Broadstairs CT10	15 A5
Marlborough CI, New Romney TN28	38 D3
Marlborough Rd, Gillingham ME7	18 D4
Marlborough Rd, Margate CT9	36 B4
Marlborough Rd, Ramsgate CT11	43 A4
Marley Rd ME17	30 C1
Marley Works ME17	32 A4
Marlfield TN12	51 B2
Marlhurst TN8	24 B2
Marlowe Arc CT1	16 C4
Marlowe Av CT1	16 B4
Marlowe Rd, Ashford TN23	12 B4
Marlowe Rd, Margate CT9	19 B5
Marlpit CI TN8	24 C2
Marr CI ME12	37 A3
Marriott Rd DA1	21 A5
Marsh Cres TN28	38 B3
Marsh La CT14	22 A2
Marsh St, Dartford DA1	21 D1
Marsh St, Dartford DA1	21 D2
Marsh St, Rochester ME2	52 D4
Marshall Cres, Broadstairs CT10	15 A4
Marshall Gdns TN11	17 B5
Marshalls Land TN30	54 C4
Marsham CI ME17	30 C2
Marsham St ME14	35 C3
Marston Dr ME14	35 D3
Martello Rd CT20	26 D4
Martin Ho DA11	28 A6
Martin Rd ME12	37 D4
Martindown Rd CT5	59 A5
Martins CI TN30	54 C4
Martyrs Field Rd CT1	16 A6
Marwell TN16	57 B5
Mary Dukes PI ME15	35 C4

Mary Magdalene Ho TN9	55 B4
Mary Rd CT14	22 A5
Maryland Ct ME8	42 A6
Mascalls Court Rd TN12	40 C5
Mascalls Pk TN12	40 B5
Masefield Rd DA11	39 C6
Masons Rise CT10	15 B3
Matfield Cres ME14	35 D2
Matthews CI CT14	22 B2
Maugham Ct CT5	59 A4
Maxine Gdns CT10	15 A3
Maxwell PI CT14	22 C4
Maxwell Rd ME7	18 C2
May Rd, Gillingham ME7	27 A4
May Rd, Rochester ME1	44 D6
May St ME6	49 D2
Mayes CI BR8	53 E4
Mayfair CI ME2	52 D2
Mayfair Rd DA1	21 A1
Mayfair Rd CT6	32 C3
Mayfields DA10	29 E3
Mayhew CI TN23	12 B6
Maynard Av CT9	58 F3
Maynard PI ME5	27 B6
Maynards TN12	34 B5
Mayors PI*, Burgess Row TN30	54 A6
Mayville Rd CT10	15 A2
McCabe CI TN12	51 B4
McDermott Rd TN15	13 B5
Mdw Walk ME6	49 B3
Mead CI BR8	53 E4
Mead Cres DA1	21 B5
Mead Rd, Dartford DA1	21 B5
Mead Rd, Gravesend DA11	28 B5
Meades CI TN12	34 A5
Meadow Bank Rd ME4	18 C4
Meadow CI TN13	46 A3
Meadow Ct TN9	19 A5
Meadow Hill Rd TN1	56 C5
Meadow La TN8	24 B2
Meadow Rd, Ashford TN23	12 A2
Meadow Rd, Gravesend DA11	28 A5
Meadow Rd, Margate CT9	58 E2
Meadow Rd, Northfleet DA11	39 B5
Meadow Rd, Southborough TN4	50 C2
Meadow Rd, Tonbridge TN9	55 A4
Meadow Rd, Tunbridge Wells TN1	56 C1
Meadow Walk, Maidstone ME15	35 C4
Meadow Walk, Whitstable CT5	59 A6
Meadow Way TN12	34 C5
Meadowside DA1	21 B5
Medway CI ME10	48 A3
Medway Enterprise Centre ME2	44 D1
Medway Rd, Gillingham ME7	27 A1
Medway Rd, Rainham ME8	42 B1
Medway Rd, Sheerness ME12	47 C3
Medway Road Camp ME4	18 D1
Medway St, Chatham ME4	18 B3
Medway St, Maidstone ME14	35 B4
Medway Trading Est ME16	35 A5
Medway Wharf Rd TN9	55 B3
Meeting House La ME4	18 B4
Meeting St CT11	43 B4
Megan CI TN9	34 C1
Melbourne Rd ME4	18 C5
Melbury Mws TN28	38 C1
Mellanby CI CT1	14 D3
Melsetter CI CT1	14 F2
Melville Ct ME4	18 B2
Melville Rd ME15	35 C4
Mendip Ho DA11	39 C2
Mendfield St ME13	25 C2
Menzies CI ME12	37 A4
Mercer Dr ME17	30 D1
Mercers TN18	31 B2
Mercers CI TN12	40 B4
Mercery La CT1	16 C3

Merchant PI TN12	34 B5
Mercury CI ME1	44 A6
Mere Gate CT9	36 B4
Meresborough La ME8	42 C5
Meresborough Rd ME8	42 C5
Mereworth Rd TN4	50 C5
Meridian Pk ME2	18 A2
Merlewood TN13	46 B3
Merlin CI ME10	48 C4
Mermaid CI DA11	39 D3
Merrivale Heights CT10	15 C5
Merryfields ME2	52 B2
Merryweather CI DA1	21 C3
Meyrick Rd ME12	47 D2
Michael Av CT11	43 C2
Michelle Gdns CT9	58 D3
Mickleburgh Av CT6	32 D3
Mickleburgh Hill CT6	32 C2
Mid Kent Bsns Centre ME6	49 C4
Middle Deal Rd CT14	22 A3
Middle Garth TN17	20 C5
Middle Row, Faversham ME13	25 D2
Middle Row, Maidstone ME14	35 B4
Middle St, Deal CT14	22 D1
Middle St, Deal CT14	22 D1
Middle St, Gillingham ME7	18 C2
Middle Wall CT5	59 A2
Middleburg Sq CT20	26 C3
Middlefields ME8	42 C2
Middleton CI ME8	42 A6
Middleway ME10	48 D4
Middlings Rise TN13	46 A6
Middlings Wood TN13	46 A6
Midsummer Rd ME6	49 A2
Mierscourt CI ME8	42 C2
Mierscourt Rd ME8	42 A5
Milburn Rd ME7	27 A1
Mile Town Ind Est ME12	47 B3
Miles PI ME1	44 D5
Miles Way CT7	14 C2
Military Rd, Canterbury CT1	16 D2
Military Rd, Chatham ME4	18 B4
Military Rd, Dover CT17	23 B2
Military Rd, Hythe CT21	33 A3
Military Rd, Ramsgate CT11	43 B5
Mill Bay CT20	26 D2
Mill CI, Maidstone ME17	32 C6
Mill CI, Rochester ME2	52 D2
Mill CI, Sandwich CT13	45 C1
Mill Cres TN9	55 C2
Mill Ct, Ashford TN24	12 D5
Mill Ct, Sittingbourne ME10	48 C4
Mill Fld CT10	15 B2
Mill Hill, Deal CT14	22 A6
Mill Hill, Edenbridge TN8	24 C6
Mill Hill, Sheerness ME12	37 E3
Mill Hill Cotts TN8	24 C6
Mill La, Birchington CT7	14 C3
Mill La, Canterbury CT1	16 C2
Mill La, Dover CT16	23 C2
Mill La, Hythe CT21	33 C3
Mill La, Maidstone ME14	35 A2
Mill La, Margate CT9	36 C3
Mill La, Romney Marsh TN29	34 C2
Mill La, Sevenoaks TN14	46 D1
Mill La, Snodland ME6	49 D2
Mill La, Tenterden TN30	54 C3
Mill La, Tonbridge TN9	55 C2
Mill La, Westerham TN16	57 C6
Mill Mws CT14	22 B4
Mill Pond CI, Rochester ME2	52 D3
Mill Pond CI, Sevenoaks TN14	46 D2
Mill Pond Rd DA1	21 C2
Mill Rd, Deal CT14	22 B4
Mill Rd, Gillingham ME7	18 D2
Mill Rd, Gravesend DA11	39 D3

Mill Rd, Hythe CT21 33 C3
Mill Rd, Rochester ME2 52 C2
Mill Rd, Romney Marsh TN29 34 C2
Mill Row CT7 14 C4
Mill St, Maidstone ME15 35 B4
Mill St, Snodland ME6 49 D2
Mill St, Westerham TN16 57 D5
Mill Stream Pl TN9 55 D1
Mill Vw, Ashford TN26 60 A1
Mill Vw, Tonbridge TN11 17 A5
Mill Way ME10 48 B2
Millbank TN27 31 A4
Millbrook Cl ME15 35 A6
Milldale Cl CT14 22 B4
Millen Rd ME10 48 A2
Millennium Way ME12 47 C2
Miller Cl TN24 12 D4
Miller Ct ME12 37 A4
Millers Ct CT5 59 A5
Millfield, Dover CT15 41 B4
Millfield, Folkestone CT20 26 C3
Millfield, Sittingbourne ME10 48 C4
Millfield Dr DA11 39 D5
Millfield Manor CT5 59 B3
Millmead Av CT9 19 C5
Millmead Gdns CT9 19 C5
Millmead Rd CT9 19 A4
Mills Cl ME12 37 A3
Mills Ter ME4 18 C5
Millside Ind Est DA1 21 A1
Millstead Cl ME14 35 D3
Millstream Cl, Faversham ME13 25 C2
Millstream Cl, Whitstable CT5 59 B3
Millstrood Rd CT5 59 B3
Millwall Pl CT13 45 D2
Milner Rd ME7 27 B1
Milroy Av DA11 39 D5
Milsted Cl ME12 47 C5
Milstock Ter ME15 35 A6
Milton Av, Gravesend DA12 28 D4
Milton Av, Margate CT9 36 C3
Milton Cl DA12 28 C5
Milton Hall Rd DA12 28 D4
Milton Pl DA12 28 C2
Milton Rd, Ashford TN23 12 B4
Milton Rd, Gillingham ME7 27 A5
Milton Rd, Gravesend DA12 28 C2
Milton Rd, Sittingbourne ME10 48 B2
Milton Rd, Swanscombe DA10 29 E2
Milton Rd Bsns Pk DA12 28 C3
Milton St DA10 29 D3
Minerva Rd ME2 52 B3
Minnis Bay CT7 14 A2
Minnis Rd CT7 14 A2
Minster Cl CT10 15 C6
Minster Dr, Herne Bay CT6 32 A2
Minster Dr, Sheerness ME12 37 C2
Minster Rd, Sheerness ME12 37 A3
Minster Rd, Westgate-on-Sea CT8 58 C3
Minterne Av ME10 48 A5
Minters Ind Est CT14 22 B2
Minters Orch TN15 13 D5
Miranda Ct ME12 47 C4
Mirror Ct DA10 29 E2
Miskin Rd DA1 21 A3
Mitchell Av, Chatham ME4 18 B6
Mitchell Av, Gravesend DA11 39 C5
Mitchell Cl, Dartford DA1 21 B6
Mitchell Cl, Maidstone ME17 32 C6
Mitchell Walk DA10 29 E3
Mitre Ct TN9 55 C2
Mitre Rd ME1 44 C5
Moat Rd TN27 31 A5
Moat Sole CT13 45 D2
Moat Way ME11 41 B1
Mockett Dr CT10 15 A1
Modesty Cotts TN4 50 A2
Moles Mead TN8 24 B4
Molyneux Park Gdns TN4 56 A3

Molyneux Park Rd TN4 56 A2
Monastery St CT1 16 D4
Moncktons Av ME14 35 A1
Moncktons Dr ME14 35 A1
Moncktons La ME14 35 A1
Monks Cl ME13 25 B2
Monks Orch DA1 21 A6
Monks Walk TN27 17 B2
Monkton Rd TN15 13 B6
Monson Rd TN1 56 C2
Monson Way TN1 56 C3
Mont St Aignan Way TN8 24 C5
Montacute Gdns TN4 56 A6
Montague Cl BR8 53 D3
Montague Ct ME12 47 C4
Montague Rd CT11 43 B3
Montague St CT6 32 A1
Montefiore Av CT11 43 C1
Montfort Rd ME2 52 C4
Montgomery Rd, Gillingham ME7 27 A5
Montgomery Rd, Tunbridge Wells TN4 50 D4
Montpelier Av CT5 59 A5
Montpelier Bsns Pk TN23 12 A5
Monypenny Cl TN11 17 B5
Moor Park Cl ME8 42 C2
Moor Rd TN14 46 C1
Moor St ME8 42 D2
Moore Rd DA10 29 E3
Moore St ME2 52 C3
Moray Av CT7 14 D1
Mordaunt Av CT8 58 B3
Morden St ME1 44 C5
Morel Ct TN13 46 C3
Morella Walk ME17 32 B5
Morello Cl BR8 53 B3
Moreton Cl BR8 53 D2
Moreton Ind Est BR8 53 F4
Morewood Cl TN13 46 A4
Morgan Cl ME8 42 A6
Morgan Rd ME2 52 C3
Morhen Cl ME6 49 A4
Morland Dr ME2 52 C2
Morley Rd TN9 55 D3
Morris Gdns DA1 21 D2
Morrison Rd CT20 26 E1
Mortimer St CT6 32 B1
Mortuary Rd ME12 47 B2
Moss End Mws CT11 15 A6
Mossy Glade ME8 42 A4
Mostyn Rd ME14 35 D3
Mote Av ME15 35 C4
Mote Rd ME15 35 C4
Moultain Hill BR8 53 E3
Mount Cl TN13 46 A3
Mount Edgecombe Rd TN4 56 A4
Mount Ephraim TN1 56 A3
Mount Ephraim Ct TN4 56 A3
Mount Ephraim Rd TN1 56 B2
Mount Fld, Faversham ME13 25 B3
Mount Fld, Queenborough ME11 41 B1
Mount Harry Rd TN13 46 B4
Mount Pleasant, Chatham ME5 18 D5
Mount Pleasant, Cranbrook TN18 31 A3
Mount Pleasant, Tenterden TN30 54 C4
Mount Pleasant, Tonbridge TN12 40 B3
Mount Pleasant Av TN1 56 C3
Mount Pleasant Rd, Dartford DA1 21 C3
Mount Pleasant Rd, Folkestone CT20 26 D2
Mount Pleasant Rd, Tunbridge Wells TN1 56 C4
Mount Rd ME4 18 B5
Mount Sion TN1 56 B5
Mount St CT21 33 B4
Mountfield TN15 13 C6
Mountfield Ct TN1 56 C4
Mountfield Gdns TN1 56 C4
Mountfield Pk TN9 55 C5
Mountfield Rd, New Romney TN28 38 C4
Mountfield Rd, Tunbridge Wells TN1 56 C4
Mountfield Rd Ind Est TN28 38 C4
Mountfield Way CT8 58 A4
Mounts Cl CT14 22 A3
Mounts Rd DA9 29 B2
Moyle Cl ME8 42 A6
Moyle Tower Rd CT21 33 C5
Mozart Ct ME4 18 A6

Muddy La TN26 60 B2
Muir Rd, Maidstone ME15 35 C5
Muir Rd, Ramsgate CT11 43 C2
Mulberry Cl CT11 43 C3
Mulberry Fld CT13 45 C1
Munday Works Est TN9 55 C3
Munford Rd DA10 29 F4
Murston Rd ME10 48 B2
Murthwaite Ct ME12 37 A4
Murton Neale Cl TN18 31 C1
Museum St ME14 35 B3
Musgrave Rd ME10 48 B1
Musgrove TN23 12 B6
Mutrix Gdns CT9 58 E2
Mutrix Rd CT9 58 E2
Mutton La ME13 25 A4
Myrtle Rd DA1 21 B5

Nacholt Cl CT5 59 D2
Nags Head La ME1 44 D4
Napier Ct ME14 35 B1
Napier Gdns CT21 33 B4
Napier Rd, Broadstairs CT10 15 A2
Napier Rd, Gillingham ME7 27 B5
Napleton Rd ME13 25 C2
Napoleon Dr TN12 34 B5
Napoleon Walk ME17 32 B5
Nash Court Gdns CT9 36 C5
Nash Court Rd CT9 36 C5
Nash Gardens CT10 15 D4
Nash La CT9 36 C5
Nash Rd CT9 36 B5
Nasmyth Rd CT7 14 D1
Natal Rd ME4 18 C6
Nativity Cl ME10 48 A3
Nautilus Cl ME12 37 B4
Nautilus Dr ME12 37 B4
Naylands CT9 36 A3
Neale St ME4 18 B6
Neame Rd CT7 14 E2
Nelson Av, Sheerness ME12 37 D4
Nelson Av, Tonbridge TN9 55 A3
Nelson Cl ME12 47 B4
Nelson Cres CT11 43 B5
Nelson Ct CT7 14 B2
Nelson Gdns ME13 25 C4
Nelson Ho DA9 29 D2
Nelson Pl CT10 15 D3
Nelson Rd, Gillingham ME7 27 A4
Nelson Rd, Whitstable CT5 59 A3
Nelson St, Deal CT14 22 C1
Nelson St, Faversham ME13 25 C4
Nelson Ter ME13 25 C4
Neptune Bsns Est ME2 18 A1
Neptune Cl ME2 18 A1
Neptune Way ME2 18 A1
Ness Rd TN29 34 C2
Nether Av TN28 38 E4
Nevill Pl ME6 49 C4
Nevill Rd ME6 49 C4
Nevill St TN2 56 B6
Neville Rd ME4 18 A6
New Barn Rd BR8 53 D1
New Bri CT16 23 C2
New Covenant Pl ME1 44 D4
New Cross St CT9 36 B2
New Cut ME4 18 A6
New England Rd TN4 50 D5
New House La, Ashford TN27 31 A6
New House La, Gravesend DA11 28 A6
New Hythe La ME20 49 D6
New La TN29 34 B2
New Prospect Rd CT21 33 B4
New Rd, Ashford TN27 31 C5
New Rd, Chatham ME4 18 A4
New Rd, Cranbrook TN17 20 A5
New Rd, Gravesend DA11 28 B2
New Rd, Hythe CT11 33 A1
New Rd, Hythe CT21 33 B4
New Rd, Minster ME12 37 C4
New Rd, Rochester ME1 44 D4
New Rd, Sheerness ME12 47 B5
New Rd, Swanley BR8 53 D2
New Rd, Tonbridge TN12 40 C4

New Rd Ind Est ME12 47 B3
New Rents TN24 12 C4
New Road Av ME1 18 A4
New Romney TN28 38 D3
New Romney Pl CT13 45 D2
New Ruttington La CT1 16 D1
New St, Ashford TN24 12 B3
New St, Canterbury CT1 16 A6
New St, Chatham ME4 18 A5
New St, Deal CT14 22 C1
New St, Dover CT16 23 C2
New St, Folkestone CT20 26 D2
New St, Gravesend DA12 28 C2
New St, Herne Bay CT6 32 C1
New St, Margate CT9 36 B2
New St, Maidstone ME15
New St, Romney Marsh TN29 34 C2
New St, Sandwich CT13 45 D2
New St, Sheerness ME12 47 C3
New St, Westerham TN16 57 C5
New Stairs ME4 18 B2
New Swan Yd DA12 28 B2
New Wharf Rd TN9 55 B3
Newark Yd ME2 52 C4
Newbury Cl CT7 14 E3
Newcastle Hill CT11 43 B4
Newcomen Rd, Sheerness ME12 47 D2
Newcomen Rd, Tunbridge Wells TN4 50 C6
Newgate Lower Prom CT9 36 D1
Newgate Prom CT9 36 D1
Newhouse Ter TN8 24 B3
Newington Mdw CT21 33 C3
Newland Rd ME12 47 B5
Newlands Rd, Ramsgate CT12 43 A1
Newlands Rd, Tunbridge Wells TN4 50 D5
Newlands Rise TN4 50 D5
Newlands Way TN4 50 D4
Newlyn Dr TN12 51 C1
Newmans Cl CT10 15 C1
Newnham St ME4 18 C5
Newton Abbot Rd DA11 28 A5
Newton Cl ME16 35 A4
Newton Gdns TN12 40 B3
Newton Rd, Faversham ME13 25 D3
Newton Rd, Tunbridge Wells TN1 56 C2
Newtown Grn TN24 12 D6
Newtown Rd TN24 12 D5
Nicholls Av CT10 15 B6
Nicolson Way TN13 46 D3
Nightingale Cl, Gillingham ME8 42 A4
Nightingale Cl, Gravesend DA11 39 D6
Nightingale Gro DA1 21 D1
Nightingale Pl CT9 36 D2
Nightingale Rd ME13 25 C3
Nightingale Way BR8 53 C3
Nile Rd ME7 27 A4
Nine Acres TN24 12 D1
Nine Elms Gro DA11 28 A3
Noakes Mdw TN23 12 A6
Nobel Ct ME13 25 B3
Noble Gdns CT9 58 E3
Nore Cl ME12 47 D3
Norfolk Cl ME14 37 A3
Norfolk Dr TN23 21 D2
Norfolk Rd, Gravesend DA12 28 D2
Norfolk Rd, Margate CT9 19 A2
Norfolk Rd, Tonbridge TN9 55 A3
Norfolk Rd, Tunbridge Wells TN1 56 C5
Norfolk St CT5 59 A4
Norman Cl ME14 35 D1
Norman Rd, Broadstairs CT10 15 A2
Norman Rd, Canterbury CT1 16 C6
Norman Rd, Dartford DA1 21 B5
Norman Rd, Dover CT15 41 D4

Norman Rd, Faversham ME13
Norman Rd, Snodland ME6
Norman Rd, Tunbridge Wells TN1
Norman Rd, Westgate-on-Sea CT8
Norman Rise TN17
Norman St CT17
Normanhurst Rd TN15
Normans Cl DA11
Norreys Rd ME8
Norrie Rd CT7
Norstead Gdns TN4
North Av CT11
North Bank Cl ME2
North Barrack Rd CT14
North Ct, Deal CT14
North Ct, Maidstone ME15
North Down TN12
North Foreland Av CT10
North Foreland Rd CT10
North Gate ME1
North Kent Av CT11
North La, Canterbury CT2
North La, Faversham ME13
North Lea CT14
North Military Rd CT17
North Rd, Chatham ME4
North Rd, Dover CT17
North Rd, Hythe CT21
North Rd, Queenborough ME11
North Rd West CT21
North St, Ashford TN24
North St, Biddenden TN27
North St, Dartford CT14
North St, Deal CT14
North St, Folkestone CT19
North St, Gravesend DA12
North St, Headcorn TN27
North St, Herne Bay CT6
North St, New Romney TN28
North St, Strood ME2
Northbourne Way CT9
Northbrooke TN24
Northbrooke La TN24
Northcliffe Gdns CT10
Northcote Rd, Deal CT14
Northcote Rd, Strood ME2
Northcote Rd, Tonbridge TN9
Northdown TN24
Northdown Av CT9
Northdown Cl, Maidstone ME14
Northdown Cl, Tonbridge TN12
Northdown Hill CT10
Northdown Park Rd CT9
Northdown Rd, Clifftonville CT9
Northdown Rd, Margate CT9
Northdown Way CT9
Northdowns Vw ME17
Northern By-Pass TN27
Northfleet Ind Est DA11
Northgate CT1
Northgrove Rd TN18
Northumberland Rd DA12
Northumberland Av, Gillingham ME8
Northumberland Av, Margate CT9
Northview BR8
Northview Rd TN14
Northwall Cl CT14
Northwall Mws CT14
Northwall Rd CT14
Northwood Dr ME10
Northwood Rd CT5
Norton Rd TN14
Norway Ter ME14
Norwood Ct DA1

ood Gdns TN23 12 B4
ood Rise ME12 37 C2
ood St TN23 12 C4
ngham Rd CT7 14 D4
ery Flds CT1 16 C6
ery Rd CT1 16 C6
ery Cl,
  enoaks TN13 46 C3
ery Cl,
  nley BR8 53 A1
ery Cl,
  tstable CT5 59 D3
ery Rd TN12 40 B2
erylands CT6 32 B3
elds ME10 48 D4
ey Cl TN24 12 D3

Av,
  ngham ME7 27 C2
Av,
  erness ME12 37 F3
End Cl TN4 50 C1
Farm Gdns TN27 31 B4
Hall Pass CT21 33 B3
La, Ashford TN27 31 C5
La,
  nney Marsh TN29 34 B2
erness ME12 37 F3
odge La TN16 57 D4
odge Rd TN28 38 C2
Rd,
  vesend DA12 28 C6
Rd,
  hester ME2 52 A5
Rd,
  sterham TN16 57 D4
St CT14 22 D2
ree Cl TN12 34 B5
ree Gro CT9 58 E3
ree Rd TN23 12 A6
w TN8 24 B4
Walk CT21 33 B3
ale Rd CT6 32 D3
lene Rd TN13 46 B5
eld TN18 31 B1
eld La DA1 21 A6
eld Park Rd DA1 21 B6
eld Rd TN8 24 B1
elds TN27 31 B4
ill Rd TN13 46 B5
ands Rd TN18 31 B2
ea Rd TN12 40 C4
eigh Cl BR8 53 C2
Rd TN30 54 B5
rm Ct ME4 18 D6
vood Dr,
  enoaks TN13 46 B4
vood Dr,
  tstable CT5 59 D2
Rd ME13 25 C1
Ct, Margate CT9 36 D1
Ct,
  ngbourne ME10 48 B5
view ME8 42 C2
n Hill CT1 16 D6
n Hill Pl CT1 16 D5
eld Cl TN17 20 B4
eld Dr TN17 20 B4
pation Rd TN25 60 D5
n Cl CT14 62
n Ter ME12 37 E3
n Vw CT10 43 D1
ey La TN18 31 B1
ey Rd TN18 31 B1
Rd CT17 23 A1
s Dr TN12 51 B3
y Cl CT5 19 C4
tigh Rd TN25 60 C5
e Rd CT9 19 A4
ash CT17 24 C1
Ashford Rd,
  iford TN27 17 B3
Ashford Rd,
  dstone ME14 32 D6
Boundary Rd CT8 58 D1
Bridge Rd CT5 59 B3
Cannon Wharf TN9 55 C3
Castle Walk ME8 42 A6
Crossing Rd CT9 58 E2
Dover Rd CT1 59 A6
Farm Cl CT5 59 A6
Farm Gdns BR8 53 D2
Farm Rd CT7 14 B2
Gate Rd ME13 25 B2
Green Rd,
  adstairs CT10 15 B1
Green Rd,
  rgate CT9 19 B5
Ham La ME17 32 A6
Kent Rd TN12 40 C4
Kingsdown Cl
0 15 A5
ain ME17 30 D2
ondon Rd TN10 55 C1

Old Manor Dr DA12 28 C4
Old Otford Rd TN14 46 C1
Old Pattens La ME1 44 D6
Old Perry St DA11 39 D5
Old Pond Rd TN23 12 A5
Old Railway Works
  Ind Est TN24 12 D6
Old Rd ME4 18 B4
Old Rd East DA12 28 B4
Old Rd West DA11 28 A4
Old Ruttington La CT1 16 D3
Old Saltwood La CT21 33 A2
Old School Cl ME17 32 C6
Old School Ct BR8 53 C2
Old School Gdns CT9 36 D4
Old School Pl ME14 35 C3
Old Tannery Cl TN30 54 A6
Old Tovil Rd ME15 35 B6
Old Vicarage Gdns
  TN25 60 C5
Old Vinters Rd ME14 35 C3
Olive Rd DA1 21 A5
Oliver Cl ME4 18 D6
Oliver Rd,
  Swanley BR8 53 B2
Oliver Rd,
  Tonbridge TN12 51 B3
Oliver Twist Cl ME1 44 B5
Omer Av CT9 19 B3
One Tree Hill ME15 35 D5
Onslow Rd ME1 44 D6
Orange St CT1 16 C3
Orange Ter ME1 44 D4
Orch Cl TN8 24 A4
Orchard Av, Deal CT14 22 A3
Orchard Av,
  Rochester ME2 52 B2
Orchard Bsns Centre
  TN9 55 D3
Orchard Cl,
  Maidstone ME15 35 C5
Orchard Cl,
  Sevenoaks TN14 46 D1
Orchard Cl,
  Sheerness ME12 37 A3
Orchard Cl,
  Whitstable CT5 59 C1
Orchard Dr,
  Ashford TN23 12 A2
Orchard Dr,
  Edenbridge TN8 24 A4
Orchard Dr,
  Hythe CT21 33 B4
Orchard Dr,
  New Romney TN28 38 E3
Orchard Dr, Wye TN25 60 C6
Orchard Gdns CT9 58 E2
Orchard Glade TN27 31 C5
Orchard Gro ME12 37 C3
Orchard Heights TN25 12 A1
Orchard Pl,
  Faversham ME13 25 D3
Orchard Pl,
  Maidstone ME16 35 A4
Orchard Pl,
  Sittingbourne ME10 48 C4
Orchard Rd,
  Gravesend DA11 39 B5
Orchard Rd,
  Herne Bay CT6 32 C3
Orchard Rd,
  Margate CT9 58 E2
Orchard Rd,
  Swanscombe DA10 29 F2
Orchard St,
  Tenterden TN30 54 B1
Orchard St,
  Dartford DA1 21 B3
Orchard St,
  Gillingham ME8 42 A3
Orchard St,
  Maidstone ME15 35 C5
Orchard Villas ME4 18 B5
Orchard Way,
  Cranbrook TN17 20 A6
Orchard Way,
  Snodland ME6 49 B3
Ordnance Rd DA12 28 C2
Ordnance St ME4 18 A5
Ordnance Ter ME4 18 A4
Oriel Rd TN23 12 A2
Orient Pl CT2 16 B1
Ormonde Rd,
  Folkestone CT20 26 E1
Ormonde Rd,
  Hythe CT21 33 B5
Osborne Cl ME13 25 A2
Osborne Rd,
  Broadstairs CT10 15 B4
Osborne Rd,
  Gillingham ME7 27 A3
Osborne Ter CT9 36 C3
Osbourn Av CT8 58 B3
Oscar Rd CT9 15 C4
Osprey Av ME5 27 B6
Osprey Ct ME10 48 C4

Ospringe Pl ME13 25 B4
Ospringe Rd ME13 25 B3
Ospringe St ME13 25 A3
Osterberg Rd DA1 21 C1
Ostlers Ct ME6 49 C2
Otford Rd TN14 46 C1
Otterham Quay La
  ME8 42 D2
Otway St,
  Chatham ME4 18 C5
Otway St,
  Gillingham ME7 27 A2
Otway Ter ME4 18 C5
Outnalls ME12 47 D3
Overcliffe DA11 28 A2
Overmead BR8 53 C4
Overy St DA1 21 C3
Owen Sq CT14 22 B6
Owens Way ME7 27 D1
Ox La TN30 54 C3
Oxenden Park Dr CT6 32 A2
Oxenden Sq CT6 32 A1
Oxenden St CT6 32 A1
Oxenturn Rd TN25 60 C6
Oxfield TN18 24 C3
Oxford Rd ME7 27 B5
Oxford St,
  Margate CT9 36 C3
Oxford St,
  Snodland ME6 49 C3
Oxford St,
  Whitstable CT5 59 A3
Oxford Ter CT20 26 C3
Oxney Cl CT7 14 D3
Oyster Cl ME10 48 B1

Pacific Cl DA10 29 E2
Packers La CT11 43 B3
Paddlesworth Rd ME6 49 A2
Paddock Cl TN29 34 B2
Paddock Rd,
  Birchington CT7 14 D3
Paddock Rd,
  Sheerness ME12 47 B2
Paddock Vw CT5 59 B5
Pads Hill ME15 35 C4
Padsole La ME15 35 C4
Paget St ME7 27 A3
Pagitt St ME4 18 A6
Painters Ash La DA11 39 C6
Palace Av ME15 35 B4
Palace Ct ME5 27 B6
Palace St CT1 16 C3
Palm Bay Av CT9 19 B2
Palm Bay Gdns CT9 19 B5
Palmer Cres CT9 19 B5
Palmers Brook TN11 17 C4
Palmerston Av,
  Broadstairs CT10 15 C5
Palmerston Av,
  Deal CT14 22 B5
Palmerston Rd CT14 22 D6
Palmerston Rd ME4 18 B6
Palmerston St TN19 26 C1
Palting Way CT20 26 A3
Papyrus Way ME20 49 D6
Paradise CT11 43 A4
Paradise Row CT13 45 C1
Paragon CT11 43 A5
Paragon St CT11 43 A5
Parham Rd ME4 18 B6
Parish Rd ME12 37 B4
Park Av,
  Birchington CT7 14 D3
Park Av,
  Broadstairs CT10 15 A6
Park Av, Deal CT14 22 B3
Park Av, Dover CT16 23 B1
Park Av,
  Edenbridge TN8 24 B4
Park Av,
  Gillingham ME7 27 B6
Park Av,
  Gravesend DA12 28 C4
Park Av,
  Maidstone ME14 35 C2
Park Av,
  Northfleet DA11 39 D4
Park Av,
  Queenborough ME11 41 B2
Park Av,
  Sittingbourne ME10 48 A5
Park Av,
  Whitstable CT5 59 D3
Park Chase CT10 15 A6
Park Cotts TN18 31 C1
Park Crescent Rd CT9 36 D3
Park Dr ME10 48 A6
Park Gate CT10 15 A6
Park House Gdns TN4 50 C2
Park La,
  Birchington CT7 14 D3
Park La, Margate CT9 36 D3
Park La,
  Sevenoaks TN13 46 C4
Park Lea CT11 22 B3

Park Pl, Dover CT16 23 B1
Park Pl,
  Gravesend DA12 28 C2
Park Pl, Margate CT9 36 B3
Park Rd,
  Birchington CT7 14 E3
Park Rd,
  Broadstairs CT10 15 D2
Park Rd, Dartford DA1 21 D4
Park Rd,
  Faversham ME13 25 D3
Park Rd,
  Gravesend DA11 39 D6
Park Rd,
  Gravesend DA11 28 B5
Park Rd,
  Herne Bay CT6 32 B2
Park Rd, Hythe CT21 33 B5
Park Rd, Margate CT9 36 D3
Park Rd,
  New Romney TN28 38 E4
Park Rd,
  Queenborough ME11 41 A1
Park Rd,
  Ramsgate CT11 43 A3
Park Rd,
  Sittingbourne ME10 48 A4
Park Rd, Swanley BR8 53 D3
Park Rd,
  Swanscombe DA10 29 E3
Park Rd,
  Tunbridge Wells TN4 50 C2
Park Rd,
  Tunbridge Wells TN4 50 D6
Park Rd Ind Est BR8 53 D3
Park Rd North TN24 12 C3
Park St, Ashford TN24 12 C4
Park St, Deal CT14 22 C2
Park St, Dover CT16 23 B1
Park St,
  Romney Marsh TN29 34 B2
Park Ter DA9 29 C2
Park View CT18 24 B4
Park Villas TN11 17 C5
Park Vw Ter TN30 54 A5
Park Way ME15 35 C6
Park Wood Cl CT10 15 A6
Parker Cl,
  Ashford TN26 30 B6
Parker Cl,
  Gillingham ME8 42 A5
Parkfield Ct CT19 26 B1
Parkland Ct CT10 15 B2
Parklands TN4 50 B3
Parkside Ct TN30 54 A6
Parkwood Cl CT10 43 B1
Parr Av ME7 27 B2
Parrock Av DA12 28 C4
Parrock Rd DA12 28 C4
Parrock St DA12 28 B3
Parsonage Chase
  ME12 37 A4
Parsonage Rd CT6 32 C3
Partridge La ME13 25 D2
Pasley Rd ME7 18 C2
Pasley Rd East ME4 18 D1
Pasley Rd North ME4 18 D1
Pasley Rd West ME4 18 C1
Pattenden La TN12 34 A4
Patterson Ct DA1 21 D2
Pavilion Ct CT20 26 E3
Pavilion Rd CT19 26 C1
Payers Pk CT20 26 D2
Payton Cl CT9 36 D6
Peach Cft DA11 39 D6
Peacock St DA12 28 C3
Pear Tree Cl,
  Cranbrook TN17 20 C6
Pear Tree Cl,
  Swanley BR8 53 D3
Pearman Cl ME8 42 C1
Pearson Way DA1 21 C6
Pearsons Way CT10 19 D6
Peckham Cl ME2 52 D3
Pedham Pl Ind Est
  BR8 53 E4
Peel St ME14 35 B2
Peelers Ct CT2 16 B1
Pegasus Cl DA12 28 C6
Pelham Rd DA11 28 A4
Pelham Ter DA11 28 A3
Pemberton Gdns BR8 53 E4
Pemberton Rd TN24 12 D4
Pembroke Av CT9 58 E2
Pembroke Ct CT20 26 E1
Pembroke Gdns ME8 42 A6
Pembroke Mws,
  New Romney TN28 38 C2
Pembroke Mws,
  Sevenoaks TN13 46 C5
Pembroke Rd,
  Sevenoaks TN13 46 C5
Pembroke Rd,
  Tonbridge TN9 55 A3
Pembury Gro TN9 55 C4
Pembury Rd TN9 55 B4
Pembury St ME10 48 B3
Pencester Rd CT16 23 C4

Pencroft Dr DA1 21 A3
Pendennis Rd TN13 46 C4
Penderel Mws TN30 54 B4
Penenden St ME14 35 B2
Penfold Rd CT19 26 F1
Penlee Cl TN8 24 C4
Penn Cl ME10 48 D5
Penney Cl DA1 21 A4
Pennine Way,
  Ashford TN24 12 C2
Pennine Way,
  Gravesend DA11 39 D6
Pennington Pl TN4 50 C1
Pennington Rd TN4 50 C1
Pennyfields TN17 20 C6
Penshurst Rd CT11 43 C3
Penshurst Rise ME13 25 B3
Pentstemon Dr DA10 29 E2
Pepper Hill DA11 39 B6
Pepper Hill La DA11 39 B6
Pepys Av ME12 47 C2
Pepys Cl,
  Dartford DA1 21 D1
Pepys Cl,
  Gravesend DA11 39 C6
Pepys Way ME2 52 B3
Percy Av,
  Broadstairs CT10 15 B3
Percy Rd, Margate CT9 36 D1
Percy Rd,
  Ramsgate CT11 43 A3
Percy Ter TN4 50 C5
Peregrine Dr ME10 48 C4
Periwinkle Cl ME10 48 A2
Perkins Av CT9 36 C4
Perry Gro DA1 21 D1
Perry St,
  Chatham ME4 18 A5
Perry St,
  Maidstone ME14 35 B2
Perryfield St ME14 35 B2
Peter St, Deal CT14 22 C1
Peter St, Dover CT14 23 B1
Peter St,
  Folkestone CT20 26 D1
Peter St,
  Gravesend DA12 28 C3
Petfield Cl ME12 37 D3
Pett La TN27 17 C2
Pettits Row ME13 25 B3
Pettman Ct CT6 32 C3
Philip Av BR8 53 B3
Philip Corby Cl CT9 19 B3
Phillips Rd CT7 14 D3
Phoenix Cl DA1 21 B4
Phoenix Ind Est ME2 44 D1
Phoenix Pl DA1 21 B4
Pickwick Cres ME1 44 C6
Pickwick Gdns DA11 39 C6
Pier App CT10 15 D4
Pier Approach Rd
  ME7 27 B1
Pier Av,
  Herne Bay CT6 32 B1
Pier Av,
  Whitstable CT5 59 D1
Pier Chine CT6 32 B2
Pier Rd,
  Gillingham ME7 27 B1
Pier Rd,
  Greenhithe DA9 29 B1
Pier Rd,
  Queenborough ME11 47 A6
Pierpoint Rd CT5 59 A5
Pierremont Av CT10 15 C4
Pile La TN12 51 D2
Pilgrims Ct,
  Ashford TN27 17 B3
Pilgrims Ct,
  Dartford DA1 21 D1
Pilgrims Lakes ME17 30 C1
Pilgrims Rd DA10 29 E1
Pilgrims Vw DA9 29 C3
Pilgrims Way,
  Ashford TN27 17 C2
Pilgrims Way,
  Maidstone ME17 32 B5
Pilgrims Way,
  Rochester ME2 52 A6
Pilgrims Way,
  Westerham TN16 57 B2
Pilots Av CT14 22 A4
Pin Hill CT1 16 A5
Pine Av DA12 28 D4
Pine Cl BR8 53 D3
Pine Gro,
  Edenbridge TN8 24 B4
Pine Gro,
  Maidstone ME14 35 C1
Pine Needle La TN13 46 C4
Pine Rd ME2 52 B5
Pinetree Cl,
  Birchington CT7 14 E3
Pinetree Cl,
  Whitstable CT5 59 C1
Pinewood Cl TN12 40 C4

Pinewood Ct TN4 50 C2
Pinewood Gdns TN4 50 C2
Pink Alley TN2 56 A6
Pinks Hill BR8 53 C4
Pinnock La TN12 51 A5
Pinnocks Av DA11 28 B4
Pioneer Way BR8 53 C2
Pit La TN8 24 B2
Pittlesden TN30 54 A5
Pittlesden PI TN30 54 A5
Pittock Ho CT14 22 B5
Place La TN26 60 B1
Plain Rd TN12 34 B6
Plains of Waterloo CT11 43 B4
Plane Av DA11 39 C3
Plantation La TN12 34 A5
Plantation Rd ME13 25 C3
Platt Ind Est TN15 13 D3
Platt Mill CI TN15 13 D5
Pleasant Row ME4 18 B2
Plenty Brook Dr CT6 32 B3
Pleydell Gdns CT20 26 C4
Plough Walk TN8 24 C3
Ploughmans Way ME8 42 A4
Plover CI TN8 24 C3
Plover Rd ME12 37 B4
Pluckley Gdns CT9 19 D3
Pluckley Rd TN27 17 B3
Plum Tree Gdns TN26 60 B3
Plymouth CI TN13 46 C5
Plymouth Pk TN13 46 D5
Poets Corner CT9 36 B3
Pond Dr ME10 48 C4
Pondmore Way TN25 12 A2
Pontoise CI TN13 46 A3
Poona Rd TN1 56 D5
Pope Dr TN12 51 B3
Poplar CI ME2 52 B6
Poplar La TN29 34 C1
Poplar Rd,
Broadstairs CT10 15 A2
Poplar Rd,
Ramsgate CT11 43 A4
Poplar Rd,
Rochester ME2 52 A6
Poppy CI ME7 27 C3
Poppy Mdw TN12 40 D4
Porchfield CI DA12 28 C5
Port Av DA9 29 B3
Port Rise ME4 18 B5
Porter CI ME12 37 B3
Portland Av DA12 28 B5
Portland CI CT21 33 A4
Portland Mws ME10 48 A1
Portland PI ME6 49 C2
Portland Rd,
Gillingham ME7 27 C2
Portland Rd,
Gravesend DA12 28 B4
Portland Rd,
Hythe CT21 33 B4
Portland Rd,
Northfleet DA11 39 C2
Portland St ME4 18 C6
Portman Pk TN9 55 C1
Portree Mws ME7 27 C5
Post Barn Rd ME4 18 B5
Post Office Rd TN18 31 B1
Postern La TN11 55 D3
Postley Rd ME15 35 C6
Postmill Dr ME15 35 A6
Potter St CT13 45 D1
Poulders Gdns CT13 45 B3
Poulders Rd CT13 45 A2
Poulsen Ct ME10 48 D3
Pound La,
Canterbury CT1 16 B2
Pound La,
Sevenoaks TN13 46 C5
Pound Way CT20 26 D3
Pout Rd ME6 49 B4
Povey Av ME2 52 D1
Powder Mill La,
Dartford DA1 21 B6
Powder Mill La,
Tunbridge Wells TN4 50 D4
Powell Cotton Dr CT7 14 E3
Powlett Rd ME2 52 D2
Poyntell Rd TN12 51 C3
Prestedge Av CT11 43 B1
Preston Gro ME13 25 D4
Preston La ME13 25 D4
Preston Pk ME13 25 D3
Preston Rd,
Gravesend DA11 39 D4
Preston Rd,
Tonbridge TN9 55 A3
Preston St ME13 25 D3
Pretoria Rd,
Chatham ME4 18 B6
Pretoria Rd,
Gillingham ME7 27 A5
Prices Av CT9 19 A3
Pridmore Rd ME6 49 B2
Priestfield Rd ME7 27 B3

Priestfields ME1 44 B6
Primrose Walk TN12 40 C5
Prince Andrew Rd CT10 15 A1
Prince Arthur Rd ME7 18 D2
Prince Charles Av ME12 37 D4
Prince Charles Rd CT10 15 A1
Prince of Wales Ter CT14 22 D2
Princes Av ME12 37 D3
Princes CI CT7 14 B2
Princes Cres CT9 36 C3
Princes Gdns CT9 19 B3
Princes Par CT21 33 D4
Princes Rd,
Dartford DA1 21 A5
Princes Rd,
Ramsgate CT11 43 A2
Princes St, Deal CT14 22 C1
Princes St, Dover CT17 23 C2
Princes St,
Gravesend DA11 28 B2
Princes St,
Maidstone ME14 35 C2
Princes St,
Margate CT9 36 C2
Princes St,
Rochester ME1 44 C5
Princes Vw DA1 21 D5
Princes Walk CT9 19 C2
Princess Anne Rd CT10 15 A1
Princess Margaret Av CT9 19 D3
Princess Mary Av ME4 18 D1
Prioress Cres DA9 29 C1
Priory CI,
Broadstairs CT10 15 B5
Priory CI, Dartford DA1 21 A2
Priory CI,
New Romney TN28 38 A3
Priory Ct ME8 27 D6
Priory Gate ME14 35 B3
Priory Gate Rd CT17 23 B2
Priory Gdns,
Canterbury CT1 16 D6
Priory Gdns,
Dartford DA1 21 A2
Priory Gdns,
Folkestone CT20 26 D3
Priory Gro,
Dover CT17 23 B1
Priory Gro,
Tonbridge TN9 55 B4
Priory Hill,
Dartford DA1 21 A2
Priory Hill, Dover CT17 23 A1
Priory PI,
Dartford DA1 21 B3
Priory PI,
Faversham ME13 25 C1
Priory Rd,
Dartford DA1 21 B1
Priory Rd,
Dover CT17 23 B1
Priory Rd,
Faversham ME13 25 C2
Priory Rd,
Gillingham ME8 27 D6
Priory Rd,
Maidstone ME15 35 B4
Priory Rd,
Ramsgate CT11 43 A5
Priory Rd,
Strood ME2 52 B5
Priory Rd,
Tonbridge TN9 55 B4
Priory Row ME13 25 C1
Priory St, Dover CT16 23 B2
Priory St,
Tonbridge TN9 55 B4
Priory Station Approach Rd CT17 23 A2
Priory Walk TN9 55 B4
Priory Wy TN30 54 C5
Promenade,
Broadstairs CT10 15 C4
Promenade, Deal CT14 22 D4
Promenade,
Dover CT16 23 D3
Prospect Av ME2 52 D3
Prospect CI CT8 58 B3
Prospect Gro DA12 28 D3
Prospect Hill CT6 32 C1
Prospect Pk TN4 50 B2
Prospect PI,
Broadstairs CT10 15 C4
Prospect PI,
Dartford DA1 21 B3
Prospect PI,
Gravesend DA12 28 D3
Prospect PI,
Maidstone ME16 35 A5
Prospect Rd,
Birchington CT7 14 D2

Prospect Rd,
Broadstairs CT10 15 C4
Prospect Rd,
Hythe CT21 33 B4
Prospect Rd,
Sevenoaks TN13 46 C3
Prospect Rd,
Southborough TN4 50 B2
Prospect Rd,
Tunbridge Wells TN1 56 D5
Prospect Row,
Chatham ME4 18 C5
Prospect Row,
Gillingham ME7 18 C2
Prospect Ter CT11 43 B5
Providence La ME1 44 C3
Providence St,
Ashford TN23 12 C6
Providence St,
Greenhithe DA9 29 A2
Puckle La CT1 16 D6
Pudding La ME14 35 B3
Pudding Rd ME8 42 C2
Purbeck Rd ME4 18 B6
Purser Way ME7 27 A1
Quaker CI TN13 46 D4
Quaker Dr TN17 20 C3
Quaker La TN17 20 C3
Quakers Hall La TN13 46 C3
Quantock Dr TN24 12 B3
Quarry CI CT21 33 B3
Quarry Cotts TN13 46 A4
Quarry Gdns TN9 55 B4
Quarry Hill Rd,
Tonbridge TN9 55 A5
Quarry Hill Rd,
Tonbridge TN9 55 A5
Quarry La CT21 33 A3
Quarry Rd ME15 35 B6
Quarry Rise TN9 55 A5
Quarry Sq ME14 35 C2
Quay La,
Faversham ME13 25 D2
Quay La,
Greenhithe DA9 29 B1
Quay La,
Sandwich CT13 45 D2
Quebec Av TN16 57 C5
Queen Anne Rd ME14 35 C3
Queen Berthas Av CT7 14 F2
Queen Elizabeth Av CT9 19 C4
Queen Elizabeth Rd CT16 23 E1
Queen St,
Ashford TN23 12 C4
Queen St,
Chatham ME4 18 C4
Queen St, Deal CT14 22 C2
Queen St, Dover CT16 23 C2
Queen St,
Folkestone CT20 26 D2
Queen St,
Gravesend DA12 28 B2
Queen St,
Herne Bay CT6 32 B1
Queen St,
Ramsgate CT11 43 B4
Queen St,
Rochester ME1 44 C4
Queen St,
Rochester ME1 44 D4
Queenborough
Bsns Centre ME11 41 A3
Queenborough Dr ME12 37 B3
Queenborough Rd ME12 41 C1
Queens Av,
Birchington CT7 14 A2
Queens Av,
Broadstairs CT10 15 C2
Queens Av,
Margate CT9 36 C3
Queens Av,
Snodland ME6 49 C2
Queens Ct,
Ashford TN24 12 C3
Queens Ct,
Cranbrook TN18 31 C1
Queens Ct,
Edenbridge TN8 24 C5
Queens Ct,
Hythe CT21 33 B4
Queens Dr TN14 46 C1
Queens Gdns,
Broadstairs CT10 15 D5
Queens Gdns,
Dover CT16 23 C2
Queens Gdns,
Herne Bay CT6 32 C2
Queens Gdns,
Margate CT9 36 D1

Queens Gdns,
Tunbridge Wells TN4 50 D5
Queens Mws,
Cranbrook TN18 31 C1
Queens Mws,
Deal CT14 22 C2
Queens Prom CT9 19 A2
Queens Rd,
Ashford TN24 12 C3
Queens Rd,
Broadstairs CT10 15 C4
Queens Rd,
Cranbrook TN18 31 C1
Queens Rd,
Faversham ME13 25 B3
Queens Rd,
Gillingham ME7 27 A4
Queens Rd,
Gravesend DA12 28 C6
Queens Rd,
New Romney TN28 38 D4
Queens Rd,
Ramsgate CT11 43 C3
Queens Rd,
Romney Marsh TN29 34 B2
Queens Rd,
Sheerness ME12 37 D3
Queens Rd,
Snodland ME6 49 C2
Queens Rd,
Tunbridge Wells TN4 50 C6
Queens Rd,
Westgate-on-Sea CT8 58 D2
Queens Way ME12 47 B5
Queensway TN29 34 B2
Quern Rd CT14 22 A6
Quested Way ME17 30 A2
Questor Trading Est
DA1 21 C6
Quex Rd CT8 58 C3
Quex View Rd CT7 14 D4
Quince Orch TN26 30 B5
Quinnell St ME8 42 B1
Quixote Cres ME2 52 C2
Radley CI CT10 15 C2
Radnor Bridge Rd
CT20 26 E1
Radnor Park Av CT19 26 A1
Radnor Park Cres CT19 26 B2
Radnor Park Gdns
CT19 26 B1
Radnor Park Rd CT19 26 B2
Radnor Pk West CT19 26 A2
Radnor St CT19 26 E2
Raggatt PI ME15 35 D6
Raglan PI CT10 15 C4
Railway Av CT5 59 B3
Railway PI DA11 28 B2
Railway Rd ME12 47 C3
Railway St,
Chatham ME4 18 B4
Railway St,
Gillingham ME7 27 A3
Railway St,
Gravesend DA11 39 A1
Railway Ter,
Margate CT9 36 B3
Railway Ter,
Queenborough ME11 41 A1
Railway Ter,
Westerham TN16 57 D4
Rainham Rd ME5 27 A6
Rammell Mws TN17 20 C5
Rampart Rd CT21 33 B4
Ramsgate Rd,
Broadstairs CT10 15 B5
Ramsgate Rd,
Margate CT9 36 C4
Ramsgate Rd,
Sandwich CT13 45 D1
Rancorn Rd CT9 58 F2
Randall St ME14 35 B2
Randolph Cotts ME2 52 D2
Randolph Rd ME7 27 A3
Ranelagh Gro CT10 15 A3
Ranelagh Rd,
Deal CT14 22 D3
Ranelagh Rd,
Sheerness ME12 47 D2
Range Rd CT21 33 A5
Range Rd Ind Est
CT21 33 A5
Ransome Way CT9 14 D4
Raphael Rd DA12 28 D3
Rathmore Rd DA11 28 B3
Ravenscourt Rd CT14 22 C3
Ravenswood Av ME2 52 D2
Rawdon Rd ME15 35 C5
Rayfield CI ME6 49 C2
Rayford CI DA1 21 A2
Rayham Rd CT5 59 D4

Rayners Ct DA11
Reach CI CT15
Reach Mdw CT15
Reach Rd CT15
Readers Bridge Rd
TN30
Reading Street Rd
CT10
Rec Av ME6
Recreation La ME14
Recreation Ground Rd
TN30
Rectory CI,
Ashford TN26
Rectory CI,
Snodland ME6
Rectory Flds TN17
Rectory La,
Cranbrook TN17
Rectory La,
Hythe CT21
Rectory La,
Maidstone ME17
Rectory La,
Broadstairs CT13
Rectory Rd, Deal CT14
Rectory Rd,
Sittingbourne ME10
Rectory Rd,
Swanscombe DA10
Rectory Walk TN26
Rectory Way TN24
Reculver Av CT7
Reculvers Rd CT8
Redcliffe La ME14
Rede Court Rd ME2
Redfern Av ME7
Redhill Rd CT8
Redlands Rd TN13
Redpoll Walk TN13
Redsull Av CT14
Redvers Rd ME4
Reedland Cres ME13
Reeves CI TN12
Reeves Cres BR8
Reform Rd ME4
Regency CI CT5
Regency Ct ME10
Regency Hall TN2
Regent Rd ME7
Regent St CT5
Regents PI TN23
Reginald Rd ME16
Rembrandt Dr DA11
Rendezvous St CT20
Repton CI CT10
Repton Manor Rd
TN23
Reservoir Rd CT5
Reynolds CI CT6
Reynolds La TN4
Rheims Way CT1
Rhodaus CI CT1
Rhodaus Town CT1
Rhode St ME4
Rhodes Gdns CT10
Ribston Gdns TN12
Richard St,
Chatham ME4
Richard St,
Rochester ME1
Richardson Rd TN4
Richborough Dr ME2
Richborough CI CT13
Richborough Rd,
Westgate-on-Sea CT8
Richmond Av CT9
Richmond Dr TN28
Richmond Rd,
Gillingham ME7
Richmond Rd,
Ramsgate CT11
Richmond St CT6
Riddlesdale Av TN4
Ridge Way,
Edenbridge TN8
Ridge Way,
Gillingham ME7
Ridgeway Av DA12
Ridley Rd ME1
Ringden Av TN12
Ringway TN24
Ringwood CI ME8
Rising Rd TN23
Ritch Rd ME6
River Bank CI ME15
River Dr ME2
River Lawn Rd TN9
River St ME7
River Vw,
Maidstone ME15
River Vw,
Queenborough ME11
River Walk TN9

rdale Ind Est
, 55 D4
head Cl CT9 19 B4
s Walk ME17 32 B5
sdale DA11 39 D6
side TN8 24 C5
side Ct,
nbridge TN8 24 C5
side Ct,
bridge TN9 55 C3
rside Est ME2 18 A2
rside Ind Est,
ford TN24 12 D4
rside Ind Est,
ford DA1 21 B1
rside One ME2 18 A2
rside Three ME2 18 A2
rside Two ME2 18 A2
side Way DA1 21 B2
view Rd DA9 29 A2
h St ME2 52 C4
t of Remembrance
0 26 D3
Ct ME2 52 A3
rt St CT14 22 C1
rts Rd,
ngham ME8 42 A2
rts Rd,
dland ME6 49 B2
n Hood La TN29 34 C3
n La TN29 34 C3
na Ct BR8 53 E4
nia Av DA11 39 C3
ns Av ME17 32 B6
ns Cl ME17 32 B6
rns Way,
nbridge TN8 24 C6
rns Way,
enoaks TN13 46 A2
ort Rd ME6 49 C3
ester Av ME1 44 C5
ester Bri ME2 44 C2
ester Rd DA1 44 C5
ester St ME4 18 A6
Av ME7 27 A4
Rd,
dstone ME14 35 C1
Rd,
enoaks TN15 13 B5
Rd,
ngbourne ME10 48 A3
Villa Rd TN1 56 B2
dale Rd TN13 46 C6
y Hill ME16 35 A4
ner Cl ME12 37 C2
ney St CT11 43 A5
uck Rd,
ersham ME13 25 A3
uck Rd,
hester ME1 44 C4
horne Gdns
0 54 C4
n Rd ME1 44 C6
rs Ct BR8 53 E3
rsmead TN30 54 A5
 La TN28 38 B3
enden Rd,
hester ME2 52 D1
enden Rd,
terden TN30 54 A6
an Cl CT14 22 A2
an Heights ME14 35 D1
an Rd,
ersham ME13 25 C3
an Rd,
vesend DA11 39 B6
dland ME6 49 B2
an Sq ME10 48 B3
an Way CT15 41 B5
an Way Ind Est
2 44 A4
e Rd TN28 38 B3
ney Cl CT7 14 D3
ney Ct ME10 48 A1
ney Marsh Rd,
ford TN23 12 C5
ney Marsh Rd,
street TN26 30 B6
ney Pl ME15 35 C4
ney Rd,
ford TN26 30 B6
ney Rd,
vesend DA11 39 D6
kery Hill ME6 49 B3
nagh Ct ME10 48 A5
n Walk,
tham ME4 18 B3
n Walk,
nbrook TN17 20 B4
er Cl CT2 16 A1
er Rd CT2 16 A2
r Gdns CT7 14 D4
r Hill CT11 43 B4
a CT1 16 C4

Rose St,
Gravesend DA11 39 A2
Rose St,
Rochester ME1 44 D5
Rose St,
Sheerness ME12 47 C3
Rose St,
Tonbridge TN9 55 C4
Rose Yd ME14 35 B3
Roseacre Ct CT9 19 D3
Rosebank Gdns DA11 39 D4
Rosebery Av CT11 43 C2
Rosebery Ct DA11 28 A4
Rosebery Rd,
Chatham ME4 18 A6
Rosebery Rd,
Gillingham ME7 27 B1
Rosedale Rd CT9 36 D3
Rosedene Ct DA1 21 A3
Rosefield TN13 46 A5
Rosehill Walk TN1 56 B3
Roselawn Gdns CT9 58 E3
Roselea Av CT6 32 C3
Rosemary Av CT10 15 B6
Rosemary Gdns,
Broadstairs CT10 15 B6
Rosemary Gdns,
Whitstable CT5 59 D4
Rosemary La CT1 16 A4
Rosemead Gdns TN27 31 A4
Rosemount Ct ME2 52 B2
Rosherville Way DA11 39 D2
Ross St ME1 44 D4
Rossendale Gdns
CT20 26 E1
Rossendale Rd CT20 26 E1
Rossetti Rd CT7 14 D2
Rosslare Cl TN16 57 C4
Rothley CT10 54 C4
Rothsay Ct*,
Argyll Dr CT10 43 B1
Rouge La DA12 28 B4
Roundel Way TN12 34 B5
Rowan Cl TN12 40 B4
Rowan Cres DA1 21 A5
Rowan Ct CT20 26 D1
Rowan Rd BR8 53 B3
Rowan Walk ME4 18 A5
Rowe Cl CT9 36 C5
Rowena Rd CT8 58 B2
Rowfield TN8 24 C3
Rowland Cl ME16 35 A4
Roxburgh Rd CT8 58 C2
Royal Av TN9 55 C4
Royal Chase TN4 56 A1
Royal Cl CT10 15 A4
Royal Cres,
Margate CT9 36 A3
Royal Cres,
Ramsgate CT11 43 A5
Royal Eagle Cl ME2 18 A1
Royal Engineers Rd
ME14 35 B1
Royal Esp CT9 58 D2
Royal Par CT11 43 B5
Royal Pier Rd DA12 28 C2
Royal Rd,
Ramsgate CT11 43 A5
Royal Rd,
Sheerness ME12 47 D2
Royal Rise TN9 55 C4
Royal Sovereign Av
ME4 18 D1
Royal Victoria Pl
Shopping Centre
TN1 56 C2
Royston Gdns CT15 41 B5
Royton Av ME17 32 C5
Ruckinge Rd TN26 30 B5
Rugby Cl CT10 15 A3
Rugby Gdns TN23 12 D6
Rule Ct ME12 47 C4
Runnymede Mws
ME13 25 C3
Rural Vale DA11 39 D3
Ruscombe Cl TN14 50 C1
Rushdean Rd ME2 52 A6
Rushenden Cl ME11 41 A3
Rushenden Rd ME11 41 A3
Rushford Cl TN17 31 B5
Russell Av ME8 42 C2
Russell Ct ME4 18 D5
Russell Rd DA12 28 D2
Russell St,
Dover CT16 23 C2
Russell St,
Sheerness ME12 47 C3
Russells Yd TN17 20 C5
Russett Cl DA12 28 A3
Russett Way BR8 53 B1
Rutherford Rd TN24 12 C1
Rutland Av CT9 19 B3
Rutland Cl DA1 21 B3
Rutland Gdns,
Birchington CT7 14 C2

Rutland Gdns,
Margate CT9 19 B3
Ruxton Cl BR8 53 C2
Rycault Cl ME16 35 A4
Rydal Cl TN4 50 A6
Rydal Dr TN4 50 A6
Ryders Av CT8 58 A2
Rye Rd TN18 31 B2
Ryland Ct CT20 26 E1
Ryland Pl CT20 26 E1
Rylands Rd TN24 12 D2
Rype Cl TN29 34 B3
Rysted La TN16 57 C5
Ryswick Mws TN28 38 C2

Sacketts Gap CT9 19 C2
Sackville Cl TN13 46 B2
Sackville Cres TN23 12 A4
Sackville Rd DA2 21 B6
Saddington St DA12 28 B3
Saddleton Gro CT5 59 A4
Saddleton Rd CT5 59 A4
Saffrons Pl CT20 26 E1
Sage Rd ME1 44 B5
Sail Makers Ct ME4 18 D6
St Agnes Gdns ME12 47 D4
St Albans Cl,
Gillingham ME7 27 C1
St Albans Cl,
Gravesend DA12 28 D6
St Albans Gdns DA12 28 D6
St Albans Rd DA1 21 D3
St Albans Walk ME4 18 A5
St Alphege La CT1 16 C2
St Ambrose Grn TN25 60 C5
St Andrews Cl,
Canterbury CT1 16 A5
St Andrews Cl,
Herne Bay CT6 32 C2
St Andrews Cl,
Margate CT9 36 C5
St Andrews Cl,
Tonbridge TN12 40 C3
St Andrews Cl,
Whitstable CT5 59 B5
St Andrews Cl,
Swanley BR8 53 B3
St Andrews Cl,
Tunbridge Wells TN4 50 C2
St Andrews Lees CT13 45 D2
St Andrews Park Rd
TN4 50 C2
St Andrews Rd,
Deal CT14 22 C2
St Andrews Rd,
Gillingham ME7 27 B1
St Andrews Rd,
Gravesend DA12 28 C3
St Andrews Rd,
New Romney TN28 38 E4
St Andrews Rd,
Ramsgate CT11 43 C2
St Andrews Rd,
Tonbridge TN12 40 C4
St Annes Ct ME16 35 A3
St Annes Dr CT6 32 A2
St Annes Gdns CT9 36 C5
St Annes Rd CT5 59 C1
St Anns Rd ME13 25 B3
St Anthonys Way CT9 19 B4
St Augustines Av CT9 36 C5
St Augustines Rd CT11 43 A5
St Barnabas Cl ME7 27 B5
St Bartholomews
CT17 23 A1
St Barts Rd CT13 45 C3
St Benedict Rd ME6 49 A3
St Benedicts Lawn
CT11 43 A5
St Benets Ct TN30 54 B4
St Benets Rd CT8 58 C4
St Benets Wy TN30 54 B4
St Botolphs Av TN13 46 B4
St Botolphs Rd,
Gravesend DA11 39 C6
St Botolphs Rd,
Sevenoaks TN13 46 B5
St Brelades CT18 24 A3
St Catherines Ct*,
Argyll Rd CT10 43 B1
St Catherines Dr ME13 25 D4
St Christopher Cl CT9 19 C5
St Christophers Grn
CT10 15 B3
St Clement Way DA9 29 A2
St Clements CT13 45 D2
St Clements Rd CT8 58 B2
St Crispins Rd CT8 58 C3
St Davids Cl,
Birchington CT7 14 F2
St Davids Cl,
Whitstable CT5 59 C4
St Davids Rd,
Deal CT14 22 C2
St Davids Rd,
Ramsgate CT11 43 C2

St Davids Rd,
Tunbridge Wells TN4 50 D5
St Dunstans Rd CT9 36 D3
St Dunstans St CT2 16 A2
St Dunstans Walk TN17 20 C5
St Eanswythes Way
CT20 26 D2
St Edmunds Rd,
Canterbury CT1 16 B4
St Edmunds Rd,
Dartford DA1 21 D1
St Edmunds Way ME8 42 D1
St Faiths St ME14 35 B3
St Francis Cl,
Maidstone ME14 35 D1
St Francis Cl,
Margate CT9 19 C5
St Georges Av ME12 47 C5
St Georges Cl CT5 59 B5
St Georges Ct ME12 47 C4
St Georges La CT1 16 C5
St Georges Lees CT13 45 D2
St Georges Pl,
Canterbury CT1 16 D4
St Georges Pl,
Dover CT15 41 B5
St Georges Pl,
Sandwich CT13 45 E2
St Georges Rd,
Broadstairs CT10 15 C4
St Georges Rd,
Deal CT14 22 C2
St Georges Rd,
Gillingham ME7 27 A2
St Georges Rd,
Ramsgate CT11 43 C2
St Georges Rd,
Sandwich CT13 45 D2
St Georges Rd,
Sevenoaks TN13 46 C3
St Georges Rd,
Swanley BR8 53 D3
St Georges Sq TN24 12 C4
St Georges St CT1 16 C4
St Georges Ter CT8 58 B5
St Hildas Rd CT21 33 B5
St James Av CT10 15 A3
St James Ct TN1 56 D1
St James Park Rd CT9 58 D2
St James Pl DA1 21 B3
St James Rd TN13 46 C2
St James Rd TN13 23 C2
St James Ter CT7 14 F2
St James's Av DA11 28 A2
St James's Rd DA11 28 A2
St James's St DA11 28 A2
St Jeans Rd CT8 58 B4
St Johns Church Rd
CT19 26 B1
St Johns Hill TN13 46 C2
St Johns La,
Ashford TN23 12 C4
St Johns La,
Canterbury CT1 16 B4
St Johns Pk TN4 50 C3
St Johns Pl CT1 16 D1
St Johns Rd,
Dover CT17 23 A2
St Johns Rd,
Faversham ME13 25 D3
St Johns Rd,
Gillingham ME7 27 A5
St Johns Rd,
Gravesend DA12 28 D3
St Johns Rd,
Margate CT9 36 C3
St Johns Rd,
New Romney TN28 38 A4
St Johns Rd,
Sevenoaks TN13 46 C2
St Johns Rd,
Tunbridge Wells TN4 50 C6
St Johns St CT20 26 D2
St Katherines La ME6 49 B3
St Leonards Av ME4 18 B6
St Leonards Cl CT14 22 A4
St Leonards Ct CT21 33 B4
St Leonards Mws
CT21 33 B4
St Leonards Rd,
Deal CT14 22 A4
St Leonards Rd,
Hythe CT21 33 B5
St Lukes Av,
Maidstone ME14 35 C5
St Lukes Cl,
Ramsgate CT11 43 A2
St Lukes Cl,
Swanley BR8 53 B2
St Lukes Rd,
Westgate-on-Sea CT8 58 C3
St Lukes Rd,
Whitstable CT5 59 B5

St Lukes Rd,
Maidstone ME14 35 C2
St Lukes Rd,
Ramsgate CT11 43 B3
St Lukes Rd,
Tunbridge Wells TN4 50 D5
St Magnus Cl CT7 14 D1
St Margarets Bank
ME1 44 D4
St Margarets Mws
ME1 44 D4
St Margarets Rd,
Dover CT15 41 C6
St Margarets Rd,
Gravesend DA11 39 D5
St Margarets Rd,
Westgate-on-Sea CT8 58 C3
St Margarets St,
Canterbury CT1 16 B4
St Margarets St,
Rochester ME1 44 C4
St Marks Cl CT5 59 B4
St Martins Gdns CT17 23 B2
St Martins Path CT17 23 B4
St Martins Rd,
Dartford DA1 21 C3
St Martins Rd,
New Romney TN28 38 C4
St Martins Steps CT17 23 B3
St Marys Av CT9 19 C4
St Marys Cl,
Ashford TN26 30 B5
St Marys Cl,
Gravesend DA12 28 C5
St Marys Cl,
Herne Bay CT6 32 B3
St Marys Cl,
Westerham TN16 57 C5
St Marys Gdns ME4 18 D1
St Marys Pass CT16 23 C2
St Marys Rd,
Faversham ME13 25 D3
St Marys Rd,
Gillingham ME7 27 A2
St Marys Rd,
New Romney TN28 38 C2
St Marys Rd,
Strood ME2 52 C4
St Marys Rd,
Swanley BR8 53 B3
St Marys Rd,
Tonbridge TN9 55 B5
St Marys Row ME12 37 A3
St Marys St CT1 16 B4
St Michaels Av CT9 19 C5
St Michaels Cl,
Chatham ME4 18 B5
St Michaels Cl,
Sittingbourne ME10 48 C3
St Michaels Ct ME2 52 D3
St Michaels Cl,
Sittingbourne ME10 48 A3
St Michaels Cl,
Tunbridge Wells TN4 50 D5
St Michaels St CT20 26 D2
St Michaels Ter TN30 54 B1
St Mildreds Av,
Birchington CT7 14 B2
St Mildreds Av,
Broadstairs CT10 15 B4
St Mildreds Cl TN30 54 B5
St Mildreds Gdns CT8 58 C1
St Mildreds Rd,
Margate CT9 19 A4
St Mildreds Rd,
Westgate-on-Sea CT8 58 B2
St Nicholas Dr TN13 46 C6
St Nicholas Gdns ME2 52 B3
St Nicholas Rd,
Faversham ME13 25 A3
St Nicholas Rd,
Hythe CT21 33 A4
St Nicholas Rd,
New Romney TN28 38 D3
St Patricks Cl CT5 59 B5
St Patricks Rd,
Deal CT14 22 C2
St Patricks Rd,
Ramsgate CT11 43 C2
St Pauls Av ME13 25 A3
St Pauls Rd CT9 29 F3
St Pauls St ME10 48 A2
St Pauls Ter CT1 16 D4
St Peter St,
Maidstone ME16 35 A4
St Peter St,
Rochester ME1 44 D4
St Peters Cl DA10 29 F3
St Peters Ct,
Broadstairs CT10 15 B3
St Peters Ct,
Faversham ME13 25 A3
St Peters Footpath
CT9 36 C3
St Peters Gro CT1 16 A3

St Peters La CT1 16 B3
St Peters Park Rd CT10 15 B3
St Peters Pl CT1 16 A3
St Peters Rd,
Broadstairs CT10 15 A3
St Peters Rd,
Margate CT9 36 C4
St Peters St,
Canterbury CT1 16 B2
St Peters St,
Sandwich CT13 45 D1
St Peters St,
Whitstable CT5 59 A2
St Philips Av ME15 35 C5
St Radigunds Pl CT1 16 C1
St Radigunds St CT1 16 C2
St Richards Rd CT14 22 A5
St Stephens Rd CT2 16 B1
St Stephens Sq ME15 35 A6
St Stephens St TN9 55 B4
St Theresas Cl TN24 12 B3
St Thomas Rd DA11 39 D5
St Thomas's Av DA11 39 D5
St Vincents Av DA1 21 D2
St Vincents Cl CT5 59 B5
St Vincents Rd DA1 21 D4
St Welcumes Way
ME17 30 C2
St Williams Way ME1 44 D6
Salem Pl DA11 39 C3
Salem St ME15 35 C5
Salisbury Av,
Broadstairs CT10 15 B5
Salisbury Av,
Ramsgate CT11 43 B3
Salisbury Av,
Swanley BR8 53 E3
Salisbury Rd,
Chatham ME4 18 C5
Salisbury Rd,
Deal CT14 22 B6
Salisbury Rd,
Dover CT15 41 C5
Salisbury Rd,
Maidstone ME14 35 C1
Salisbury Rd,
Whitstable CT5 59 A4
Sally Port ME7 18 C2
Sally Port Gdns ME7 18 C2
Salmestone Rd CT9 36 C5
Salmon Cres ME12 37 A3
Salt Marsh La CT5 59 A2
Salters La ME13 25 D6
Saltings Rd ME6 49 C4
Salts Cl CT5 59 A3
Salts Dr CT10 15 A3
Saltwood Gdns CT9 19 D3
Saltwood Rd ME15 35 B6
Samuel Mws TN29 34 C1
Sanctuary Cl,
Broadstairs CT10 15 B6
Sanctuary Cl,
Dartford DA1 21 A3
Sanctuary Rd ME8 27 D5
Sanders Ct ME12 37 A4
Sanderson Way TN9 55 D3
Sandgate Cl ME8 42 B6
Sandgate Rd CT20 26 A4
Sandles Rd CT7 14 C2
Sandling Rd,
Hythe CT21 33 A1
Sandling Rd,
Maidstone ME14 35 B2
Sandown Dr CT6 32 A2
Sandown Rd,
Deal CT14 22 C1
Sandown Rd,
Sandwich CT13 45 E2
Sandpit Rd DA1 21 A1
Sandway Rd ME17 30 C3
Sandwich By-Pass
CT13 45 A2
Sandwich Ind Est
CT13 45 E1
Sandwich Rd CT13 45 A3
Sandwood Rd,
Ramsgate CT11 43 C1
Sandwood Rd,
Sandwich CT13 45 C2
Sandy Bank Rd DA12 28 C4
Sandy La,
Sevenoaks TN13 46 D3
Sandy La,
Snodland ME6 49 A4
Sandy La,
Tenterden TN30 54 B5
Sandy La,
Westerham TN16 57 D4
Sandy Ridge TN15 13 C5
Sandycroft Rd ME2 52 B2
Sanger Cl CT13 36 B4
Sanspareil Av ME12 37 A4
Sappers Walk ME7 27 A3
Sara Cres DA9 29 B1
Sarah Gdns CT9 19 C5
Sarre Pl CT13 45 D2

Saunders Cl DA11 39 D5
Saunders St,
Chatham ME4 18 B5
Saunders St,
Gillingham ME7 27 A2
Saunders Way DA1 21 C6
Savoy Rd DA1 21 A2
Sawyers Ct ME4 18 C6
Saxon Av ME12 37 B3
Saxon Cl,
Gravesend DA11 39 C6
Saxon Cl,
Rochester ME2 52 B2
Saxon Pl ME2 52 B6
Saxon Rd,
Faversham ME13 25 C3
Saxon Rd,
Westgate-on-Sea CT8 58 C2
Saxon St CT17 23 B2
Saxons Dr ME14 35 D1
Saxton St ME7 18 D3
Sayer Cl DA9 29 A2
Sayer Rd TN27 17 B2
Sayers La TN30 54 B5
Scanlons Bridge Rd
CT21 33 A3
Scarborough Dr ME12 37 B1
School App TN15 13 B5
School Av ME7 27 B4
School Fld TN8 24 B4
School La,
Ramsgate CT11 43 B4
School La,
Staplehurst TN12 51 C3
School La,
Swanley BR8 53 F1
School La,
Tonbridge TN11 17 B6
School Rd,
Ashford TN27 17 B2
School Rd,
Faversham ME13 25 B3
School Rd,
Gravesend DA12 28 C6
School Rd,
Hythe CT21 33 A2
School Rd,
Sandwich CT13 45 C1
School Rd,
Sittingbourne ME10 48 D4
School Ter TN18 31 B1
Scocles Rd ME12 37 C4
Scott Av ME8 42 C2
Scott St ME14 35 B2
Scotteswood Av ME4 18 B6
Scotton St TN25 60 C5
Scotts Terr ME4 18 B6
Scrapsgate ME12 37 A3
Sea App CT10 15 D4
Sea Cl CT8 58 A2
Sea St, Dover CT15 41 B5
Sea St, Herne Bay CT6 32 A2
Sea St, Whitstable CT5 59 A2
Sea View Av CT5 14 B1
Sea View Rd,
Birchington CT7 14 B1
Sea View Rd,
Broadstairs CT10 15 C2
Sea View Rd,
Dover CT15 41 C6
Sea View Sq CT6 32 B1
Sea View Ter CT9 36 A3
Sea Wall CT5 59 A2
Seabrook Rd,
Hythe CT21 33 D3
Seabrook Rd,
Tonbridge TN10 55 A1
Seacroft Rd CT10 15 C6
Seafield Rd CT10 15 B4
Seagrave Cres CT19 26 F1
Seal Hollow Rd TN13 46 C5
Seal Rd TN14 46 C2
Seapoint Rd CT10 15 D5
Seaside Av ME12 37 C2
Seathorpe Av ME12 37 D2
Seaton Av CT21 33 A3
Seaton Rd ME7 27 B5
Seaview Rd ME7 27 A4
Second Av,
Gillingham ME7 27 C5
Second Av,
Margate CT9 19 A2
Second Av,
Queenborough ME11 41 A3
Second Av,
Sheerness ME12 37 B3
Seeshill Cl CT5 59 B4
Segrave Rd CT19 26 F1
Selah Dr BR8 53 A1
Selborne Rd CT19 19 A5
Selborne Rd ME7 27 B1
Selway Ct CT14 22 B5
Selwyn Dr CT10 15 A3
Semaphore Rd CT7 14 C2
Semple Gdns ME4 18 A6
Sene Pk CT21 33 D2

Sermon Dr BR8 53 A2
Serpentine Ct TN13 46 D3
Serpentine Rd TN13 46 D4
Setterfield Rd CT9 36 C4
Seven Stones Dr CT10 43 D2
Sevenacre Rd ME13 25 C1
Sevenoaks TN13 46 A5
Sevenoaks Bsns Centre
TN14 46 C1
Sevenoaks Rd TN15 13 A5
Sewell Cl CT7 14 D3
Sexburga Dr ME12 37 B1
Sextant Pk ME2 18 A2
Seymour Ct,
Margate CT9 58 D2
Seymour Av,
Whitstable CT5 59 B3
Seymour Rd ME5 18 D5
Seymour Walk DA10 39 C4
Shaftesbury Ct CT14 22 C6
Shaftesbury Rd,
Tunbridge Wells TN4 50 C6
Shaftesbury Rd,
Whitstable CT5 59 A3
Shaftsbury St CT11 43 C4
Shakespeare Rd,
Birchington CT7 14 D2
Shakespeare Rd,
Gillingham ME7 27 A5
Shakespeare Rd,
Margate CT9 36 C3
Shakespeare Rd,
Sittingbourne ME10 48 D3
Shakespeare Ter CT20 26 B3
Sharland Rd DA12 28 C5
Sharnal La ME6 49 C4
Sharps Fld TN27 31 C5
Shaw Cross TN24 12 D1
Shaws Way ME1 44 C6
Sheafe Dr TN17 20 B4
Sheals Cres ME15 35 C6
Shears Cl DA1 21 A6
Shears Green Ct DA11 28 A5
Shearwater Ct ME12 47 C4
Sheerways ME13 25 A3
Sheet Glass Rd ME11 41 B3
Sheffield Gdns CT14 22 C4
Sheffield Rd TN4 50 C1
Shelden Dr ME8 42 B2
Shellons St CT20 26 C2
Shenley Rd DA1 21 D3
Shepherd St DA11 39 C3
Shepherds Gate CT2 16 A1
Shepherds La DA1 21 A3
Sheppey Cl CT7 14 D3
Sheppey St ME12 47 B2
Sheppy Pl DA12 28 B3
Shepway Cl CT19 26 C1
Sherbourne Dr ME2 52 C2
Sheridan Cl BR8 53 D3
Sheridan Ct DA1 21 D1
Sheron Cl CT14 22 A3
Sherway Cl TN27 31 C5
Sherwood Cl,
Faversham ME13 25 B1
Sherwood Cl,
Whitstable CT5 59 A6
Sherwood Gdns CT11 43 B1
Sherwood Rd CT7 14 C4
Ship La CT21 18 A4
Ship St CT19 26 C1
Shipbourne Rd TN10 55 C1
Shipwrights Lee CT5 59 A2
Shirley Av CT11 43 B1
Shirley Cl DA1 21 A1
Shorefields ME8 42 D1
Shoreham La TN30 54 A1
Shorncliffe Rd CT20 26 A2
Short St,
Chatham ME4 18 D5
Short St,
Sandwich CT13 45 D2
Short St,
Sheerness ME12 47 C2
Shortlands Rd ME10 48 D3
Shorts Reach ME1 44 B4
Shorts Way ME1 44 A6
Shottendane Rd CT9 19 B1
Shottenden Rd ME7 27 B1
Shrubbery Rd DA12 28 C4
Shrubcote TN30 54 C5
Shrublands Ct TN9 55 C2
Shrubsole Av ME12 47 D3
Shurland Av,
Sheerness ME12 37 B3
Shurland Av,
Sittingbourne ME10 48 B6
Shurlock Av BR8 53 B2
Shutler Rd CT10 15 D3
Shuttle Cl TN27 13 C2
Sidney Rd ME7 27 A1
Signal Ct ME8 42 C1
Silk Mills Cl TN14 46 D2
Silver Av CT7 14 E4
Silver Cl TN9 55 A6

Silver Hill,
Chatham ME4 18 B5
Silver Hill,
Tenterden TN30 54 C3
Silver St CT14 22 D1
Silverdale Av ME12 37 A3
Silverdale Dr ME8 42 B3
Silverspot Cl ME8 42 B3
Simon Av CT9 19 C3
Simone Weil Av TN24 12 B2
Simpson Rd ME6 49 B4
Sinclair Cl ME8 42 A6
Singapore Dr ME7 18 C3
Singlewell Rd DA11 28 B6
Sion Hill CT11 43 B5
Sir Davids Pk TN4 50 B3
Sir John Hawkins Way
ME4 18 B4
Sir John Moore Av
CT21 33 A3
Sir Thomas Longley Rd
ME2 18 A1
Siskin Gdns CT9 19 C3
Sissinghurst Rd TN27 13 A2
Sittingbourne Ind Pk
ME10 48 B2
Sittingbourne Rd
ME14 35 C3
Six Bells La TN13 46 C6
Six Flds Path TN30 54 B6
Six Penny Cl TN8 24 C5
Skeme Cl ME8 42 D1
Skeynes Rd TN8 24 B5
Skinner Rd TN29 34 C2
Skinner St,
Chatham ME4 18 B5
Skinner St,
Gillingham ME7 27 A3
Skinners La TN8 24 C3
Skinners Ter TN9 55 B4
Skippers Cl DA9 29 B1
Slaney Rd ME12 51 C3
Slatin Rd ME2 52 C3
Slicketts Hill ME4 18 C4
Slip Mill Rd TN18 31 A1
Slip Pass CT17 23 C2
Slipway Rd ME12 47 B1
Smack Alley ME13 25 D2
Smallhythe Rd TN30 54 A6
Smarden Rd TN27 31 D5
Smarden Walk ME8 42 D1
Smarts Rd DA12 28 C6
Smeed Cl ME10 48 D3
Smetham Gdns ME2 52 C2
Smith St ME2 52 C5
Smithers Cl TN11 17 C5
Smithyfield TN8 24 D3
Smugglers TN18 31 C2
Smugglers Way CT7 14 B4
Smugglers Wharf DA9 29 B1
Snargate St CT17 23 B3
Snodland By-Pass
ME6 49 C1
Snodland Rd ME6 49 A4
Snowdon Av ME14 35 D3
Snowdon Par ME14 35 D3
Solomans La ME13 25 D3
Solomon Ho CT14 22 B5
Solomon Rd ME8 42 C1
Solomons Rd ME4 18 B4
Somerhill Rd TN9 55 D4
Somerset Rd,
Ashford TN24 12 C4
Somerset Rd,
Deal CT14 22 B5
Somerset Rd,
Tunbridge Wells TN4 50 C5
Somerville Gdns TN4 56 A2
Somerville Rd DA1 21 C3
Sondes Rd CT14 22 C3
Sopers La TN18 31 A1
Sorrell Cl TN8 24 C3
Sort Mill Rd ME6 49 D3
South Av ME10 48 C4
South Bank,
Tonbridge TN12 51 B4
South Bank,
Westerham TN16 57 C5
South Bush La ME8 42 D5
South Cl CT1 16 C3
South Cliff Par CT10 15 C6
South Ct CT14 22 D2
South Eastern Rd,
Ramsgate CT11 43 A4
South Eastern Rd,
Rochester ME2 52 D3
South Gro TN1 56 B5
South Hill Rd DA12 28 C4
South Kent Av DA11 39 B2
South Lodge Cl CT5 59 B1
South Military Rd CT17 23 A4
South Par CT14 22 D2
South Park Rd ME15 35 D6
South Pk TN13 46 B6
South Rd,
Chatham ME4 18 C1

South Rd, Dover CT17 17
South Rd,
Faversham ME13
South Rd,
Herne Bay CT6
South Rd, Hythe CT21
South Rd,
Tonbridge TN12
South St, Deal CT14
South St,
Folkestone CT20
South St,
Gravesend DA12
South St,
Queenborough ME11
South St,
Romney Marsh TN29
South St,
Whitstable CT5
South Stour Av TN23
South View Rd CT5
South Wall CT14
Southbourne Rd CT19
Southern Pl BR8
Southern Way CT20
Southfield Rd TN4
Southfields ME1
Southfields Way TN4
Southgate Rd TN30
Southill Rd ME4
Southsea Av ME12
Southsea Dr CT6
Southview Cl BR8
Southview Gdns
ME12
Southwall Rd Ind Est
CT14
Southwold Pl CT8
Southwood Av TN4
Sovereign Way TN9
Sovereigns Way TN12
Sowell St CT10
Spa Cl TN11
Spanton Cres CT14
Speedwell Cl,
Edenbridge TN8
Speedwell Cl,
Gillingham ME7
Speke Rd CT10
Speldhurst Rd TN3
Spencer Mws, Berkeley
Tunbridge Wells TN1
Spencer Mws, Camden
Tunbridge Wells TN1
Spencer Rd CT7
Spencer Sq CT11
Spencer St DA11
Spenser Rd CT6
Spielman Rd DA1
Spillett Cl ME13
Spinners Cl TN27
Spire Av CT5
Spire Cl DA12
Spital St DA1
Spitalfield La TN28
Sports Fld ME14
Spring Gro DA12
Spring Vale DA9
Spring Vale North DA1
Spring Vale South DA1
Spring Walk CT5
Springfield Av,
Maidstone ME14
Springfield Av,
Swanley BR8
Springfield Av,
Tenterden TN30
Springfield Cl CT11
Springfield Ind Est
TN18
Springfield Pass CT21
Springfield Rd,
Edenbridge TN8
Springfield Rd,
Gillingham ME7
Springfield Rd,
Margate CT9
Springfield Rd,
Sittingbourne ME10
Springfield Rd,
Tunbridge Wells TN4
Springfield Ter ME4
**Springhead
Enterprise Pk** DA11
Springhead Rd,
Faversham ME13
Springhead Rd,
Gravesend DA11
Springvale ME10
Springvale Ct DA11
Springwell Rd TN9
Springwood Ct TN28
Sprucedale Cl BR8
Square Hill ME15
Square Hill Rd ME15

Tryes Mede TN16 57 B6
e Ct ME13 25 D3
CITN30 54 C4
s Cotts TN12 40 B5
y Rd TN10 55 A1
ys St ME14 35 B2
field TN8 24 C3
St CT21 33 B4
rd Cl,
ford TN23 12 A4
rd Cl,
nhithe DA9 29 A2
rd Rd TN9 55 B2
rd St ME7 27 A3
rdshire St CT11 43 B4
haw Cl ME15 35 C6
es Pl,
dstairs CT10 15 D3
es Pl,
erbury CT1 16 C4
ys Acre TN15 13 A5
ys Rd TN15 13 A6
ridge Rd TN8 24 B4
len St TN4 50 C6
Quarry Rd
5 13 A5
rove Ct TN8 24 B4
rove Rd TN8 24 B5
ope Av ME10 48 C4
ope Rd,
CT14 22 C2
ope Rd,
od ME2 52 C3
ope Rd,
nscombe DA10 29 F2
ey Av,
enborough ME11 41 B2
ey Av,
erness ME12 37 E3
ey Cl TN12 51 B3
ey Gdns CT6 32 C3
ey Pl CT11 43 A3
ey Rd,
dstairs CT10 15 B2
ey Rd,
CT14 22 D3
ey Rd,
ngham ME7 27 A2
e Bay CT6 32 C2
ey Rd,
den TN12 34 C5
ey Rd,
gate CT9 36 D2
ey Rd,
sgate CT11 43 A3
ey Rd,
nscombe DA10 29 F2
ey Rd,
ridge TN11 50 D6
ey Rd,
stable CT5 59 A5
y Sykes Cl CT9 19 A5
e Cl ME10 48 A1
e Dr TN12 51 C3
e Ford Ct TN13 46 A4
ehurst Av CT10 15 C6
ehurst Rd ME10 48 A1
Hill ME1 44 D4
t Cl ME5 27 B6
Mill La ME5 27 B6
oard Av DA9 29 C3
es Ct ME14 35 B3
n App,
ford TN27 31 C5
n App,
ington CT7 14 D2
n App,
nbridge TN8 24 C4
n App,
dstone ME16 35 A4
n App,
y Romney TN28 38 D4
n App,
enoaks TN15 13 B5
n App,
elehurst TN12 51 B1
n App,
nley BR8 53 C3
n App,
ridge TN12 40 C3
n Approach Rd
43 A3
n Chine CT6 32 B2
n Ct TN15 13 B5
on Ind Est
0 54 A5
n Par,
ington CT7 14 D2
n Par,
enoaks TN13 46 B4
n Pl ME10 48 B3
n Rd,
ford TN23 12 C5
n Rd,
hington CT7 14 D2

Station Rd,
Charing TN27 17 B3
Station Rd,
Dover CT15 41 B4
Station Rd,
Edenbridge TN8 24 B2
Station Rd,
Faversham ME13 25 D3
Station Rd,
Gillingham ME8 42 B2
Station Rd,
Gravesend DA11 39 A1
Station Rd,
Gravesend DA13 39 A6
Station Rd,
Greenhithe DA9 29 A1
Station Rd,
Harrietsham ME17 30 B1
Station Rd,
Headcorn TN27 31 B5
Station Rd,
Herne Bay CT6 32 B1
Station Rd,
Hythe CT21 33 C3
Station Rd,
Lenham ME17 32 B6
Station Rd,
Maidstone ME14 35 B3
Station Rd,
Margate CT9 36 A3
Station Rd,
New Romney TN28 38 C3
Station Rd,
Romney Marsh TN29 34 C2
Station Rd,
Sevenoaks TN15 13 B5
Station Rd,
Staplehurst TN12 51 B1
Station Rd,
Strood ME2 52 D3
Station Rd,
Swanley BR8 53 D3
Station Rd,
Tenterden TN30 54 A5
Station Rd,
Tonbridge TN12 40 C3
Station Rd,
Westgate-on-Sea CT8 58 C2
Station Rd,
Whitstable CT5 59 B1
Station Rd East CT1 16 A5
Station Rd West CT2 16 A2
Station Road Mws
TN30 54 A5
Station St ME10 48 B3
Stede Hill ME17 30 C1
Steele Av DA9 29 A2
Steele St ME2 52 C3
Steerforth Cl ME1 44 C6
Steers Pl TN11 17 B4
Stella Cl TN12 34 B5
Stembrook CT16 23 C2
Step Style ME10 48 D5
Stephen Cl CT10 15 C4
Stephens Cl,
Faversham ME13 25 B2
Stephens Cl,
Margate CT9 58 E3
Stephens Rd TN4 50 D6
Sterling Cl CT10 15 A3
Sterling Rd ME11 41 B1
Sterndale Rd DA1 21 C4
Stevens Cl ME6 49 C2
Stevenson Cl ME15 35 B5
Stiles Cl ME12 37 A3
Still La TN4 50 C1
Stirling Cl,
Gillingham ME8 42 A6
Stirling Cl,
Rochester ME1 44 A6
Stockbury Gdns CT9 19 D3
Stockdale Gdns CT14 22 B4
Stockland Green Rd
TN3 50 A2
Stonar Cl,
Ramsgate CT11 43 B1
Stonar Cl,
Sandwich CT13 45 D1
Stonar Gdns CT13 45 E1
Stonar Rd CT13 45 E1
Stone Barn Av CT7 14 E3
Stone Cross Lees
CT13 45 D3
Stone Rd CT10 15 D3
Stone St,
Cranbrook TN17 20 C4
Stone St,
Faversham ME13 25 C3
Stone St,
Gravesend DA11 28 B2
Stone St,
Tunbridge Wells TN1 56 D1
Stonebridge Rd DA11 39 A1
Stonebridge Way
ME13 25 B3
Stonedane Ct ME13 25 C2

Stonegate TN25 60 C5
Stonehorse La ME2 52 C1
Stones Cross Rd BR8 53 A4
Stonewood Cl TN4 50 C3
Stoney Alley ME5 18 D5
Stoney Path CT14 22 C4
Stoneyfield TN8 24 C3
Stopford Rd ME7 27 A5
Stour Cl ME2 52 A4
Stour Ct CT13 45 C1
Stour St CT1 16 A4
Stour Villas CT1 16 B4
Strand St CT13 45 C1
Strangford Rd CT5 59 C2
Stratford La ME8 42 C2
Stratton Ter TN16 57 C5
Straw Mill Hill ME15 35 A6
Strawberry Flds BR8 53 C1
Strawberry Vale TN9 55 C4
Stream Walk CT5 59 B2
Streatfield TN8 24 C3
Streete Court Rd CT8 58 C3
Streete Ct CT8 58 C3
Streetfield Rd ME8 42 B1
Stringer Dr CT7 14 E4
Strode Cres ME12 47 D2
Strond St CT17 23 B3
Strover Rd ME7 27 A1
Stuart Cl ME14 35 D1
Stuart Rd,
Gillingham ME7 27 B5
Stuart Rd,
Gravesend DA11 28 B2
Sturdee Av ME7 27 B4
Sturdy Cl CT21 33 C4
Sturges Rd TN24 12 C3
Sturla Rd ME4 18 C6
Style Cl ME8 42 A6
Sudbury Pl CT8 58 B3
Suffolk Av,
Gillingham ME8 42 B1
Suffolk Av,
Westgate-on-Sea CT8 58 B3
Suffolk Cl ME8 42 B1
Suffolk Dr TN23 12 B5
Suffolk Rd,
Dartford DA1 21 B3
Suffolk Rd,
Gravesend DA12 28 D2
Suffolk St CT5 59 A4
Suffolk Way TN13 46 C5
Sugar Loaf Hill ME5 27 A6
Summer Cl TN30 54 D4
Summerfield Av CT5 59 C2
Summerhill Av TN4 50 B2
Summerhill Rd DA1 21 B4
Summerville Av ME12 37 A4
Supper Way ME13 25 A2
Sun La,
Gravesend DA12 28 C5
Sun La, Hythe CT21 33 C3
Sun Rd DA10 29 F3
Sun St CT1 16 C3
Sunburst Cl TN12 34 B5
Sunderland Cl ME1 44 A6
Sunderland Dr ME8 42 C2
Sunderland Quay
ME2 52 B2
Sundew Gro CT11 43 B3
Sunningdale Cl ME8 42 A4
Sunningdale Gdns ME15 35 D4
Sunningdale Dr ME8 42 A4
Sunninghill DA11 39 D5
Sunny Bank ME10 48 D2
Sunnyfields Cl ME8 42 D2
Sunnymead Av ME7 27 C3
Sunnyside TN8 24 B2
Sunnyside Av ME12 37 B4
Sunnyside Gdns
CT13 45 B3
Surrenden Rd TN12 51 B3
Surrey Gdns CT7 14 D2
Surrey Rd CT9 19 B2
Susans Hill TN26 60 A1
Sussex Av,
Ashford TN24 12 C3
Sussex Av,
Margate CT9 36 C4
Sussex Gdns,
Birchington CT7 14 C3
Sussex Gdns,
Westgate-on-Sea CT8 58 C2
Sussex Mws TN2 56 A6
Sussex Rd,
Dartford DA1 21 D4
Sussex Rd,
Folkestone CT19 26 C1
Sussex Rd,
New Romney TN28 38 A3
Sussex Rd,
Tonbridge TN9 55 A4
Sussex St CT11 43 B3
Sutherland Cl CT21 33 A4
Sutherland Dr CT7 14 E3
Sutherland Gdns ME8 42 A4

Sutherland Rd,
Deal CT14 22 B2
Sutherland Rd,
Tunbridge Wells TN1 56 C5
Sutton Cl ME8 42 C2
Sutton Ct TN12 34 B5
Sutton Forge TN12 34 B5
Swadelands Cl ME17 32 C5
Swaffield Rd TN13 46 D3
Swain Cl ME2 52 A3
Swain Rd TN30 54 C1
Swale Av,
Queenborough ME11 41 A3
Swale Av,
Sheerness ME12 47 C3
Swallow Cl CT9 36 A4
Swallowfields DA11 39 D6
Swan Cl ME10 48 D3
Swan La TN8 24 B2
Swan Ridge TN8 24 C2
Swanfield Rd CT5 59 A3
Swanley By-Pass BR8 53 A1
Swanley La BR8 53 D2
Swanley Village Rd
BR8 53 F1
Swanmead Way TN9 55 D2
Swanscombe
Bsns Centre DA10 29 E1
Swanscombe St DA10 29 F3
Swanstree Av ME10 48 D5
Swanzy Rd TN14 46 D1
Sweetlands La TN12 51 D2
Sweyn Rd CT9 36 D2
Sweyne Rd DA10 29 F3
Swifts Vw TN17 20 C3
Swinburne Av CT10 15 B5
Swinford Gdns CT9 19 C5
Sycamore Cl,
Gravesend DA12 28 D3
Sycamore Cl,
Margate CT9 36 B5
Sycamore Cl,
Romney Marsh TN29 34 C1
Sycamore Dr,
Deal CT14 22 B4
Sycamore Dr,
Swanley BR8 53 C2
Sycamore Gdns TN12 40 C5
Sycamore Grange
CT11 43 C1
Sycamore Rd,
Dartford DA1 21 A4
Sycamore Rd,
Rochester ME2 52 A6
Sydenham Rd CT14 22 C1
Sydenham St CT5 59 A2
Sydney Rd,
Chatham ME4 18 C5
Sydney Rd, Deal CT14 22 A6
Sydney Rd,
Ramsgate CT11 43 C3
Sydney Rd,
Whitstable CT5 59 B4
Sydney St TN23 12 C6
Symmonds Dr ME10 48 C1
Symons Av ME4 18 B6

Taddy Gdns CT9 19 C5
Tadworth Rd TN24 12 D1
Tainter Rd TN11 17 B5
Talbot Pl DA11 28 B2
Talbot Rd,
Margate CT9 19 A4
Talbot Rd,
Sevenoaks TN15 13 B4
Tamar Dr ME2 52 A5
Tams Gdns ME12 37 E3
Tangmere Cl ME7 27 D3
Tankerton Heights
CT5 59 B1
Tankerton Mws CT5 59 B1
Tankerton Rd CT5 59 B1
Tanners Hill CT21 33 B2
Tanners Hill Gdns
CT21 33 B2
Tanners Mead TN8 24 B5
Tanners St ME13 25 C3
Tannery La TN23 12 C4
Tannery Rd TN9 55 C3
Tar Path CT14 22 B2
Tarbutts TN17 20 C5
Taswell Cl CT16 23 C1
Taswell Rd ME8 42 C1
Taswell St ME8 23 C1
Tates TN18 31 B2
Tatsfield Cl ME8 27 D6
Taunton Vale DA12 28 D6
Tavern Cl TN15 13 A5
Taverners Rd ME8 42 A3
Tavistock Cl ME8 42 B3
Tavistock Rd CT11 43 A1
Taylor Cl ME17 30 B2
Taylor Rd ME6 49 B3
Taylor St TN4 50 C3
Taylors La ME2 52 D4

Taylors Yd TN25 60 C5
Teardrop Ind Est
BR8 53 F4
Teasels TN27 13 C2
Tedder Rd TN4 50 D4
Telegraph Rd CT14 22 B6
Telford St CT6 32 B1
Templar St CT17 23 A1
Templar Way TN23 12 A2
Templars Ct TN8 24 C3
Temple Gdns,
Sittingbourne ME10 48 D4
Temple Gdns,
Strood ME2 52 B5
Temple Hill DA1 21 D2
Temple Hill Sq DA1 21 D2
Temple Ind Est ME2 52 C5
Tennyson Rd ME7 27 A5
Tennyson Walk DA11 39 C6
Tensing Av DA11 39 D6
Tenterden Rd TN27 13 C2
Tenterden Way CT9 19 B5
Terrace Rd,
Maidstone ME16 35 A4
Terrace Rd,
Sittingbourne ME10 48 D3
Terrace St DA12 28 B2
Terrys La CT5 59 A2
Teynham Dr CT5 59 C2
Teynham Rd CT5 59 C2
Thames Av,
Gillingham ME8 42 A2
Thames Av,
Sheerness ME12 47 C3
Thames Gate DA1 21 D1
Thames Way,
Gravesend DA11 28 A2
Thames Way,
Northfleet DA11 39 C4
Thanet Place Gdns
CT10 15 D2
Thanet Rd,
Broadstairs CT10 15 C4
Thanet Rd,
Margate CT9 36 C3
Thanet Rd,
Ramsgate CT11 43 C3
Thanet Way,
Westgate-on-Sea CT8 58 B2
Thanet Way,
Herne Bay CT6 32 A3
Thanet Way,
Whitstable CT5 59 A6
Thatch Barn Rd TN27 31 C4
Thatcher Rd TN12 51 B2
The Abbots CT17 23 A1
The Acorns TN13 46 B4
The Avenue,
Deal CT14 22 C1
The Avenue,
Dover CT15 41 B4
The Avenue,
Gravesend DA11 28 A4
The Avenue,
Greenhithe DA9 29 B1
The Avenue,
Hythe CT21 33 C4
The Avenue,
Margate CT9 36 D3
The Avenue,
Sevenoaks TN15 13 B4
The Avenue,
Tonbridge TN9 55 B2
The Avenue,
Westerham TN16 57 A1
The Banks CT10 15 B2
The Bayle CT20 26 D3
The Beach CT14 22 D5
The Beeches TN29 34 D1
The Bines TN12 40 C5
The Birches,
Swanley BR8 53 C1
The Birches,
Tonbridge TN9 55 B5
The Borough CT1 16 C2
The Bridge App CT5 59 B2
The Broadway,
Broadstairs CT10 15 B3
The Broadway,
Herne Bay CT6 32 A1
The Broadway,
Sheerness ME12 37 B1
The Brook ME4 18 B3
The Burrs ME10 48 C4
The Butts,
Sandwich CT13 45 C1
The Butts,
Sittingbourne ME10 48 B3
The Causeway,
Canterbury CT1 16 B1
The Causeway,
Sandwich CT13 45 A1
The Cedars TN12 40 C3
The Chain CT13 45 D2
The Chase,
Ramsgate CT11 43 C1

77

The Chase,
Tunbridge Wells TN2 56 D5
The Cherry Orch TN11 17 B5
The Chestnuts TN18 31 A3
The Churchlands
TN28 38 B3
The Circus CT6 32 A3
The Cloisters,
Maidstone ME17 32 B5
The Cloisters,
Ramsgate CT11 43 A5
The Cloisters,
Sittingbourne ME10 48 A3
The Close,
Ashford TN25 60 C6
The Close,
Faversham ME13 25 C4
The Close, Hythe CT21 33 B2
The Close,
Rochester ME1 44 C5
The Close,
Sevenoaks TN15 13 B4
The Cobs TN30 54 A6
The Cockpit TN12 34 B5
The Colonnade TN18 31 B1
The Common ME1 44 C2
The Courts CT9 22 B5
The Courtyard CT14 22 B5
The Creek DA11 39 B1
The Crescent,
Dover CT15 41 C6
The Crescent,
Greenhithe DA9 29 C2
The Crescent,
Sandwich CT13 45 C4
The Crescent,
Sevenoaks TN15 13 B4
The Crescent,
Tonbridge TN9 55 B2
The Crest TN17 20 C5
The Croft,
Swanley BR8 53 A2
The Croft,
Tenterden TN30 54 B5
The Crofters ME8 42 B3
The Curlews DA12 28 D5
The Dell DA9 29 B1
The Derings TN29 34 A2
The Downage DA11 28 A5
The Drive, Deal CT14 22 C3
The Drive,
Sevenoaks TN13 46 B5
The Drive,
Tonbridge TN9 55 B5
The Droveway CT15 41 C5
The Durlocks CT19 26 E2
The Fairings TN30 54 B5
The Fairway,
Gravesend DA11 28 B6
The Fairway,
Hythe CT21 33 C4
The Fairway,
New Romney TN28 38 E3
The Fairway,
Sittingbourne ME10 48 B6
The Fairways TN4 50 D4
The Ferns TN15 13 D5
The Fieldings ME10 48 B5
The Finches ME10 48 C4
The Flats DA9 29 C2
The Flyers Way TN16 57 D4
The Forstal,
Ashford TN25 60 C5
The Forstal,
Tonbridge TN11 17 C6
The Forum ME10 48 B3
The Freedown CT15 41 C4
The Freehold TN11 17 B5
The Friars CT1 16 B3
The Front CT15 41 D6
The Gateway CT16 23 D2
The Glade TN13 46 B3
The Glen,
Sheerness ME12 37 B2
The Glen,
Sheerness ME12 37 C2
The Glen,
Tunbridge Wells TN4 50 D1
The Graylings ME1 44 B6
The Green,
Hythe CT21 33 A1
The Green,
Romney Marsh TN29 34 B3
The Green,
Sevenoaks TN13 46 D2
The Green,
Westerham TN16 57 C5
The Green,
Woodchurch TN26 60 B1
The Green, Wye TN25 60 C5
The Greenways TN12 40 B5
The Grove,
Deal CT14 22 B2
The Grove,
Gravesend DA12 28 C3

The Grove,
Swanley BR8 53 D3
The Grove,
Swanscombe DA10 29 F2
The Grove,
Tonbridge TN9 55 C2
The Grove,
Westgate-on-Sea CT8 58 C2
The Groves ME6 49 B3
The Halt CT5 59 D5
The Haydens TN9 55 C1
The Hedgerows DA11 39 D5
The High St TN27 17 B3
The Hill, Ashford TN27 17 C2
The Hill,
Cranbrook TN17 20 C5
The Hill,
Gravesend DA11 39 C2
The Homestead DA1 21 A3
The Hoystings Cl CT1 16 D6
The Knole ME13 25 B2
The Landway TN15 13 B5
The Lapwings DA12 28 D5
The Larches,
Faversham ME13 25 A2
The Larches,
Whitstable CT5 59 A4
The Laxey ME15 35 A6
The Leas,
Faversham ME13 25 B2
The Leas,
Folkestone CT20 26 B4
The Lees ME12 37 C1
The Limes TN8 24 C5
The Lindens TN30 54 B4
The Lowry TN9 55 B4
The Mall ME13 25 C4
The Mallows ME14 35 A1
The Malthouses CT7 14 C2
The Maltings,
Faversham ME13 25 D1
The Maltings,
Gillingham ME8 42 C3
The Maltings,
Tonbridge TN11 17 B6
The Maples ME12 37 B3
The Meadows,
Ashford TN27 13 C2
The Meadows,
Maidstone ME15 35 A6
The Meadows,
New Romney TN28 38 C3
The Meadows,
Sittingbourne ME10 48 B5
The Meadway TN13 46 A3
The Mews,
Maidstone ME16 35 A3
The Mews,
Sevenoaks TN13 46 B4
The Mews,
Sittingbourne ME10 48 B4
The Mews,
Strood ME2 52 B4
The Mews,
Tunbridge Wells TN1 56 D1
The Mews,
Tunbridge Wells TN1 56 D4
The Middlings TN13 46 A6
The Moat TN27 17 C3
The Moorings ME15 35 B5
The Mount ME4 18 B4
The Musings TN27 13 C1
The Oaks,
Broadstairs CT10 15 B1
The Oaks,
Swanley BR8 53 C1
The Old Bailey ME17 30 C2
The Old High St CT20 26 E2
The Old Orchard
ME8 42 C2
The Orchard BR8 53 B2
The Orchards DA1 21 C3
The Paddock,
Chatham ME4 18 B4
The Paddock,
Dover CT16 23 C1
The Paddock,
Tonbridge TN11 17 B4
The Paddock,
Westerham TN16 57 C5
The Paddocks,
Ashford TN26 60 B2
The Paddocks,
Broadstairs CT10 15 B1
The Paddocks,
Sevenoaks TN13 46 D4
The Pantiles TN4 56 A6
The Parade,
Birchington CT7 14 A1
The Parade,
Broadstairs CT10 15 D4
The Parade,
Canterbury CT1 16 C3
The Parade,
Folkestone CT20 26 D3

The Parade,
Gravesend DA12 28 D5
The Parade,
Margate CT9 36 B2
The Parade,
Tonbridge TN12 51 C4
The Parkway CT7 14 E3
The Parrock DA12 28 C4
The Pathway CT10 15 C4
The Pavement TN30 54 B2
The Pavilion TN9 55 B3
The Plat TN8 24 C5
The Priory TN29 34 B2
The Promenade CT10 15 D5
The Quay CT13 45 D1
The Queen Mother Ct
ME1 44 B5
The Quern ME15 35 A6
The Rendezvous CT9 36 C1
The Retreat CT7 14 E1
The Ridgeway,
Broadstairs CT10 15 A5
The Ridgeway,
Margate CT9 19 B4
The Ridgeway,
Tonbridge TN10 55 D1
The Ridgewaye TN4 50 D2
The Ridings,
Margate CT9 19 D2
The Ridings,
Tonbridge TN12 40 C3
The Rise, Dover CT15 41 D4
The Rise,
Rochester ME1 44 D6
The Rise,
Sheerness ME12 41 D1
The Roundel ME10 48 B5
The Rowans ME12 37 B3
The Saltings,
New Romney TN28 38 F4
The Saltings,
Whitstable CT5 59 A2
The Sandpipers DA12 28 D5
The School Cl CT8 58 B2
The Shires TN12 40 C3
The Shore DA11 39 B1
The Slade TN9 55 B2
The Slip TN16 57 C5
The Spinney,
Maidstone ME15 35 D5
The Spinney,
Swanley BR8 53 C1
The Spinney,
Tonbridge TN9 55 A5
The Spires DA1 21 A6
The Square,
Birchington CT7 14 D3
The Square,
Edenbridge TN8 24 C5
The Square,
Maidstone ME17 32 D5
The Square,
Swanley BR8 53 B2
The Square,
Tonbridge TN11 17 C6
The Stade CT19 26 E3
The Staples BR8 53 F1
The Strand CT14 22 D3
The Street TN26 30 B6
The Tanyard TN17 20 C5
The Terrace,
Chatham ME4 18 C1
The Terrace,
Gravesend DA12 28 C2
The Terrace,
Rochester ME1 44 D4
The Tram Rd CT20 26 E2
The Turnstones DA12 28 D5
The Vale TN30 15 B4
The Vespers CT2 16 B1
The Viaduct CT17 23 B4
The Vine TN13 46 C5
The Vineries ME7 27 C3
The Violets TN12 40 C5
The Wall ME10 48 B2
The Warren CT5 59 A6
The Warren Dr CT8 58 A4
The Weald TN24 12 C3
The Weavers TN27 13 C2
The Wheelwrights
ME17 30 B2
The Willows ME12 37 B1
The Wynd TN27 17 D1
The Yews DA12 28 D5
Theatre Sq*,
Bells La TN30 54 B5
Theatre St CT21 33 C3
Theobalds TN18 31 B2
Theodore Pl ME7 27 A3
Theresa Rd CT13 33 B5
Thicketts TN13 46 C4
Third Av,
Gillingham ME7 27 C5

Third Av,
Margate CT9 19 A2
Thirlmere Cl,
Gillingham ME7 27 D3
Thirlmere Cl,
Rochester ME2 52 D2
Thirlmere Rd TN4 50 A6
Thirza Rd DA1 21 D3
Thistle Hill Way ME12 37 C4
Thomas Dr DA12 28 D5
Thomas Rd,
Faversham ME13 25 C2
Thomas Rd,
Sittingbourne ME10 48 D3
Thomas St,
Rochester ME1 44 D5
Thomas St,
Tunbridge Wells TN4 50 C6
Thompson Cl ME8 42 C2
Thomson Cl ME6 49 C2
Thomson Rd TN24 12 B1
Thorn Gdns CT11 43 B1
Thorn Rd TN12 34 C6
Thornbridge Rd CT14 22 A5
Thornhill Pl ME14 35 B2
Thorold Rd ME5 18 D5
Thrale Way ME8 42 A6
Three Fields Pat
TN30 54 B6
Thundersland Rd CT6 32 D3
Thurlestone Ct ME14 35 B2
Thurston Pk CT5 59 B3
Tilden Gill Rd TN30 54 C6
Tilghman Way ME6 49 D2
Tillmans TN15 13 C6
Tilsden La TN17 20 D5
Tilton Rd TN15 13 A5
Timperley Cl CT14 22 A3
Tina Gdns CT10 15 C2
Tintagel Cl ME2 52 B4
Tintagel Gdns ME2 52 B4
Tippens Cl TN17 20 C5
Tippledore La CT10 15 A3
Tithe Yd ME17 32 C6
Tivoli Brook CT9 36 B4
Tivoli Gdns DA12 28 B4
Tivoli Park Av CT9 36 B3
Tivoli Rd CT9 36 B5
Toby Gdns TN11 17 B6
Toledo Pad ME7 27 B3
Tolgate La ME2 52 C4
Toll Gate CT14 22 A4
Toll La TN27 17 D3
Tollgate Cl CT5 59 A4
Tollgate Mws TN15 13 C5
Tollgate Pl TN27 31 C5
Tolsey Mead TN15 13 C4
Tom Joyce Cl ME6 49 B4
Tomlin Cl,
Snodland ME6 49 B2
Tomlin Cl,
Tonbridge TN12 51 B2
Tomlin Dr CT9 19 C6
Tomsons Pas CT11 43 A4
Tonbridge By-Pass
TN11 55 A6
Tonbridge Rd,
Maidstone ME16 35 A4
Tonbridge Rd,
Tonbridge TN11 17 A6
Tonge Rd ME10 48 D3
Tontine St CT20 26 D2
Tookey Rd TN28 38 B4
Tooley St DA11 39 C3
Tormore Mws CT14 22 A4
Toronto Rd ME7 27 C4
Torrington Rd TN23 12 C6
Tournay Cl TN23 12 A6
Tourney Rd TN29 34 A3
Tovil Green Bsns Centre
ME15 35 A6
Tovil Hill ME15 35 A6
Tovil Rd ME15 35 A6
Tower Gdns,
Herne Bay CT6 32 B1
Tower Gdns,
Hythe CT21 33 B4
Tower Hamlets Rd
CT17 23 A1
Tower Hamlets St
CT17 23 A1
Tower Hill, Dover CT17 23 A1
Tower Hill,
Whitstable CT5 59 B1
Tower Par CT5 59 B1
Tower Rd,
Dartford DA1 21 A3
Tower Rd,
Whitstable CT5 59 B1
Tower St CT17 23 A1
Tower Way CT1 16 B3
Town Mdw TN17 20 C5
Town Walk CT20 26 C3
Townfield Cnr DA12 28 D4
Townland Cl TN27 13 C2
Townley St CT11 43 A5

Townsend Farm Rd
CT15
Townsend Rd ME6
Townwall St CT16
Trafalgar Rd,
Dartford DA1
Trafalgar Rd,
Gravesend DA11
Trafalgar St ME7
Tramways ME5
Transfesa Rd TN12
Travers Rd CT14
Trebble Rd DA10
Tree Tops TN9
Trevelyan Cl DA1
Trevithick Dr DA1
Tribune Ct ME12
Trident Cl ME2
Trinity CT9
Trinity Cres CT20
Trinity Ct CT14
Trinity Gdns,
Dartford DA1
Trinity Gdns,
Folkestone CT20
Trinity Hill CT9
Trinity Pl, Deal CT14
Trinity Pl,
Ramsgate CT11
Trinity Pl,
Sheerness ME12
Trinity Rd,
Ashford TN24
Trinity Rd,
Folkestone CT20
Trinity Rd,
Gillingham ME7
Trinity Rd,
Gravesend DA12
Trinity Rd,
Ramsgate CT11
Trinity Rd,
Sheerness ME12
Trinity Sq CT9
Tritton La TN28
Trivett Cl DA9
Trosley Av DA11
Trotts Hall Gdns ME10
Trotts La TN16
Truro Rd,
Gravesend DA12
Truro Rd,
Ramsgate CT11
Tubs Hill TN13
Tudeley La TN9
Tudor Av ME14
Tudor Cl,
Birchington CT7
Tudor Cl,
Gravesend DA11
Tudor Gro ME8
Tudor Mws CT14
Tudor Rd CT1
Tufnail Rd DA1
Tufton Rd,
Ashford TN24
Tufton Rd,
Gillingham ME8
Tufton St,
Ashford TN23
Tufton St,
Maidstone ME14
Tulip Tree Cl TN9
Tunnel Rd TN1
Tunstall Rd ME10
Tupman Cl ME1
Turkey Ct ME15
Turmine Ct ME12
Turnagain La CT1
Turnden Gdns CT9
Turner Av TN17
Turner Ct DA1
Turner Ho DA12
Turner St CT11
Turners Av TN30
Turners Ct ME12
Turnpike Cl CT21
Tutsham Way TN12
Twiss Av CT21
Twiss Gro CT21
Twiss Rd CT21
Twistleton Ct DA1
Twyford Rd TN11
Tyler Dr ME8
Tyler Gro DA1
Tyndale Pk CT6
Tysoe Ct ME12
Tyson Av CT14

Ufton La ME10
Ulcombe Rd TN27
Ulster Rd CT9
Underdown Rd CT6
Underwood Cl ME15
Union Cres CT9
Union Pl CT1
Union Rd, Deal CT14

Rd,
sgate CT11 43 C2
Rd,
rness ME12 37 D3
Row CT9 36 C2
Sq TN4 56 A6
St,
erbury CT1 16 D2
St,
ham ME4 18 C4
St, Dover CT17 23 B3
rsham ME13 25 D3
St,
stone ME14 35 B3
St,
sgate CT11 43 B4
St,
ester ME1 44 C4
St,
rness ME12 47 B2
Pl CT11 43 C3
St ME10 48 A4
ry Way ME4 18 C4
ds CI TN13 46 C6
ds Way,
noaks TN13 46 A3
ds Way,
rness ME12 41 C1
Approach Rd 15 C5
Brents ME13 25 D2
Bridge St,
ord TN25 60 C5
Bridge St,
erbury CT1 16 C5
Britton Pl ME7 18 D3
Chantry La CT1 16 D5
Dane Rd CT9 19 D4
Denmark Rd 12 C6
Dumpton Rd 43 B3
Dunstan Rd TN4 50 D5
Field Rd ME10 48 D2
Gro CT9 36 C2
Grosvenor Rd,
ridge TN11 50 D6
Grosvenor Rd,
ridge Wells TN1 56 C1
Luton Rd ME5 18 D5
Malthouse Hill 33 B3
Maltings Pl 14 C2
Rd ME15 35 C5
St Anns Rd 25 B4
Stone St ME15 35 C4
Strand St TN13 45 D2
Rd CT10 15 B3
ns TN27 31 B4
ne Dr CT8 58 A4
ne CI TN12 51 B4

Av,
hborough TN4 50 C2
Av,
ridge Wells TN1 56 B4
Ct TN4 50 C1
Pl CT11 43 A4
Rd,
dstairs CT10 15 A4
Rd,
brook TN18 31 B1
Rd,
resend DA11 39 C3
Rd,
sgate CT11 43 A4
Rd,
hborough TN4 50 C1
Rd, Tonbridge TN9 55 B3
Rd,
ridge Wells TN1 56 B4
Rd,
stable CT5 59 B4
Rise TN9 55 D4
Sq CT11 43 A5
ciennes Rd ME10 48 A4
a Way ME1 44 B4
Dr,
resend DA12 28 D6
Dr,
enoaks TN13 46 C6
Dr,
ridge TN11 17 C4
Gdns DA9 29 B3
Rd,
dstairs CT10 19 C6
Rd,
ngham ME7 27 C4
Vw,
nhithe DA9 29 B3
Vw,
ridge Wells TN4 50 D1

Vange Mws ME1 44 B4
Vauxhall Cres ME6 49 B5
Vauxhall Gdns TN11 55 C5
Vauxhall La TN11 55 C6
Vauxhall Pl DA1 21 B4
Veles Rd ME6 49 B3
Vere Rd CT10 15 C4
Vereth Rd CT11 43 A4
Vernon Pl CT1 16 D5
Vernon Rd DA10 29 F3
Vesty Ct CT8 58 C2
Vicarage Cres CT9 36 C4
Vicarage Dr DA11 39 B2
Vicarage Hill TN16 57 C5
Vicarage La,
Ashford TN23 12 C4
Vicarage La,
Dover CT15 41 B5
Vicarage La,
Faversham ME13 25 A4
Vicarage La,
Sandwich CT13 45 D1
Vicarage Rd,
Gillingham ME7 27 A3
Vicarage Rd,
Sheerness ME12 37 D3
Vicarage Rd,
Strood ME2 52 D3
Vicarage Rd,
Tunbridge Wells TN4 50 C1
Vicarage St ME13 25 D2
Victor Av CT9 19 D3
Victoria Av,
Broadstairs CT10 19 D6
Victoria Av,
Dover CT15 41 D4
Victoria Av,
Gravesend DA12 28 B3
Victoria Av,
Hythe CT21 33 A4
Victoria Av,
Margate CT9 19 A4
Victoria Av,
Westgate-on-Sea CT8 58 C3
Victoria CI TN8 24 C6
Victoria Cotts TN17 20 C4
Victoria Cres,
Ashford TN23 12 C5
Victoria Cres,
Dover CT17 23 B1
Victoria Ct ME16 35 A4
Victoria Gro CT20 26 C2
Victoria Ind Pk DA1 21 B2
Victoria Mws CT14 22 C2
Victoria Par,
Broadstairs CT10 15 D5
Victoria Par, Deal CT14 22 D2
Victoria Par,
Maidstone ME14 35 B2
Victoria Par,
Ramsgate CT11 43 C4
Victoria Pk,
Dover CT16 23 D1
Victoria Pk,
Herne Bay CT6 32 C1
Victoria Pl ME13 25 C3
Victoria Rd,
Ashford TN23 12 C5
Victoria Rd,
Broadstairs CT10 15 A2
Victoria Rd,
Chatham ME4 18 D6
Victoria Rd,
Dartford DA1 21 B2
Victoria Rd, Deal CT14 22 D3
Victoria Rd,
Edenbridge TN8 24 C6
Victoria Rd,
Folkestone CT19 26 B2
Victoria Rd,
Hythe CT21 33 B4
Victoria Rd,
Margate CT9 36 C3
Victoria Rd,
New Romney TN28 38 E4
Victoria Rd,
Ramsgate CT11 43 B3
Victoria Rd,
Sevenoaks TN13 46 C6
Victoria Rd,
Southborough TN4 50 A2
Victoria Rd,
Tonbridge TN11 17 D6
Victoria Rd,
Tunbridge Wells TN1 56 C1
Victoria Rd Ind Est
TN23 12 C5
Victoria Rd West TN8 38 E4
Victoria Row CT1 16 D1
Victoria St,
Gillingham ME7 27 A3
Victoria St,
Maidstone ME16 35 A4
Victoria St,
New Romney TN28 38 B3

Victoria St,
Rochester ME1 44 D4
Victoria St,
Sheerness ME12 47 D4
Victoria St,
Strood ME2 52 D4
Victoria St,
Whitstable CT5 59 A2
Victory Bsns Pk
ME2 44 D2
Victory Ct CT1 16 A6
Victory St ME12 47 C2
Viewlands ME5 18 D5
Viking CI CT7 14 A2
Viking Ct CT10 15 C5
Viking Rd DA11 39 B6
Villa Ct DA1 21 C5
Village Vw ME5 27 A6
Village Way TN26 30 B6
Villiers St CT17 23 A3
Vincent Ct ME12 47 D4
Vincent Gdns ME12 47 D4
Vincents Rd DA1 21 D3
Vine Av TN13 46 C5
Vine CI CT11 43 B1
Vine Court Rd TN13 46 C4
Vine Walk TN12 51 B4
Vinelands TN29 34 B2
Viners CI ME10 48 B5
Vines La ME1 44 C3
Vineyard Cres ME8 42 D1
Vineys Gdns TN30 54 C4
Vinters Rd ME14 35 D3
Virginia Rd,
Gillingham ME7 27 A1
Virginia Rd,
Whitstable CT5 59 D4
Vulcan CI CT5 59 A4

Wades CI TN12 34 C5
Wadham PI ME10 48 D5
Waghorn Rd ME6 49 C2
Waghorn St ME4 18 D6
Wagon La TN12 40 D1
Waid CI DA1 21 D3
Wainhouse CI TN8 24 C3
Wainwright PI TN24 12 D6
Wakefield Rd DA9 29 C2
Wakefield Walk CT21 33 C4
Wakefield Way CT21 33 A5
Wakeley Rd ME8 42 C1
Waldeck Rd DA1 21 D3
Waldron Rd CT10 15 C6
Waleys CI ME8 42 D1
Walker La CT7 14 A2
Wall Rd TN24 12 C3
Wallace Gdns DA10 29 E3
Wallace Way CT10 15 A4
Wallers Rd ME13 25 A3
Wallis Pk DA11 39 A1
Wallwood Rd CT11 43 C2
Walmer Gdns,
Deal CT14 22 A6
Walmer Gdns,
Sittingbourne ME10 48 A2
Walmer Rd CT5 59 B4
Walmer Way CT14 22 A6
Walmsley Rd CT10 15 B3
Walner Gdns TN28 38 C2
Walner La TN28 38 C2
Walnut CI TN12 40 C4
Walnut Tree Av DA1 21 B5
Walnut Tree CI CT7 14 D3
Walnut Way BR8 53 B1
Walpole Rd CT9 36 C2
Walters Farm Rd TN9 55 C3
Wansbury Way BR8 53 E4
Wanstall Ct CT7 14 D2
Wantsume Lees CT13 45 C1
Warblers CI ME8 42 C4
Warden House Mws
CT14 22 A4
Warden Rd ME1 44 C6
Wardona Ct DA10 29 F3
Wardour CI CT10 15 C4
Wards Hill Rd ME12 37 B2
Warehorne Rd TN26 30 A6
Warlingham CI ME8 42 D1
Warner St ME4 18 B5
Warnett Ct ME6 49 C2
Warren CI TN13 46 C5
Warren Dr CT10 15 A3
Warren La TN24 12 B2
Warren Rd,
Dartford DA1 21 C6
Warren Rd,
Folkestone CT19 26 F1
Warren Rd,
New Romney TN28 38 D3
Warren Retail Pk
TN24 12 A2
Warren Vw TN25 12 A2
Warrington Rd TN12 40 B4
Warsop Ind Est
TN8 24 D6
Warten Rd CT11 43 C1

Warwick Ct TN13 46 B6
Warwick Pk TN2 56 B6
Warwick Pl,
Gravesend DA11 39 A1
Warwick Pl,
Maidstone ME16 35 A4
Warwick Rd,
Deal CT14 22 C6
Warwick Rd,
Margate CT9 19 B3
Warwick Rd,
Tunbridge Wells TN1 56 B5
Warwick Rd,
Whitstable CT5 59 A2
Warwick Way DA1 21 C6
Wat Tyler Way ME15 35 C4
Water La,
Canterbury CT1 16 B4
Water La,
Cranbrook TN18 31 D2
Water La,
Faversham ME13 25 A6
Water La,
Hersham ME13 25 D2
Water La,
Westerham TN16 57 C6
Water Side Dr CT8 58 C2
Water Slippe TN11 17 B5
Water St CT14 22 C1
Watercress CI TN14 46 D1
Watercress Dr TN14 46 D1
Waterdales DA11 39 C5
Waterlakes TN8 24 C6
Waterloo Cres CT17 23 C3
Waterloo Hill ME12 37 D3
Waterloo P CT11 43 C4
Waterloo Pl,
Cranbrook TN17 20 C4
Waterloo Pl,
Tonbridge TN9 55 B4
Waterloo Rd,
Cranbrook TN17 20 C3
Waterloo Rd,
Gillingham ME7 27 A4
Waterloo Rd,
Sittingbourne ME10 48 A2
Waterloo Rd,
Tonbridge TN9 55 B4
Waterloo Rd,
Whitstable CT5 59 A2
Waterloo St,
Gravesend DA12 28 C3
Waterloo St,
Maidstone ME15 35 C5
Waterlow Rd ME14 35 B3
Watermans La TN12 40 C6
Watermill CI ME2 52 D3
Waters Edge ME15 35 B5
Waterside,
Faversham ME13 25 D1
Waterside,
Gravesend DA11 39 D2
Waterside,
Maidstone ME14 35 B3
Waterside Ct ME2 18 A2
Waterside Gate ME16 35 A3
Waterside La ME7 27 D1
Waterton BR8 53 B3
Watkins CI TN12 51 B2
Watling Av ME5 27 B6
Watling PI ME10 48 C4
Watling St,
Canterbury CT1 16 B4
Watling St,
Gillingham ME7 27 C6
Watling St,
Gravesend DA11 39 A5
Watling St,
Rochester ME2 52 A4
Watsons Hill ME10 48 A2
Watts Av ME1 44 C4
Watts CI ME6 49 D2
Watts St ME4 18 A5
Watts Yd CT13 45 D2
Waverley Av ME12 37 B2
Waverley Rd CT9 58 F2
Waylands BR8 53 D3
Wayne CI CT10 15 A3
Wayside TN30 54 C1
Wayside Av TN30 54 C1
Wayside Dr TN8 24 C3
Weald CE ME10 48 A5
Weald View Rd TN9 55 B5
Wealden Av TN30 54 C3
Wear Bay Cres CT19 26 F2
Wear Bay Rd CT19 26 F2
Weatherly CI ME1 44 C4
Weatherly Dr CT10 15 B6
Weavering CI ME2 52 D1
Weavers CI,
Gravesend DA11 28 A4
Weavers CI,
Tonbridge TN12 51 C2
Weavers La TN14 46 D1
Webbs Alley TN13 46 D6

Webbs Mdw TN13 46 D6
Webster Rd ME8 42 B1
Week St ME14 35 B3
Weld CI TN12 51 C3
Weldon Way DA9 29 B2
Well La CT15 41 B5
Well Rd,
Maidstone ME14 35 C2
Well Rd,
Queenborough ME11 41 A3
Well Rd,
Queenborough ME11 41 A3
Wellcome Av DA1 21 C1
Weller Av ME1 44 D6
Wellers CI TN16 57 C6
Wellesley Av CT14 22 C6
Wellesley CI,
Broadstairs CT10 15 A5
Wellesley CI,
Westgate-on-Sea CT8 58 C4
Wellesley Rd,
Ashford TN24 12 C4
Wellesley Rd,
Dover CT16 23 C2
Wellesley Rd,
Margate CT9 19 A4
Wellesley Rd,
Westgate-on-Sea CT8 58 C4
Wellington CI CT8 58 B2
Wellington Cres CT11 43 C4
Wellington Pav CT14 22 C6
Wellington Pl,
Maidstone ME14 35 B2
Wellington Pl,
Tenterden TN30 54 B4
Wellington Rd,
Dartford DA1 21 A3
Wellington Rd,
Deal CT14 22 C3
Wellington Rd,
Gillingham ME7 27 A4
Wellington Rd,
Westgate-on-Sea CT8 58 C3
Wellington St DA12 28 C3
Wellingtonia Way TN8 24 B4
Wellis Gdns CT9 36 A4
Wells CI,
New Romney TN28 38 D2
Wells CI,
Tenterden TN30 54 B4
Wells CI,
Tonbridge TN10 55 D1
Wells Way ME13 25 B1
Wellwinch Rd ME10 48 A2
Welsdene Rd CT9 58 E3
Wentworth Av CT9 58 D2
Wentworth Dr ME8 42 A4
West Cliff CT5 59 A3
West Cliff Av CT10 15 C5
West Cliff Gdns CT20 26 D3
West Cliff Prom,
Broadstairs CT10 15 C6
West Cliff Prom,
Ramsgate CT11 43 A6
West Cliff Rd,
Broadstairs CT10 15 C5
West Cliff Rd,
Ramsgate CT11 43 A5
West Crescent Rd
DA12 28 C2
West Cross TN30 54 A6
West Cross Gdns TN30 54 A6
West Cross Mws TN30 54 A6
West Dumpton La
CT11 43 B1
West End TN12 34 A5
West Fld TN13 46 C2
West Hill DA1 21 A3
West Hill Dr DA1 21 A3
West Hill Rise DA1 21 A3
West Kent Av DA11 39 B2
West La,
Sheerness ME12 47 B2
West La,
Sittingbourne ME10 48 D3
West La Trading Est
ME10 48 C2
West Lea CT14 22 B1
West Mill DA11 28 A2
West Norman Rd
CT16 23 D1
West Par CT21 33 B5
West Park Av,
Margate CT9 19 C4
West Park Av,
Tunbridge Wells TN4 50 C2
West Park Rd ME15 35 D5
West Rd ME4 18 C1
West Ridge ME10 48 A4
West Roman Ditch
CT16 23 E1
West St, Ashford TN23 12 B4
West St, Deal CT14 22 C1
West St, Dover CT17 23 A1
West St,
Faversham ME13 25 C2

79

West St, Gillingham ME7 27 B2
West St, Gravesend DA11 28 B2
West St, Maidstone ME17 30 A2
West St, New Romney TN28 38 A3
West St, Queenborough ME11 41 A1
West St, Rochester ME2 52 D2
West St, Sheerness ME12 47 B2
West St, Sittingbourne ME10 48 A3
West Ter CT20 26 C3
West View Rd, Dartford DA1 21 C3
West View Rd, Swanley BR8 53 E3
West Wood Way TN13 46 A3
Westbourne St ME10 48 B2
Westbrook Av CT9 58 D2
Westbrook Cotts CT9 36 A3
Westbrook Gdns CT9 58 F1
Westbrook Prom CT9 58 F1
Westbrook Rd CT9 36 A3
Westbrooke Cl ME4 18 C6
Westbury Rd CT8 58 C2
Westbury Ter TN16 57 B5
Westcliff Dr ME12 37 D2
Westcliff Gdns CT9 58 F1
Westcliff Rd CT9 58 F1
Westcott Av DA11 28 A6
Westcourt St ME7 18 B2
Wested La BR8 53 F4
Westergate Rd ME2 52 A2
Westerham Hill TN16 57 B1
Westerham Rd TN16 57 A6
Westerham Trade Centre TN16 57 D5
Western Av, Ashford TN23 12 B4
Western Av, Cranbrook TN18 31 B1
Western Av, Herne Bay CT6 32 A2
Western Cl CT17 23 A4
Western Cross Cl DA9 29 C3
Western Esp, Broadstairs CT10 15 C6
Western Esp, Herne Bay CT6 32 A2
Western Link ME13 25 A2
Western Rd, Cranbrook TN18 31 B1
Western Rd, Deal CT14 22 C2
Western Rd, Margate CT9 19 B5
Western Rd, Sevenoaks TN15 13 B5
Western Rd, Tunbridge Wells TN4 50 C2
Westfield Rd, Birchington CT7 14 D2
Westfield Rd, Margate CT9 58 F3
Westgate Bay CT8 58 A2
Westgate Bay Av CT8 58 A2
Westgate Gro CT2 16 A2
Westgate Hall Rd CT1 16 B2
Westgate Rd DA1 21 B3
Westgate Terr CT5 59 B2
Westharold BR8 53 B2
Westhill Cl DA12 28 B4
Westleigh Rd CT8 58 A2
Westmarsh Dr CT9 19 D3
Westmead ME20 49 D6
Westmeads Rd CT5 59 B1
Westmount Av ME4 18 B5
Weston Rd ME2 52 B4
Westonville Av CT9 58 E1
Westover Gdns CT10 15 A1
Westover Rd CT10 15 A1
Westree Ct ME16 35 A4
Westree Rd ME16 35 A4
Westrise TN9 55 A5
Westways, Edenbridge TN8 24 B4
Westways, Westerham TN16 57 C5
Westwell Ct TN30 54 A6
Westwell La TN27 17 D3
Westwood Ind Est CT9 36 D6
Westwood Pl ME13 25 D4

Wharf Rd, Gillingham ME7 27 A1
Wharf Rd, Maidstone ME15 35 A5
Wharf Rd ME10 48 B2
Wharfedale Rd CT9 36 D3
Whatman Cl ME14 35 D1
Wheatcroft Cl ME10 48 D3
Wheatcroft Gro ME8 42 B3
Wheatfield Cl TN17 20 B4
Wheatfield Dr TN17 20 B4
Wheatfield Lea TN17 20 B4
Wheatfield Way TN17 20 B4
Wheatley Cl DA9 29 A2
Wheatley Rd CT5 59 B2
Wheatsheaf Gdns ME12 47 C4
Wheelbarrow Park Est TN12 34 A4
Wheeler St, Ashford TN27 31 C5
Wheeler St, Maidstone ME14 35 C3
Wheeler Street Hedges ME14 35 C2
Wheler Rd TN27 17 B2
Whetsted Rd TN12 40 A1
Whiffens Av ME4 18 B3
Whiffens Av West ME4 18 B3
Whitby Cl DA9 29 A2
White Bear Pas TN1 56 B5
White Horse La CT1 16 B3
White Lodge Cl TN13 46 C4
White Oak Cl TN9 55 B5
White Rd ME4 18 C6
White Rock Pl ME16 35 A4
Whitecroft BR8 53 C1
Whitedyke Rd ME6 49 B1
Whitefield Rd TN4 50 C6
Whitefriars Mdw CT13 45 D2
Whitefriars Way CT13 45 D2
Whitegate Cl TN4 50 C3
Whitegate Ct ME8 42 A5
Whitehall Gdns CT2 16 A3
Whitehall Rd, Canterbury CT2 16 A3
Whitehall Rd, Sittingbourne ME10 48 A5
Whitehill La DA12 28 D6
Whitehill Par DA12 28 D6
Whitehill Rd DA12 28 C5
Whitehorse Hill ME5 18 D5
Whiteoak Cl BR8 53 C2
Whiteoak St BR8 53 C2
Whites Cl DA9 29 C3
Whites La TN4 31 C1
Whitewall Rd, Rochester ME2 44 D1
Whitewall Way ME2 44 D1
Whiteway Rd ME11 47 A6
Whitfield Av CT10 19 D6
Whitfield Cotts TN23 12 C6
Whitfield Rd TN23 12 C6
Whiting Cres ME13 25 A2
Whitstable CT5 59 A1
Whybornes Chase ME12 37 C3
Whytecliffs Par CT10 15 C6
Wickenden Rd TN13 46 C2
Wickham Av CT11 43 C2
Wickham Pl ME17 32 D5
Wickham St ME1 44 D6
Widred Rd CT17 23 A1
Wilbrough Rd CT7 14 E2
Wilderness Hill CT9 36 D2
Wildish Rd ME13 25 A2
Wiles Av TN28 38 B4
Wilfred St DA12 28 C2
Wilkes Rd CT10 15 A5
Wilkie Rd CT7 14 D2
Wilkinson Cl DA1 21 D1
Wilkinson Dr CT14 22 C5
Wilks Av DA1 21 C6
Willement Rd ME13 25 B2
Willesley Gdns TN17 20 C3
William Av CT9 19 C5
William Judge Cl TN30 54 D5
William Pitt Av CT14 22 B2
William Pitt Cl CT21 33 C3
William Rd TN23 12 B6
William St, Faversham ME13 25 D3
William St, Gillingham ME8 42 C1

William St, Gravesend DA12 28 B3
William St, Herne Bay CT6 32 C2
William St, Sittingbourne ME10 48 A3
William St, Tunbridge Wells TN4 50 C6
Willis Ct ME12 37 A4
Willow Av, Faversham ME13 25 A3
Willow Av, Swanley BR8 53 D3
Willow Cl CT9 19 C4
Willow Cres TN12 51 C1
Willow Dr TN26 30 B6
Willow Rd, Dartford DA1 21 A5
Willow Rd, Rochester ME2 52 A5
Willow Way, Maidstone ME15 35 D5
Willow Way, Margate CT9 36 A4
Willowside ME6 49 C2
Wilman Rd TN4 50 D5
Wiltie Gdns CT19 26 B1
Wilton Cl CT14 22 B3
Wilton Rd CT19 26 A1
Wimborne Ho DA12 28 D6
Wimbourne Dr ME8 42 A4
Winch Cl TN17 20 C6
Wincheap CT1 16 A6
Winchester Cres DA12 28 D6
Winchester Gro TN13 46 B4
Winchester Rd TN18 31 B1
Winchester Way ME8 42 C2
Winchs Garth TN12 51 C1
Wincliff Rd TN9 55 B4
Windermere Ct TN24 12 C2
Windmill Cl ME2 52 D2
Windmill Cotts TN17 20 C3
Windmill Ct CT5 59 A5
Windmill Rd, Chatham ME4 18 D5
Windmill Rd, Gillingham ME7 27 A5
Windmill Rd, Sittingbourne ME10 48 A1
Windmill Rise ME12 37 F3
Windmill St, Gravesend DA11 28 B2
Windmill St, Gravesend DA12 28 B3
Windmill St, Hythe CT21 33 B4
Windmill St, Rochester ME2 52 C2
Windsor Av, Chatham ME4 18 B6
Windsor Av, Margate CT9 19 A4
Windsor Cl, Broadstairs CT10 15 A3
Windsor Cl, Maidstone ME14 35 C3
Windsor Mws TN28 38 C2
Windsor Rd ME7 27 B3
Wingfield Bank DA11 39 B5
Wingfield Rd DA12 28 B3
Wingrove Dr ME2 44 C1
Wings Cl CT10 15 D2
Winstanley Cl ME7 18 C3
Winstanley Cres CT11 43 C3
Winstanley Rd ME12 47 D3
Winston Ct CT7 14 D1
Wintergarden Cres DA9 29 A4
Winterstoke Cres CT11 43 C3
Winterstoke Undercliff CT11 43 C3
Winterstoke Way CT11 43 C3
Winton Ct BR8 53 C3
Wisteria Gdns BR8 53 B1
Witham Way ME2 52 B4
Wodehouse Cl ME20 49 B6
Wollaston Rd CT14 22 C4
Wolseley Pl TN24 12 C3
Wombwell Gdns DA11 39 D5
Wood End BR8 53 A3
Wood Lodge Grange TN13 46 C3
Wood Rd CT21 33 B4
Wood St, Dover CT16 23 B1

Wood St, Gillingham ME7 18 C1
Wood St, Sheerness ME12 47 D3
Wood St, Tunbridge Wells TN1 56 D1
Woodberry Dr ME10 48 D3
Woodbridge Dr ME15 35 A6
Woodbrook TN27 17 C3
Woodbury Cl TN4 50 D6
Woodbury Gdns TN30 54 A6
Woodbury La TN30 54 A6
Woodbury Park Gdns TN4 50 D6
Woodbury Park Rd TN4 50 D6
Woodbury Rd TN18 31 B1
Woodchurch Rd TN30 54 C4
Woodcocks TN27 17 B2
Woodcourt Cl ME10 48 A5
Woodfield Av DA11 28 B4
Woodfield Rd TN9 55 B4
Woodford Av CT12 43 A2
Woodford Ct CT7 14 D2
Woodgate Cl ME13 25 C1
Woodgate Way TN11 55 D6
Woodgers Gro BR8 53 D1
Woodland Av CT7 14 E3
Woodland Dr, Edenbridge TN8 24 C3
Woodland Dr, Sheerness ME12 37 B2
Woodland Way DA9 29 A1
Woodlands, Swanley BR8 53 C2
Woodlands, Tonbridge TN12 40 B3
Woodlands Av ME6 49 B2
Woodlands Cl BR8 53 D1
Woodlands Ct TN4 50 C2
Woodlands Rd, Gillingham ME7 27 D3
Woodlands Rd, Sittingbourne ME10 48 D4
Woodlands Rd, Tonbridge TN9 55 A6
Woodlands Rise BR8 53 D2
Woodlawn St CT5 59 A2
Woodlea TN24 12 D3
Woodnesborough Rd CT13 45 A3
Woodpecker Cl TN8 24 C3
Woodside Rd, Sevenoaks TN13 46 B3
Woodside Rd, Tonbridge TN9 55 B5
Woodstock Rd, Deal CT14 22 C4
Woodstock Rd, Sittingbourne ME10 48 A6
Woodstock Rd, Strood ME2 52 B4
Woodview Rd BR8 53 B1
Woodview Rise ME2 52 B2
Woodville Pl DA12 28 B3
Woodville Rd ME15 35 C5
Woolaston Cl ME15 35 B6
Woolcomber St CT16 23 D2
Woollett St ME14 35 B3
Woolley Cl TN4 50 B2
Woolley Rd TN4 50 B2
Worcester Cl, Greenhithe DA9 29 B1
Worcester Cl, Rochester ME2 52 A3
Worcester Cl, Sheerness ME12 37 C3
Worcester Dr ME10 48 A1
Worcester Gro CT10 15 B2
Worthington St CT16 23 B2
Wreight Ct ME13 25 B1
Wright Cl DA10 29 E3
Wrights Cl TN30 54 B4
Wrotham Av CT10 15 C4
Wrotham Rd, Broadstairs CT10 15 C4
Wrotham Rd, Gravesend DA11 28 A6
Wrotham Rd, Sevenoaks TN15 13 B5
Wyatt Cl TN15 13 A6
Wyatt Pl ME2 52 B4
Wyatt St ME14 35 C3
Wye Rd, Gravesend DA12 28 D5
Wye Rd, Sevenoaks TN15 13 B4

Wyke Manor Rd ME14
Wykeham Cl ME11
Wykeham St ME2
Wyles St ME7
Wyndham Av CT9
Wyndham Rd ME4
Wynn Rd CT5
Wyvern Cl, Dartford DA1
Wyvern Cl, Snodland ME6
Wyvill Cl ME8
Yalding Cl ME2
Yardley Cl TN9
Yardley Park Rd TN9
Yarrow Cl CT10
Yeoman Gdns TN12
Yevele Cl ME13
Yew Tree Cl CT14
Yew Tree Gdns CT7
Yew Tree Mws CT14
Yew Tree Rd TN4
Yoakley Sq CT9
York Av, Gillingham ME7
York Cl CT6
York Ct ME15
York Hill ME4
York Rd, Broadstairs CT10
York Rd, Canterbury CT1
York Rd, Dartford DA1
York Rd, Deal CT14
York Rd, Gravesend DA12
York Rd, Herne Bay CT6
York Rd, Maidstone ME15
York Rd, Northfleet DA11
York Rd, Rochester ME1
York Rd, Tunbridge Wells TN1
York St, Broadstairs CT10
York St, Dover CT17
York St, Ramsgate CT11
York Ter CT7
Young Cl CT14
Zetland Av ME7
Zion Pl, Gravesend DA12
Zion Pl, Margate CT9